THE OXFORD BOOK OF TREES

BARBARA NICHOLSON
AN APPRECIATION

Barbara Nicholson died in 1978. She began her artistic career as a medical illustrator; then, in 1960, she prepared the illustrations for *The Oxford Book of Wild Flowers* followed by two more Oxford Books on garden flowers and flowerless plants. In 1972 she began a series of paintings for the British Museum (Natural History) illustrating the plants that are typical of fifteen important habitats of the British Isles. Each painting has its own particular charm and combines the highest artistic merit with accurate portrayal of the habitat and the plants within it. The series was completed in 1977. During this period she also illustrated *The Oxford Book of Food Plants* as well as *The Oxford Book of Trees*.

Barbara Nicholson's work was always preceded by field studies and, as far as possible, she painted from fresh material so that she had the rare quality of producing illustrations that were botanically precise and very beautiful.

THE OXFORD BOOK
OF TREES

Illustrations by
B. E. NICHOLSON
Text by
A. R. CLAPHAM

OXFORD   NEW YORK   TORONTO   MELBOURNE
OXFORD UNIVERSITY PRESS

Oxford University Press, Walton Street, Oxford OX2 6DP
OXFORD LONDON GLASGOW
NEW YORK TORONTO MELBOURNE WELLINGTON
KUALA LUMPUR SINGAPORE JAKARTA HONG KONG TOKYO
DELHI BOMBAY CALCUTTA MADRAS KARACHI
NAIROBI DAR ES SALAAM CAPE TOWN

ISBN 0 19 910011 X

© Oxford University Press 1975

First published 1975
Reprinted (with corrections) 1979

Filmset by BAS Printers Limited, Over Wallop, Hampshire
and printed in Spain by Heraclio Fournier, S.A., Vitoria.

Contents

INTRODUCTION

Trees and Shrubs. Woody plants have above-ground parts that persist from year to year and do not die down at the end of each growing season like those of herbaceous plants: they may continue to live for centuries or even millennia. Their main stems and branches increase in length by the outgrowth, each season, of buds at the tips. They also increase in diameter because each has an internal thickening layer or cambium which, during the growing season, adds concentric cylinders of new growth both towards the outside of the stem and towards its centre. The new growth from the inner side of the cambium undergoes chemical modification to become the hard material we call wood. Wood formed in spring is paler in colour and less hard than the dense summer wood. This makes it readily possible, there being no cambial activity in winter, to distinguish one year's wood from the next and so, by counting the annual rings on a smoothed cross-cut face (ill. 1, p. 9), to estimate the age of a main stem or any of its branches. The new growth from the outer side of the cambium includes short-lived soft layers that act as channels of transport for carbohydrates and other substances made in the green leaves and utilized in the growth of other parts of the plant. Water and mineral nutrients from the soil pass mainly up the outermost and therefore youngest layers of wood.

There are two main types of woody plants. In trees there is a single main stem or trunk passing upwards from the ground into the diffusely branching crown. Shrubs have several stems rising obliquely upwards from near ground level (ill. 2, p. 9). The distinction is not always clear-cut, and some plants, for example hazel, hawthorn, spindle tree, and some sallows, develop either as trees or as shrubs according to circumstances.

The Shapes of Trees. During winter a vigorous young sycamore, four or five years old (see diagram), has at its top end the large terminal bud that will grow out into a leafy shoot next spring and so continue the upward growth of the main stem. Below this are paired leaf-scars, each with an axillary bud just above it, the uppermost pair closely flanking the larger terminal bud. Near the base of last year's growth are the crowded scars of the bud-scales of last year's terminal bud, and a further set is to be seen lower down, at the base of the previous year's growth. The length of stem between these two sets of bud-scale scars differs from the top length in that some of the axillary buds have grown out to form side branches. These buds are usually near the top end of the year's growth, most of those towards the basal end remaining dormant. So no axillary buds grow out into branches during the first year of life;

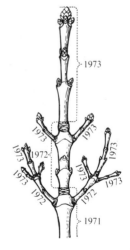

some, but by no means all, grow out in the second year, and this continues year after year on second-year lengths of branches as well as on the main stem. In the second winter of life there is a main stem and some branches; in the third winter a main stem with branches and also branches of branches—or, in other words, a main stem and two "orders" of branching. At the end of its tenth growing season a tree would then have nine orders of branching, and at the end of its 100th season 99. It is in fact rarely possible to count more than eight orders even on quite an old tree; usually there are only five or six. This is due to the distinctly limited length of life of most branches: the basal lengths of the main stem and major branches of an old sycamore are bare, but not because they have never borne branches. A search on the ground beneath any sizable tree in late summer or early autumn will usually reveal numbers of detached twigs each with a smoothly rounded basal end. Willows and poplars shed twigs up to six years old and a metre or more in length, and oaks shed lengths of up to 60 cm. The surviving branches, apart from the main supporting boughs, are the leaf-bearing twigs concentrated in the outer shell of a more or less hollow hemispherical crown. So also, if grown close together with their crowns touching, trees develop the tall branch-free trunks that delight the forester and contrast strikingly with free-standing trees which tend to retain massive old branches at no great height above the ground (ill. 3, p. 9). This branch-shedding and trunk-cleaning are not due simply to death by shading but follow an active killing of shaded branches by others that grow more vigorously because they have more light.

Variations in Tree Shape. The British army used to recognize three types of trees on the basis of crown shape: "fir trees", "bushy-top trees", and "poplars" (ill. 4, p. 9). This is a rough-and-ready classification, but it provides a useful starting-point. Fir trees are like the Norway spruce (our common Christmas tree; ill. p. 108), with a very clear distinction between a vertical main stem and rather short and more or less horizontal side branches, which may droop as they become longer and heavier. The main stem overtops all the side branches and the tree maintains the narrowly conical shape characteristic of conifers in general. Bushy-top trees have more or less rounded crowns like those of oak (ill. p. 12), beech (ill. p. 12), sycamore (ill. p. 21), and the majority of non-coniferous trees. As the crown develops the main stem eventually ceases to be distinguishable, in sharp contrast with its persistence in fir trees. Poplars are trees with the stiffly ascending side branches that give the familiar narrow outline to the Lombardy poplar (ill. p. 168), though by no means to all poplars.

That the side branches of fir trees and young bushy-top trees grow out more or less horizontally is a manifestation of what is termed "apical dominance". This is not yet fully understood but it is known that growth-controlling chemical substances are produced in all stem-tips and pass downwards from them in amounts that increase with increasing vigour of growth. The tip of the main stem is the strongest-growing of all, partly because it is vertical, and is therefore able to exert a chemical dominance over side branches, making them begin and continue to grow at an angle with the vertical. If the tip of the leader of a fir tree is cut off, damaged, or merely held horizontally, one of the uppermost side branches will turn upwards and take over as "substitute-leader" (ill. 5, p. 9). Replacement of the tip by a block of gelatine containing one of the natural growth-controlling substances of plants (indole-3-acetic acid) will often prevent the formation of a substitute-leader.

The strength of apical dominance depends upon the vigour with which a stem-tip is growing, and all stem tips seem to decline in vigour with increasing age. In general the main stems of fir trees retain both vigour and apical dominance for longer than those of bushy-top trees, though in some widely grown conifers the conical form is lost at a fairly early stage, the main stem ceasing to grow so that a rounded or even flat-topped crown results. This is true of our native Scots pine (ill. p. 76) and of both cedar of Lebanon and Atlantic cedar (both ill. p. 120). In bushy-top trees this is normal behaviour. Development of the characteristically rounded crown follows a slackening of growth of the main stem and its overtopping by upwardly curving and strong-growing side branches no longer subjected to apical dominance.

Axillary buds of trees normally remain dormant throughout the first growing season and only a few of them grow out in the second season. If, however, the stem-tip is removed, then buds grow out from the top part of the current season's growth. Their outgrowth is prevented if the stem tip is replaced by a gelatine block containing indole-3-acetic acid. It seems, therefore, that the enforced dormancy of axillary buds is another way in which apical dominance may manifest itself.

All the three aspects of growth-control to which reference has been made affect the form of the developing tree in ways that must be beneficial. The enforced dormancy of all but a few buds on the second-year stem (in shrubs some grow out in the first season), the control of the direction and rate of growth of the side branches from these few released buds, and the suppression and eventual shedding of poorly-lighted branches, all combine to secure the development of a hollow cone or hemisphere of leaf-bearing twigs that have enough light and can therefore make a positive contribution to the growth of the tree. What would happen if this strict control were lost can be inferred from "witches' brooms" (ill. 6, p. 9). These dense tangles of twigs are the result of outgrowth, because of biochemical changes induced by a parasitic fungus, of large numbers of buds that would otherwise remain dormant. If the whole crown of a tree were one enormous witch's broom, most of the leaves would be so crowded and so heavily shaded that they could survive only if supplied with food from those in the well-lighted periphery of the crown—and therefore at the expense of the growing stems and roots.

Fastigiate and Weeping Trees. It is not only Lombardy poplars that hold all their side branches so nearly erect as to give a very narrow outline to the whole tree. There are in cultivation similarly fastigiate forms of many different kinds of tree (ill. 7, p. 9), a familiar example being Irish yew; but few species are markedly fastigiate as wild plants. The converse of fastigiate growth is the weeping or pendulous form (ill. 8, p. 9), so frequent amongst trees grown in parks and gardens though again unusual in natural vegetation. The most familiar of all are the weeping willows (ill. p. 165), but there are weeping forms of ash, beech, wych elm, mountain ash, Japanese cherry, and very many others. Most of these are horticultural varieties that have appeared in nurseries and been selected and cultivated for their ornamental value, like the corresponding fastigiate forms.

Between the extremes represented by the Lombardy poplar and the weeping willow, trees show a continuous range in the angle at which branches leave the main stem and in the subsequent direction of their growth and that of their branchlets. For example, the Cornish elm (ill. p. 161) is almost fastigiate and the Huntingdon elm has quite a narrow angle of branching, like many willows and poplars; but in oak the angle is characteristically wide. In ash (ill. p. 20) and lime (ill. p. 13) the lower branches droop but their tips turn upwards, while in silver birch (ill. p. 13) the slender branchlets are often pendulous. In horse-chestnut (ill. p. 189) and ash the branchlets are few and stout, thus giving a coarse "spray" that contrasts with the fine spray of elm and beech. Such differences, in combination with differences in the general size and shape of the crown, in the pattern of branching, and in features of the bark, make identification possible even from afar and in winter (see endpapers).

External Factors and Tree Shape. The factor of the physical environment that has the strongest effect on tree shape is undoubtedly wind. Trees growing in very wind-

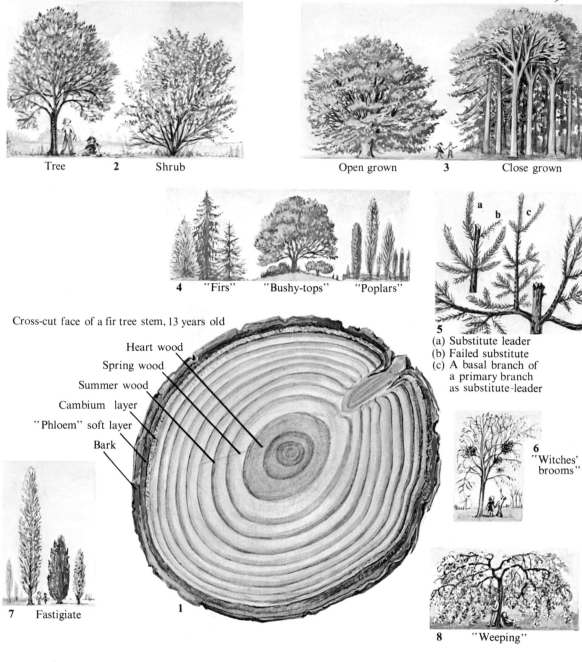

Tree   **2**   Shrub

Open grown   **3**   Close grown

4   "Firs"   "Bushy-tops"   "Poplars"

Cross-cut face of a fir tree stem, 13 years old

Heart wood

Spring wood

Summer wood

Cambium layer

"Phloem" soft layer

Bark

5
(a) Substitute leader
(b) Failed substitute
(c) A basal branch of a primary branch as substitute-leader

6 "Witches' brooms"

7 Fastigiate

1

8 "Weeping"

9 Effect of wind (on tree shape)

10 Effect of lightning (on tree shape)

11 Horizontal plane from animal grazing

Coppice   Pollard   Topiary

exposed sites have longer and better-grown branches on the side away from the prevailing wind, so that the crown seems to be streaming in the wind like a flag (ill. 9, p. 9), though this is a deceptive appearance. The main reason for the one-sided crown is that buds and young branches continually exposed to strong wind are dried out and eventually killed, though twigs may occasionally be snapped off in a purely mechanical way. The outcome is that only on the lee side can branches grow out normally, and the one-sidedness becomes more and more marked. Trees growing by the sea often show a still more pronounced wind-shaping because the desiccating effect of salt spray intensifies the direct influence of the severe winds.

Average wind speeds increase with increasing height above sea-level, so it is not surprising that trees are often absent from the tops of mountain ridges and saddles even when they grow at much greater heights on less exposed neighbouring faces. But it is a familiar fact that they grow more and more stunted and shrub-like with increasing altitude, quite apart from the effects of wind. This is because the general mountain climate becomes steadily less favourable for tree growth and, in particular, because temperatures are lower and the growing season therefore shorter. The leaves of trees have to provide food for a relatively greater amount of living but non-green stems and roots than do the leaves of herbaceous plants and therefore require a longer period each year when temperatures are favourable for food-production by leaves. It is often stated that trees require at least 100 days with mean temperatures of not less than 5 °C or, alternatively, two months with mean temperatures of not less than 10 °C, but no such simple rules cover all the facts about the altitudinal limits of tree growth. A complication is that grazing by sheep and deer has undoubtedly lowered the tree limit on many mountains. The shortened growing season explains the smaller amount of growth each year and therefore the dwarfed stature of trees at high levels on mountains. That they are also gnarled and often semi-prostrate arises from other features of the mountain climate—the strong winds, hard frosts, and heavy snowfall, all tending to damage or kill buds and shoots.

Frost and Snow. As growth slackens in early autumn our native woody plants become gradually "hardened" so that normal winter frosts have no deleterious effect, though early frosts sometimes kill the "Lammas shoots" of oaks and other trees that grow out in July and August and may not have had time to harden. Late spring frosts may kill whole opening buds or, if later and less severe, only the newly expanded leaves. Repeated loss of the terminal bud results in a stunted and misshapen tree, and if side branches are also frosted, as at high altitudes or in frost-hollows, the tree may come to resemble a much-branched shrub. Trees vary in their sensitivity to late frosts. Ash and beech have their leaves blackened and killed when birch, aspen, mountain ash, and sallow are unaffected, while oak, sycamore, and Scots pine are intermediate in sensitivity. Snow and ice can cause damage by weighing down slender main stems and branches or by causing them to break.

Lightning causes a special type of damage to trees. The characteristic features are a conspicuous deep furrow down one of the upper main branches and on down the trunk, often with a spiral course; and the die-back of the struck branch so that the tree becomes "stag-headed" (ill. 10, p. 9). Oaks are the commonest trees to suffer because over much of the country they are the large trees most frequently standing in isolation and are also deep-rooted. Such trees act as good lightning-conductors provided there is an unbroken conducting path from the top of the tree downwards to moist soil. Smooth-barked trees like beech can conduct all over their surface when it is wet, and may often do so without visible after-effects, but a rough-barked tree like oak provides no such continuous surface pathway and the lightning therefore passes inwards to the moist cylinder formed by the cambium and its recent products. The deep furrow is due to the explosive expansion of air and water-vapour close round the track of the lightning. In exceptional cases the trunk may be split open and branches broken off.

Animals and Man. Trees in parks and meadows often have the base of the crown planed level by browsing cattle (ill. 11, p. 9). Unprotected young trees become dwarfed and distorted if grazing animals repeatedly bite off their leading shoots. The shape of trees is also modified by man, most obviously by coppicing and pollarding. Coppicing is the repeated cutting of stems down to near ground level for the sake of the straight stool-shoots which then spring up in many but not all woody species (ill. 11, p. 9). Oak, ash, alder, sweet chestnut, and especially hazel have in the past been coppiced extensively; lime, hornbeam, and field maple rather less extensively; and osier-willows are still coppiced for basket-making. Pollarding differs from coppicing only in that the repeated cutting is at two metres or so above the ground (ill. 11, p. 9). Pollard willows are a familiar sight by lowland rivers. The natural forms of certain fruit trees have also been greatly modified by pruning and training to increase the yield and accessibility of fruit, and some ornamental woody plants are cut into unnatural and often grotesque shapes by devotees of the art of topiary (ill. 11, p. 9).

Bark. The activity of the internal cambium (p. 6) imposes a steadily increasing strain on the original surface-layer of a stem, which must ultimately give way. It is replaced by the products of another cambium arising just beneath the surface. This is called the "cork-cambium" because it forms on its outer side layers of more or less elastic cork. But even cork cannot be stretched beyond a certain point, so that continuous replacement is necessary. In some trees, including beech, the first cork-cambium persists throughout life—the overstretched outermost layers of cork dry and shred off and the surface remains smooth. More commonly it is replaced after a limited number of years by deeper ones. Usually these are not complete cylinders like the first but form separate overlapping plates of varying extent which are again short-lived and are replaced in their turn by others still more deeply set. The whole complex of cork-cambiums, their products, and the tissues in which they arise—collectively termed "bark"—continually dries and cracks open in its outer layers and pieces are detached in patterns which are characteristically different from one kind of tree to another. "Scale bark" is the term used for bark that flakes off in broad flat scales, as in Scots pine; and if long vertical cracks develop the bark is "fissured", as in many oaks.
Bark protects vulnerable living layers from mechanical damage, from browsing animals, insects, and various parasites, and from extremes of temperature if of short duration. At the same time it provides aerating passages at the bottom of the deep fissures and through the localized patches of spongy tissue called "lenticels".

m 35

30

20

10

0

scale for trees 1, 2, 3, 4. 5. 6, 7, 8, 9, 10, 11, & 12

1 PEDUNCULATE OAK (*Quercus robur*)   2 SESSILE OAK (*Q. petraea*)   3 EUROPEAN BEECH (*Fagus sylvatica*)
7 LARGE-LEAVED LIME (*T. platyphyllos*)   8 HORNBEAM (*Carpinus betulus*)   9 SILVER BIRCH (*Betula pendula*)
See also pp. 16–17; text pp. 14–15, 18–19

4 ENGLISH ELM (*Ulmus procera*) 5 WYCH ELM (*U. glabra*) 6 SMALL-LEAVED LIME (*Tilia cordata*)
10 HAIRY BIRCH (*B. pubescens*) 11 ALDER (*Alnus glutinosa*) 12 ASPEN (*Populus tremula*). Leaf details × ⅔.

NATIVE BRITISH TREES: Deciduous

OAKS (*Quercus*); ill. pp. 12, 16. Oaks have simple alternate leaves with early-falling stipules. Separate male and female flowers are borne on the same tree, the former in slender drooping catkins, the latter singly or in spikes. The flowers are small, inconspicuous, and wind-pollinated. The fruit is the familiar acorn, a single-seeded nut sitting in an open scaly cup. The seed-leaves remain inside the germinating acorn. There are two native species. (For non-native species see pp. 138, 159.)

1–2 **Pedunculate** or **Common Oak** (*Q. robur* (**1**) and **Sessile** or **Durmast Oak** (*Q. petraea*) (**2**). Both are deep-rooted broad-crowned deciduous trees reaching 30 m or more and have thick, deeply fissured bark. Buds are clustered at the ends of twigs. The shoot from the terminal bud is often weak and short-lived and a strong side branch continues last year's growth so that the boughs tend to become markedly zig-zag. Many buds renew growth in summer to form bright green Lammas shoots. Flowers open in April or May and the acorns, borne singly or in groups of 2–5, fall early in autumn and soon germinate if kept moist, but the first green leaves appear only in the following spring.

Both species are found all over the British Isles but natural woodland on heavy fertile lowland soils is typically of pedunculate oak while sessile oak predominates, irrespective of soil type, in the uplands of the west and north. The table below shows differences between the two, but there are some parts of the country where many individual trees may be found to combine one or more features from one column of the table with the rest from the other column, or to show some features intermediate between those given in the two columns. Reasons for this are matters of dispute: it may mean that pedunculate oak is truly native only in lowland England but has been more widely planted and has hybridized with local native populations of sessile oak.

Pedunculate oak is so-named from its long-stalked acorns, those of sessile oak being unstalked or quite short-stalked. On the whole pedunculate oak has a shorter and broader crown, with lower branches going off at a wider angle and all branches more zig-zag, but these are not clear-cut differences.

	Pedunculate Oak	Sessile Oak
Widest point of leaf	Well above middle	At or just above middle
Lobes on each side	3–5, fairly deep	5–8, shallow
Shape of leaf-base	Narrowly heart-shaped with tiny marginal lobes folded tightly back	Narrowly wedge- or heart-shaped, usually lacking folded-back lobes
Underside of leaf	Usually hairless	Always with some branched hairs along the midrib
Leaf-stalk	Very short (2–7 mm)	Fairly long (13–25 mm)
Stalk of acorn	Usually 3–9 cm	Usually less than 2 cm

BEECHES (*Fagus*); ill. pp. 12, 16. Beeches also have simple alternate leaves and early-falling stipules. Separate male and female flowers are on the same tree, the male hanging in long-stalked globular clusters and the female in pairs in a long-stalked upturned scaly cup which later closes round the 2 sharply 3-sided nuts until it splits along 4 lines to release them in autumn. For introduced species see p. 158. Only one species is native to the British Isles.

3 **European Beech** (*F. sylvatica*) is broad-crowned and deciduous, taller than oak (to 40 m) and has shallow roots and a thin smooth grey bark. The elliptical untoothed leaves, 4–9 cm long, fringed with long silky hairs when young, are borne in 2 rows, to the right and left of the twig, as are the long slender red-brown winter-buds. Most side branches are "short-shoots" with only 3–4 crowded leaves each season. Flowers open in May and the nuts are shed in October. They germinate in spring and the rounded seed-leaves, broader than long, emerge as the first green leaves. Beech grows as an evident native species only in Southern England westwards to Gloucestershire and a few localities in South Wales, but it is widely planted for its attractive foliage and beautiful autumn colours.

ELMS (*Ulmus*); ill. pp. 12, 16. Elms are deciduous trees with fissured bark and simple alternate coarsely-toothed leaves which are usually unequal-sided at the base and have early-falling stipules. The flowers, bisexual and wind-pollinated, are in dense reddish-brown clusters. They open before the leaves. The single-seeded fruits have a flat green wing all round except for an apical notch and hang in conspicuous clusters in early spring. The terminal bud dies and falls by autumn, and growth is continued next spring by the uppermost side branch. Most other side branches are quite short and go off at a wide angle. This, and the zig-zag rows of fat flower-buds, make elm shoots unmistakable in winter.

Elms are variable and difficult to name, but our three main types in woods and hedgerows may be distinguished as shown in the table below. Only leaves from short-shoots on main boughs should be examined; others may be misleadingly different. (For introduced elms see p. 162.)

	English Elm	Smooth-leaved Elm	Wych Elm
Young twigs	Hairy	Hairless or nearly so	Hairy
Leaf-stalk	About 4–6 mm	About 6–12 mm	About 3 mm
Leaf-blade	5–8 cm long	4–10 cm long	8–15 cm long
Main veins	8–14 pairs	8–14 pairs	15–20 pairs
Upper surface of leaf	Rough	Smooth	Rough

4 English Elm (*U. procera*) is a narrow-crowned tree 30–40 m high, whose tall straight trunk often has many short leafy shoots growing directly from it. Suckers are abundant. Leaves are commonly 5–8 cm long, and broadly rounded and rough above. The larger lobe of the unequal base does not hide the leaf-stalk as in wych elm. Ripe fruit and seedlings are rarely seen. This is the common and distinctive hedgerow elm of lowland England, nowhere found in natural woods, and curiously absent from ancient hedges in East Anglia. It may have arisen in a Midland county as a variant of smooth-leaved elm or from a hybrid with wych elm.

Smooth-leaved Elm (*U. minor*) ill. pp. 160–1. This tree is usually no more than 20 m high, with leaves varying considerably in size and shape but commonly intermediate in size of blade between English elm and wych elm, though usually longer-stalked than either. The leaves are often very asymmetric at the base, but some small-leaved forms are almost equal-sided; and they are usually smooth and shining above. The nut is well above the centre of the fruit-wing. This is another hedgerow elm, common in East Anglia, the East Midlands, and parts of Southern England and perhaps introduced at some early time for fodder. Naturally-occurring more or less fastigiate forms (Cornish and Jersey elms) and hybrids with wych elm are described on p. 162.

5 Wych Elm (*U. glabra*). This is a large spreading tree up to 35 m or more high with a shorter trunk and a more broadly rounded crown than English elm. It has few or no suckers. Twigs, hairy when young but smooth by the third year, bear 2 rows of leaves 8–13 cm or more long, broadest at or beyond the middle and with the tip drawn out into a long point. There are often similar long points at the "shoulders" of the leaf. Seen from above, the longer side of the unequal base hides the very short leaf-stalk. The leaf is very rough above, and more softly hairy beneath. The abundant fruits are 15–20 mm long, each with a central nut. This is our most widespread elm, commonest in the north and west and the only elm in our natural vegetation. Northern forms have narrower leaves with less unequal bases.

"Dutch elm disease" was first recognized in this country in 1927 and has recently become a devastating epidemic which by the end of 1976 had already killed about 9 million elms in Southern England out of an estimated total of 23 millions. The species chiefly affected is the English elm, and in many counties the whole aspect of the countryside has been changed by the loss of these conspicuous hedgerow trees. The wych elm and smooth-leaved elm seem less susceptible.

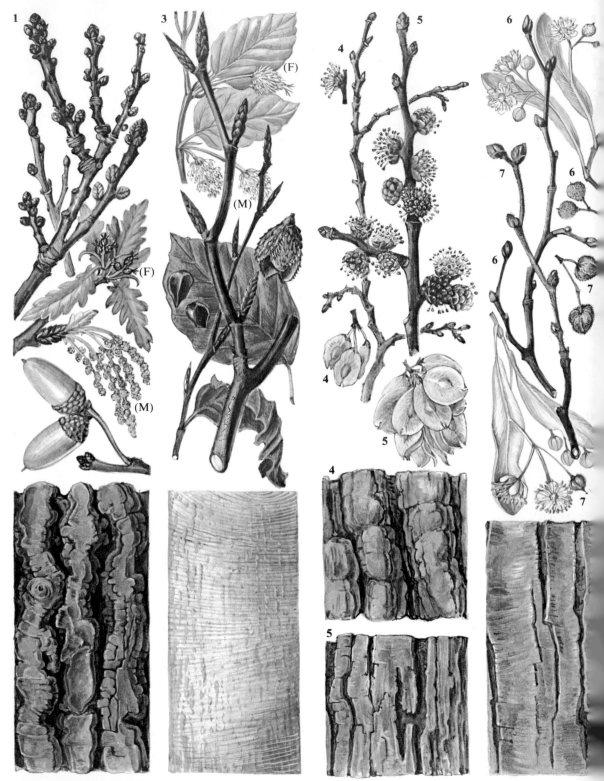

1 PEDUNCULATE OAK (*Quercus robur*)   3 EUROPEAN BEECH (*Fagus sylvatica*)   4 ENGLISH ELM (*Ulmus procera*)
8 HORNBEAM (*Carpinus betulus*)   9 SILVER BIRCH (*Betula pendula*)   10 HAIRY BIRCH (*B. pubescens*)—bark is of no. 9
Bark, winter twigs, flowers, fruits, and leaves × $\frac{2}{3}$. See also pp. 12–13; text pp. 14–15, 18–19.

17

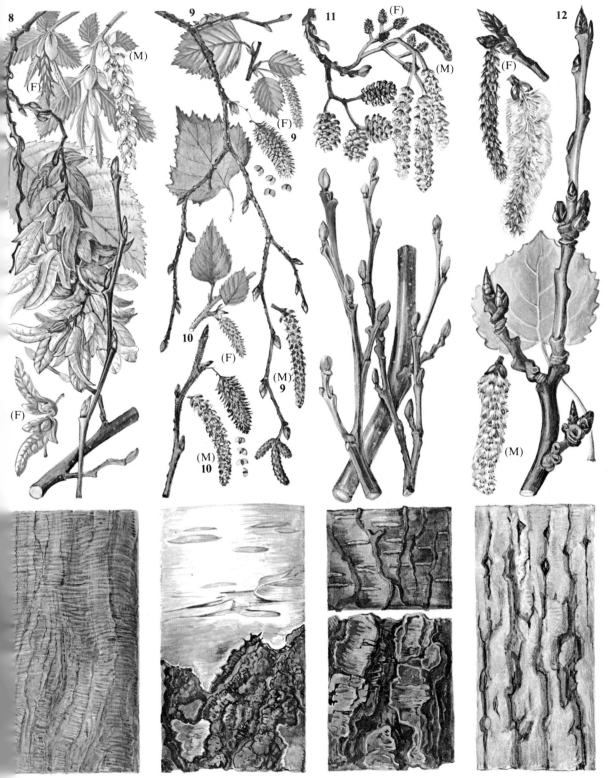

5 WYCH ELM (*U. glabra*)　　6 SMALL-LEAVED LIME (*Tilia cordata*)　　7 LARGE-LEAVED LIME (*T. platyphyllos*)
11 ALDER (*Alnus glutinosa*)—young bark above, base of tree below　　12 ASPEN (*Populus tremula*).
Numbers correspond with those on pp. 12–13.

LIMES (*Tilia*); ill. pp. 13, 16. These are deciduous trees with smooth or shallowly fissured bark and simple alternate heart-shaped leaves with toothed margins; the stipules fall early. The blunt rounded winter-buds expose only 2–3 of the outermost scales. The terminal bud dies and falls off in spring, growth being continued next spring by the uppermost side branch. Each cluster of bisexual, yellowish-white, fragrant flowers has a stalk joined for half its length with a long narrow greenish bracteole. The flowers are pollinated by honey-bees and other insects visiting them for their nectar, and the whole cluster of nutlets (each with 1–3 seeds) is wind-carried by the wing-like bracteole. The seed-leaves emerge and are unusual in having long finger-like lobes.

6–7 **Small-leaved Lime** (*T. cordata*) **(6)** and **Large-leaved Lime** (*T. platyphyllos*) **(7)**. Our two native limes are readily distinguished except where intercrossing has been active. The much-planted **Common Lime** (*T. x vulgaris*), which grows to 25 m and flowers in early July, is a fertile hybrid between them (ill. p. 192). Small-leaved lime, which grows to 25 m, is widespread and locally common in woods. It flowers in early July. Large-leaved lime, which grows to 30 m, is very rare as a native tree. It flowers in late June.

	Small-leaved Lime	Common Lime	Large-leaved Lime
Winter-buds	Only 2 scales visible	2–3 scales visible	3 scales visible
First-year twigs	Soon hairless	Soon hairless	Remaining hairy
Leaf-blade	Usually 3–6 cm long	Usually 6–10 cm	Usually 6–12 cm
Leaf underside	Blue-green, hairless, but with rusty tufts in vein angles	Light green, hairless, but with whitish tufts in vein angles	Light green, hairy, with whitish tufts in vein angles
Leaf-stalk	Slender, hairless	Intermediate	Less slender, hairy
Flower clusters	Semi-erect	Hanging	Hanging
Number of flowers	5–10	4–10	Usually 3
Fruit	6 mm, thin-walled, unribbed	8 mm, thick-walled, slightly ribbed	8–10 mm, thick-walled, strongly 3–5 ribbed

HORNBEAMS (*Carpinus*); ill. pp. 13, 17. Hornbeams are trees and shrubs with simple alternate deciduous leaves and early-falling stipules and they resemble hazels (p. 34) in having male and female flowers in separate groups on the same plant but differ in that both are in pendulous many-flowered catkins, the female initially shorter than the male but lengthening in fruit. Each scale of the male catkin has in its axil a single flower consisting merely of 3–13 split stamens with no perianth; and each scale of the female catkin has a pair of axillary flowers consisting of an ovary surmounted by a small green lobed perianth. These give rise to paired nutlets, each in a very shallow cup with its margin prolonged only on one side into a large lobed or toothed leafy wing.

8 **Hornbeam** (*C. betulus*) is a tree up to 30 m high with a markedly fluted trunk and smooth grey bark. The young twigs are brown and sparsely hairy and the buds are 5–10 mm long, pale brown, shorter and less slender than those of beech. The ovate-oblong leaves, 3–10 cm long, are rounded or heart-shaped at the base and pointed at the tip, with sharply and doubly toothed margins. They are somewhat folded along the veins. The ribbed nut, 5–10 mm long, is in a cup with 3 lobes on one side, the middle lobe much the longest. Hornbeam is a native tree only in South-eastern England northwards to south Norfolk and westwards to Chepstow. It is often coppiced or pollarded, as in Epping Forest. (See also p. 154.)

BIRCHES (*Betula*); ill. pp. 13, 17. These are deciduous trees and shrubs, usually with smooth shining bark and alternate simple leaves, with stipules falling early. Male and female flowers occur in separate drooping catkins on the same tree in April–May; they are inconspicuous and wind-pollinated. The fruits are flattened single-seeded winged nutlets; up to 3 are borne on each 3-lobed female catkin-scale, scales and ripe fruits being detached and shed separately. The seed-leaves emerge from the germinating seed. There are two native tree birches; they occur throughout the British Isles. (For introduced species see pp. 155.)

10 Silver Birch (*B. pendula*) (**9**) and **Hairy Birch** (*B. pubescens*) (**10**). Both are smallish short-lived trees: silver birch grows to 25 m, hairy birch to 20 m. They have more or less triangular leaves, usually only 2–4 cm long. They differ in several ways, as shown in the table below.

Hairy birch is the more tolerant of wet and cold and is more variable. In southern and lowland areas the twigs are distinctly hairy, but the northern form (perhaps a separate species) has almost or quite hairless twigs with brown, resinous, and sticky warts.

	Silver Birch	Hairy Birch
Bark	Silvery-white; older trees rough and black below	Silver-grey, often brownish, down to the ground
Branches	Commonly pendulous	Usually not pendulous
Twigs	Hairless, with whitish warts	Hairy or with sticky brown warts
Leaves	Triangular, long-pointed	Rounded or rhomboidal, short-pointed
Toothing of leaf-margin	Double, with small teeth on larger teeth	Single, with irregular but simple teeth
Fruit-wing	2–3 times as wide as nutlet	1–1½ times as wide as nutlet
Catkin-scale	Side lobes curving towards base	Side lobes not curving down

ALDERS (*Alnus*); ill. pp. 13, 17. Alders are related to birches and like them have simple alternate deciduous leaves with early-falling stipules and separate male and female catkins borne on the same tree. The male catkins are long and drooping. The female ones are quite short, finally becoming woody and cone-like, with each 5-lobed cone-scale bearing a pair of narrow-winged single-seeded nutlets. Seed-leaves emerge from the germinating seed. The single native species is a tree chiefly of stream-sides and fen-woods and, like other alders, has large root-nodules containing nitrogen-fixing bacteria. (For introduced species see p. 155.)

1 Alder (*A. glutinosa*) is a tree growing to 20 m or more, with a long trunk and narrow crown. Winter-buds are purplish and stalked. The leaves are 3–9 cm long, irregularly toothed, roundish, widest at or beyond the middle and with a flattened or notched end. Flowers open in February or March. The female "cones" lengthen to 1–1·5 cm and become black and woody, opening to shed the nutlets during winter. After leaf-fall the persistent black cones and numerous unopened catkins for next season make the crown notably dense and purple-tinged. The wood was formerly used for making clogs, and the charcoal for gunpowder. Alder occurs in wet places throughout the British Isles.

ASPEN

2 Aspen (*Populus tremula*); ill. pp. 13, 17. Aspen is our most widespread poplar (for other native poplars see p. 94). This is a deciduous tree to 20 m high, the greyish bark at first smooth and shining but later rough with roundish lenticels and becoming fissured towards the base of the trunk; sucker-shoots are abundant. Twigs are hairless. Buds are glossy-brown, pointed, and rather sticky. Leaves are almost circular, 2·5–6 cm, with shallow rounded teeth. Leaf-stalks are slender and flattened, so that the leaves readily flutter in the wind. Leaves on sucker-shoots are larger, heart-shaped, often long-pointed at the tip and densely hairy beneath. The wind-pollinated flowers, which appear in February–March, are in red-purple drooping catkins, male and female being borne on different trees. The small fruits open to release numerous tiny seeds with tufts of white hairs making them readily wind-carried. Aspen is a very hardy tree found in a wide range of localities from wet lowland woods to high mountain-ledges.

m 35

30

20

10

5

0

scale for trees 1, 2, 3, 4, 5, 6, 7, 8, & 9

1 WILD CHERRY (*Prunus avium*)   2 COMMON WHITEBEAM (*Sorbus aria*)   3 MOUNTAIN ASH (*S. aucuparia*)
7 SWEET CHESTNUT (*Castanea sativa*)   8 SCOTS PINE (*Pinus sylvestris*)   9 YEW (*Taxus baccata*).

4 EUROPEAN ASH (*Fraxinus excelsior*)   5 SYCAMORE (*Acer pseudoplatanus*)   6 FIELD MAPLE (*A. campestre*)
Leaf details × $\frac{2}{3}$ (whole ash leaf × $\frac{1}{4}$). See also pp. 24–5; text pp. 22–3, 26–7

NATIVE BRITISH TREES: Deciduous and Evergreen

PLUMS and CHERRIES (*Prunus*); ill. pp. 20, 24. These are trees and shrubs with simple alternate leaves and stipules that may or may not persist. The flowers are bisexual, with white or pink petals, numerous stamens, and a single ovary ripening to a fleshy fruit with a large single-seeded stone. They are conspicuous and insect-pollinated and are often self-sterile, setting fruit only if pollen comes from a different plant. The seed-leaves emerge during germination.

1 **Wild Cherry** or **Gean** (*P. avium*) is a deciduous tree growing to 25 m or more high. Its smooth, glossy, purplish-brown bark has horizontally-elongated lenticels and peels in horizontal papery strips. Suckers are frequent. Leaves are 6–15 cm long, mostly on short-shoots, rather limp and drooping, elliptical, long-pointed, with toothed margins and pale hairy undersides. Leaf-stalks are 2–5 cm long with 2 large glands close to the top end; stipules fall early. The white flowers are borne on short-shoots in hanging umbels of 2–6; they open in April–May and are self-sterile. The fruit is almost round, 1 cm across, dark red and sweet when ripe in July–August. The seeds require winter-chilling before they will germinate. Wild cherry occurs in woods on good fertile soil throughout the British Isles (although less in Northern Scotland). It is one of our loveliest trees, both in flower and when the autumn leaves turn first yellow and then crimson. Cultivated sweet cherries are derived mainly from this wild cherry. The **Sour Cherry** (*P. cerasus*), from which the Morello cherries originate, is usually a hedgerow shrub and differs further in its smaller (5–8 cm long), firmer, and non-drooping leaves, its smaller flowers, and acid fruit. It is found throughout the British Isles but is rare in Northern England and Eastern Scotland. The fruit ripens in July.

WHITEBEAMS, SERVICE TREES, and MOUNTAIN ASHES (*Sorbus*); ill. pp. 20, 24. These are deciduous trees, related to apples and hawthorns, with alternate simple or compound leaves and early-falling stipules. The small white flowers, massed in flat-topped clusters in May–June, are followed, in September, by small berry-like fruits, usually red, orange, or brown, each with 2–5 single-seeded compartments. Seeds germinate only after winter-chilling, and the seed-leaves emerge during germination. (For introduced species see p. 175.)

2 **Common Whitebeam** (*S. aria*) is a wide-crowned tree 20 m or more high, with simple oval or elliptical leaves 5–12 cm long, their margins rather irregularly toothed or shallowly lobed, except near the base, and the underside densely felted with white hairs, as also are the young twigs. The fruit is crimson, globular or longer than broad, 8–15 mm. The bark is dark grey with shallow fissures. Whitebeam is found in woods and scrub on chalk and limestone south of a line from Hertfordshire to the Wye Valley, but much planted elsewhere. The opening leaf-buds are stiffly erect and resemble white magnolia flowers. Besides the rather variable *S. aria* there are several other whitebeams mostly confined to quite small areas and differing from *S. aria* and from each other in details of the shape and marginal toothing of the leaves and the size, shape, colour, and lenticel-pattern of the fruit. The most widespread is the **Cliff Whitebeam** (*S. rupicola*) (ill. p. 72), of limestone cliffs in the north and west. Its leaves are widest beyond the middle, blunt-ended and with a long-tapering wedge-shaped base, there being no marginal teeth in the lower third to half of the leaf. The fruit is broader than long, 12–15 mm. This and the other local whitebeams are apomictic, yielding fruit without being pollinated, and therefore much less variable than *S. aria* itself which has to be pollinated in the ordinary way.

Wild Service Tree (*S. torminalis*); ill. p. 173. This is a broad-crowned tree to 25 m with dark-grey fissured bark and twigs white-felted only when young. The leaves are 7–10 cm, about as broad as long, with 3–4 pairs of finely-toothed, long-pointed, triangular lobes, the lowest pair deeper and more wide-spreading than the others; the underside of the leaf becomes hairless or nearly so. The fruit is 12–16 mm, longer than broad, brown when ripe. This is a rather local tree of woods on clay or limestone from Cumbria and Lincolnshire southwards. The autumn leaves turn through yellow to orange and finally terracotta. Whitebeams in South-western England and Ireland with distinctly lobed leaves, greyish rather than white beneath, and with orange-brown fruits, may have originated from crosses between true whitebeam and wild service tree.

3 Mountain Ash or **Rowan** (*S. aucuparia*) is a narrow-crowned tree to 15 m or more high, with greyish shining bark. The leaves are 10–25 cm long, pinnately compound, usually with 6–7 pairs of finely-toothed oblong leaflets. They differ from those of true ash in being alternate (not in opposite pairs) and in the deeper toothing of the leaflets. The winter-buds are 10–15 mm long, asymmetrically pointed, purplish-brown, hairy. The small bright-red fruits are ripe in September, when they are taken greedily by birds. Rowan-berry jelly is often eaten with game. Mountain ash is found all over the country in woods and hedgerows on a wide range of soils from calcareous to very poor and acid. It is frost-resistant and can thrive on high mountain ledges if out of reach of sheep and deer. It was formerly planted to protect dwellings from witches and is now widely grown as an ornamental tree. Crosses with whitebeam are not infrequent and may have given rise to some of the very local populations with pinnate-lobed leaves, grey-felted beneath, and scarlet berries.

ASHES (*Fraxinus*); ill. pp. 20, 24. Ashes are deciduous trees with fissured bark and usually pinnately compound leaves borne in opposite and decussate pairs; they have no stipules. The flowers have both sepals and petals, sepals only, or neither; and there are usually separate male and female flowers, either on the same or different trees, but some bisexual flowers are also found in several species. There are only 2 stamens. The fruit is a 1 (–2)-seeded nut with a long narrow wing from its top end. The seed-leaves emerge from the germinating seed. The only native species is:

4 European Ash (*F. excelsior*). This tree reaches 25 m or more, its grey bark smooth at first but soon acquiring shallow vertical fissures. The upper branches ascend to form a rounded crown, but the lower tend to curve downwards, sometimes almost vertically, then to turn upwards near their tips. The twigs are a pale slightly greenish-grey but can appear gold-tinged in winter sunshine. They are characteristically stout and are distinctly flattened close to the "nodes" where pairs of leaves or leaf-scars with their axillary buds are borne. The plane of flattening at any node is parallel to the line through its two buds, and is therefore at right angles to the plane at the next nodes above and below it. The leaves are up to 30 cm long with a terminal and 3–6 pairs of lateral leaflets, each about 7 cm long, elliptical and shallow-toothed. The leaves open late and fall early while still green, the leaflets separating from the central stalk. The flowers are in purplish clusters, opening in April–May before the leaves and having neither sepals nor petals. Some trees bear chiefly male and others chiefly female flowers, but some have about equal numbers of each and there may be some bisexual flowers. The crowded purple-black stamens make the newly exposed male clusters resemble ripe blackberries. Pollination is by wind and the fruits develop into the familiar "keys", at first green but later brown, that hang down in dense clusters from "female" trees until they are detached and blown away during winter and early spring. They are said to germinate at once if gathered green, but most germinate only in the second spring after shedding, a few in the first spring.

Ash grows throughout the country on a wide range of soils except the poorest and most acid, but it is especially characteristic of woods and scrub on moist well-drained fertile soils and on calcareous soils that are not too dry: it is a frequent colonist of limestone screes. The timber is tough, resilient, and readily bent, and was valued for making ploughs, harrows, and oars; it is still much used for furniture. It coppices freely and stool-shoots make excellent tool handles and hockey-sticks. Leafy branches used formerly to be given to stock as fodder, a practice still continued in parts of the Lake District, where pollarded ashes are a not uncommon sight. The leaves of ash are readily blackened and killed by late spring frosts. (For introduced ashes see p. 198.)

24

1 WILD CHERRY (*Prunus avium*)   2 COMMON WHITEBEAM (*Sorbus aria*)   3 MOUNTAIN ASH (*S. aucuparia*)
7 SWEET CHESTNUT (*Castanea sativa*)   8 SCOTS PINE (*Pinus sylvestris*)   9 YEW (*Taxus baccata*).
Bark, winter twigs, flowers, fruits, and leaves × ⅔. See also pp. 20–1; text pp. 22–3, 26–7

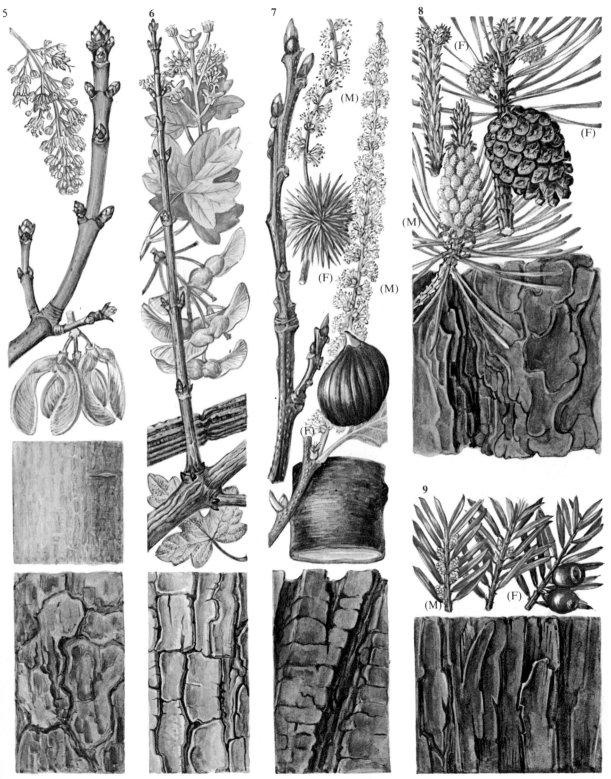

4 EUROPEAN ASH (*Fraxinus excelsior*)   5 SYCAMORE (*Acer pseudoplatanus*)   6 FIELD MAPLE (*A. campestre*)
Note: Two aspects of bark are shown where young bark (above) differs from older bark (below). (M)=male; (F)=female.

MAPLES (*Acer*); ill. pp. 21, 25. Maples are deciduous trees and shrubs with the often palmately-lobed leaves borne in opposite and decussate pairs; they have no stipules. The green or yellowish flowers may appear to be bisexual but some have non-opening stamens and some non-functional ovaries. In most maples the flowers produce nectar and pollination is by insects, but box elder (*A. negundo*—ill. p. 188) has male and female flowers on different trees and pollination is by wind. The fruit is of 2 single-seeded winged halves, still attached when shed so that the 2 twisted wings cause the whole to rotate and descend slowly, meanwhile being carried by the wind to varying distances from the parent tree: the halves separate later. The long narrow seed-leaves emerge during germination.

5–6 **Sycamore** (*A. pseudoplatanus*) (**5**) and **Field Maple** (*A. campestre*) (**6**). Of the two maples found in natural vegetation in this country only field maple is truly native; the sycamore, though now very widespread, appears to have been introduced only during late mediaeval times, perhaps in the thirteenth or fourteenth century and perhaps first in Scotland. The field maple is usually a small tree though occasionally reaching 25 m, but the sycamore can be a magnificent tree with a dense broadly rounded crown and a height of 30 m or more. Their main differences are shown in the table below.

Field maple is scattered in woods and scrub on good fertile soils, whether calcareous or non-calcareous, and also in hedgerows on a rather wider range of soil types. It seems native throughout England from Cumbria and Durham southwards but is rare in the north and in Cornwall, rather local in Wales, and probably only planted in Scotland and Ireland. Sycamore appears to have been planted extensively from the late sixteenth century but only as an ornamental tree in parks and gardens, and it was not until the end of the eighteenth century that it was much planted in woods. Since then it has become thoroughly naturalized and even a troublesome weed of cleared and open woodland. It thrives best on well-drained fertile soils but is found on any but the poorest and most acid. It is more tolerant of exposure to strong wind and to salt spray than most native trees and has been much planted to give shelter to houses and farm buildings in the uplands of the north and west, where there are many fine specimens. The whitish shining wood is easy to work and is used in furniture-making and turnery. Leaves are often disfigured with black patches caused by a fungus, *Rhytisma acerinum*. This "tar-spot" disease is less severe where there is heavy industrial air-pollution.

	Field Maple	Sycamore
Bark	Pale grey, smooth, but later developing shallow fissures	Grey, smooth, later scaling to reveal buff or orange underbark
Twigs	Pale brown, hairy, but later often developing corky ridges	Pale brown, hairless, not developing corky ridges
Winter-buds	5 mm, brown	Up to 12 mm, greenish
Leaf-blade	4–7 cm, pale green and hairy beneath, with (3–) 5 blunt lobes, untoothed or nearly so	7–16 cm, bluish and hairless beneath, with 5 pointed irregularly toothed lobes
Leaf-stalk	2–8 cm long, with milky juice	10–20 cm long, no milky juice
Flowers	10–20 in an open, erect, branching cluster, opening in May–June	60–100 in a dense, hanging, catkin-like panicle, opening in April–June
Fruit	Usually hairy, with wings straight and aligned	Hairless, with wings at an angle of 50–60°

SWEET CHESTNUT

7 Sweet or **Spanish Chestnut** (*Castanea sativa*); ill. pp. 21, 25. The sweet chestnuts are closely related to beech and oak and are deciduous trees with simple alternate leaves whose stipules fall early. Sweet chestnut is the only European species. It seems to have been introduced into this country in Roman times and is now well established, especially in the south-eastern counties. It is a large broad-crowned tree up to 30 m, with fissured grey-brown bark, the fissures often running spirally down the trunk. The twigs are olive-brown, more or less hairless, angled. The winter-buds are 4–5 mm long, plump and blunt. The leaves are 10–25 cm, oblong-elliptical with a long-pointed tip, large regular sharply pointed marginal teeth, and both surfaces hairless in the mature leaf; the leaf-stalk is up to 3 cm long. The conspicuous yellowish obliquely erect catkins are 12–20 cm long and open in July. The lower catkins on a fertile shoot are of male flowers only, each with 12–20 golden-yellow stamens; the upper catkins have a few female flowers at the base, the rest being male. The female flowers are in groups of 3, each group in a cup covered with long prickly scales. Pollination is by insects seeking pollen and attracted by the pleasant smell, not by wind as in the earlier-flowering oak and beech. The single-seeded fruits, up to 3 per cup, are the familiar brown chestnuts, released when the prickly green cup splits into 2–4 lobes. The seed-leaves remain inside the seed, as in oak. The ripe fruits, which appear in July, are formed here only in good warm summers and more often in South-eastern England than elsewhere. Sweet chestnut is not much grown for large timber but is coppiced extensively for poles used in particular for making split-chestnut fencing.

SCOTS PINE

8 Scots Pine (*Pinus sylvestris*); ill. pp. 21, 25. This is our only native pine. It formed forests over much of the country until about 8000 years ago. Native pine forests are now confined to the Scottish Highlands (pp. 78–9), though trees of true Scottish stock have been planted extensively during recent decades. In the broad sense Scots pine is an evergreen tree reaching 40 m or more, with bark dark below but scaling off to leave the upper parts of trunk and main branches a very distinctive reddish-orange colour. The leaves or "needles" are in pairs on short-shoots and are 3–7 cm long, blue-green, and twisted. The small male cones are massed in oval clusters and the female are in groups of 2–5 at the ends of strong shoots, each only 3–4 mm long at first, erect and crimson. After pollination at the end of May the cone-scales, separated until then, enlarge at their ends and so seal the cone which soon becomes directed downwards. It turns green and grows to about 12 mm long by the end of the season, resuming growth in the following spring to reach a final length of 3–7 cm. During the second growing season it is easy to see, at the exposed end of the cone-scale, a brownish transversely diamond-shaped central area, developed during the first season and surrounded by the green addition of the current season. Fertilization takes place in June of the second year and then the cone becomes woody, drying out and turning brown by autumn. During winter and early spring the winged seeds, 2 on each cone-scale, are gradually released when the cone-scales gape open in dry spells. The dozen or so seed-leaves, long and very narrow, emerge from the germinating seed. True Scots pine (*P. sylvestris* var. *scotica*) retains a pyramidal crown for longer than the central European forms, becoming rounded rather than flattened in old trees. Both leaves and cones are short, only about 4 cm long. (For introduced pines see pp. 114–15, 123.)

YEW

9 Yew (*Taxus baccata*); ill. pp. 21, 25. This is our only other native tree-conifer; juniper is at best a tall shrub and may be almost prostrate. Yew is a long-lived, evergreen, short-trunked tree which can reach 20 m in height, though it is usually not so tall. The reddish-brown bark of the short thick trunk is thin and scaly. The short-stalked leaves are 1–3 cm long, narrow and abruptly short-pointed, dark glossy green above, paler beneath. They are borne all round the green shoots but are twisted into 2 horizontal rows. Male and female cones are usually on different trees. The male are tiny clusters of "stamens" each bearing 5–9 pollen-sacs, and the pollen is shed in March or April; the female are small spindle-shaped ovules with enclosing scales, directed downwards from the undersides of shoots. By October the olive-brown seeds are each surrounded by a bright crimson fleshy cup which attracts birds. The 2 seed-leaves emerge from the germinating seed. The leaves, bark, and seeds (but not the fleshy cup) are poisonous to man and livestock.
Yew grows in woods and scrub especially on chalk and limestone but also on some good non-calcareous soils: locally it is the main or only component of woods (p. 70). It is especially characteristic of cliff-faces and cliff-edges on limestone. (Horticultural varieties are described on p. 135.)

scale for trees 1, 2, 3, 4, 5, 6, 7, & 8

1 MIDLAND HAWTHORN (*Crataegus laevigata*) 2 COMMON HAWTHORN (*C. monogyna*) 3 SLOE (*Prunus spinosa*)
7 SEA BUCKTHORN (*Hippophaë rhamnoides*) 8 SPINDLE TREE (*Euonymus europaeus*).

4   6   7   8

(M)

(F)

(F)

(M)

BIRD CHERRY (*P. padus*)   5 CRAB APPLE (*Malus sylvestris*)   6 PURGING BUCKTHORN (*Rhamnus catharticus*)

(M) = male flowers; (F) = female flowers. Details of bark, winter twigs, flowers, fruit, and leaves × ⅔. Text pp. 30–1

NATIVE BRITISH SHRUBS AND SMALL TREES: Deciduous

HAWTHORNS (*Crataegus*); ill. p. 28. Hawthorns are deciduous shrubs and small trees with rough brown bark and simple alternate stipulate leaves, which are usually lobed and toothed. They commonly have spine-tipped lateral branches of varying lengths. The white or pink bisexual flowers are in corymbs and are insect-pollinated. They usually have about 20 stamens and 1–5 styles. The ripe fruits appear in August–October: they are red to orange, berry-like but with 1–5 stones, each single-seeded. The remains of the sepals are at the top end of the fruit. There are two native species. (For introduced hawthorns see p. 174.)

1–2 **Midland Hawthorn** (*C. laevigata*) (**1**) and **Common Hawthorn**, **Whitethorn**, or **May** (*C. monogyna*) (**2**). The Midland hawthorn is chiefly a woodland shrub, growing occasionally in hedges. It is much the less common of the two, rare in the north and west and doubtfully native in Scotland. Hybrids between the two are frequent near woods where Midland hawthorn grows. Garden plants with double red or pink flowers are usually forms of Midland hawthorn. Common hawthorn, which usually flowers about a week later than Midland hawthorn, in May–June, is an abundant component of woodland and scrub all over the country and is by far our commonest hedgerow shrub (pp. 98–9). Both species may grow either as shrubs or as trees, occasionally as much as 10 m high. The strong spines afford some protection against grazing animals (p. 58). It has long been regarded as unlucky to bring hawthorn blossom into a house.

The table below shows the chief differences (leaves from short-shoots should be examined).

	Midland Hawthorn	Common Hawthorn
Leaves:		
lobes	Rarely reaching halfway to midrib; rounded, wider than long, toothed	Usually reaching more than halfway to midrib; pointed, longer than wide, untoothed or hardly toothed
underside	No tufts of hairs in vein-angles	Tufts or hairs in vein-angles
main veins	Straight or curving upwards	Curving downwards
base	Margins usually somewhat convex	Margins straight or slightly convex
size	1·5–5 cm	1·5–3·5 cm
Flowers:		
number in corymb	Rarely more than 10	Up to 16—sometimes more
length of petal	5–8 mm	4–6 mm
Styles, and stones in fruit	2, occasionally 3	Usually 1

SLOE and BIRD CHERRY

3 **Sloe** or **Blackthorn** (*Prunus spinosa*); ill. p. 28. This and the bird cherry (**4**) belong to different sections of the large genus *Prunus* (see also pp. 22, 142–3, 178–9, 182). Sloe is a spiny shrub which can reach 4 m high but is usually smaller. It suckers freely and often forms large thickets. The twigs soon become hairless and dark-coloured, almost black, and their short lateral branches develop spiny tips. The leaves are 2–4 cm long, short-stalked, elliptical or obovate, with shallow marginal teeth. The pure white flowers cover the bushes in March or April, before the leaves appear, and arise singly or in pairs from buds along the side branches. The petals are 5–8 mm long. The fruit is almost globular, 10–15 mm across, blue-black with a whitish bloom, the flesh greenish and very acid; it ripens in September–October. In some parts of the country the **Bullace** (*P. domestica* subspecies *institia*) is much naturalized in hedgerows but can be distinguished from sloe by its densely hairy young twigs and larger leaves and fruit, the latter commonly 2–5 cm across and sometimes red, yellow, or green when ripe. Both sloe and bullace occur throughout the British Isles. Seedlings from garden plums (*P. domestica*) often occur in hedges.

4 **Bird Cherry** (*P. padus*); ill. p. 29. This is a deciduous shrub or small tree, occasionally growing up to 15 m high, with dark brown peeling bark. The leaves are 5–10 cm long, elliptical or obovate, long-pointed, rounded at the base, sharp-toothed, usually hairless; they are characteristically dull and wrinkled above. The leaf-stalk is 1–2 cm long, with a pair of glands close to the leaf-blade. Sub-erect or drooping racemes, 7–15 cm long, each with 10–40 flowers, appear in May or June: the petals are white, 4–6 mm long, and jagged-toothed. The cherry-like fruit is 6–8 mm long, egg-shaped, black, and astringent; it ripens in July–August. Bird cherry occurs in woods, scrub, and hedgerows in Scotland, Northern England, and Wales but is rare and local elsewhere. It is very attractive during its short flowering period and strikingly different from our other cherries in its long racemes of flowers. The leaves turn red in autumn.

CRAB APPLE

5 **Crab Apple** (*Malus sylvestris*); ill. p. 28. This is one of the ancestors of cultivated apples. It is a small deciduous tree growing to 10 m high, or sometimes a shrub, with cracking and scaling grey-brown bark. The twigs are reddish-brown and have many short-shoots. The leaves are 3–4 cm long, ovate, toothed; the leaf-stalk is up to 2 cm. The flowers are white, usually pink-tinged, appearing in umbel-like clusters of 4–7 in May. The fruit, which ripens in October, is almost globular, 2 cm or more across, green but flushed and streaked with red, with the persistent sepals at the top end. It usually sets fruit only if cross-pollinated. Crab apple occurs in woods, scrub, and hedgerows throughout the country. The true crab apple differs from descendants of cultivated apples in being thorny, having hairless leaves, flower-stalks, sepals, and fruit, having petals only 2 cm long or less, and bearing very acid apples only about 2 cm across. Established seedlings from orchard apples are rarely thorny, have leaves persistently hairy beneath, densely hairy flower-stalks, sepals, and young fruits, and have larger and sweeter fruits. (For ornamental crab apples see p. 183.)

BUCKTHORNS and SEA BUCKTHORN

6 **Purging Buckthorn** (*Rhamnus catharticus*); ill. p. 29. This is a thorny deciduous shrub or small tree, commonly reaching 4–6 m, with the bark of old stems fissured and scaling. A knife-cut parallel to the surface reveals an orange-coloured under-bark. The branches are in nearly opposite pairs almost at right angles to the main stem, many of them short-shoots and some ending in spines. The short-stalked stipulate leaves vary from alternate to almost opposite but most are crowded on short-shoots. They are simple, 3–6 cm long, ovate or elliptical, with toothed margins and with their main side veins curving upwards towards the leaf tip: they turn yellow or brownish before falling in autumn. The greenish and inconspicuous flowers, only 4 mm across, are usually in axillary clusters, male and female on different plants; they appear in May–June. In male flowers the 4 stamens are opposite the 4 tiny green petals. Pollination is by insects and the black berry-like fruits, which appear in October–November, are 6–10 mm across with 3–4 stones, each single-seeded: the seed-leaves emerge during germination. The fruits, like the bark, are strongly purgative. Purging buckthorn is native in woodland, scrub, and hedgerows on calcareous soils and fen-peat over much of England, Wales, and Ireland, but rare in Northern England and doubtfully native in Scotland.

Alder Buckthorn (*Frangula alnus*), which grows to 4–5 m, is a related shrub but shows a lemon-yellow under-bark when slashed, and has untoothed leaves widest well beyond the middle, and bisexual greenish flowers in May–June. The seed-leaves remain within the germinating seed. The wood yields the best charcoal for making gunpowder. For illustrations and ecological notes see pp. 80–3. Alder buckthorn is local in England and Wales, rare in Ireland, and absent from Scotland.

7 **Sea Buckthorn** (*Hippophaë rhamnoides*); ill. p. 29. This is a thorny deciduous shrub up to 3 m high, which suckers freely. The simple alternate leaves are up to 8 cm long, very narrow, untoothed, almost sessile. They are covered on both sides with silvery scales. The greenish flowers appear before the leaves in March–April and are very small, with separate male and female flowers on different plants. The male flowers have 4 stamens. Pollination is by wind and the bright orange fruits, which appear from September onwards, are 6–8 mm across, berry-like but enclosing the single-seeded ovary. A colonist of fixed sand-dunes, it is native along the east coast from Berwickshire to Kent but much planted elsewhere. It is attractive both for the silvery willow-like leaves and the clusters of orange fruits, the setting of which depends on the proximity of a male plant. The roots of sea buckthorn have nitrogen-fixing organisms in nodules like those of leguminous plants.

SPINDLE TREE

Spindle Tree (*Euonymus europaeus*); ill. p. 29. Usually a shrub, but occasionally a small tree reaching 6 m, this has opposite deciduous leaves and smooth grey bark. The twigs and winter-buds are green and 4-angled. The leaves are simple, 3–8 cm long, more or less elliptical, with shallow rounded teeth; the leaf-stalk is 6–12 mm long. Flowers are borne in May–June in long-stalked axillary cymes of usually 3; each is about 1 cm across and has 4 green petals. They are mostly bisexual, 4 stamens alternating with the petals, their bases in a fleshy nectar-secreting ring round the ovary. They are insect-pollinated. The ripe fruits, which appear in September–October, are flattened, 4-lobed, pink, 10–15 mm across, splitting open to reveal seeds each enclosed in a fleshy orange coat. Spindle tree occurs in woods and scrub, especially on calcareous soil, throughout the British Isles but is rare in Northern England and in Scotland reaches only the midland valley. The wood was formerly used for spindles for wool-spinning and for butchers' skewers.

scale for trees 1, 2, 3, 4, 5, 6, & 7

m 4

3

2

1

0

1

2

3

4

(F)

(M)

(M)
2

(F)
2

(M)
3

(F)
3

1 HAZEL (*Corylus avellana*)   2 GREAT SALLOW (*Salix caprea*)   3 COMMON SALLOW (*S. cinerea*)
7 GUELDER ROSE (*V. opulus*).   (M) = male catkins; (F) = female catkins. Details of bark, winter twigs, flowers, fruits,

4 DOGWOOD (*Cornus sanguinea*) and leaves × ⅔. Text pp. 34–5   5 ELDER (*Sambucus nigra*)   6 WAYFARING TREE (*Viburnum lantana*)

NATIVE BRITISH SHRUBS AND TREES: Deciduous

HAZELS (*Corylus*); ill. p. 32. These are deciduous shrubs and trees with simple alternate leaves and early-falling stipules. The winter-buds are usually blunt and expose many stipular scales. Male and female flowers are in separate groups on the same plant, the male in slender drooping many-flowered catkins, the female in short erect few-flowered and bud-like spikes with only their red styles visible beyond the enclosing scales. The male flowers are borne singly in the axils of the catkin-scales, each with 4–8 split stamens but neither sepals nor petals. The female are in pairs and consist of an ovary surmounted by a small lobed perianth. Pollination is by wind. The fruit is a hard-shelled nut in a green leafy cup, variously cut or lobed. The seed-leaves remain within the germinating seed.

1 Hazel (*C. avellana*). Although most familiar as a coppiced shrub up to about 6 m, hazel is sometimes seen as a small tree with smooth brown bark peeling in thin strips. The young twigs are densely covered with reddish hairs and the buds are plumply ovoid, about 4 mm long. The leaves are 5–12 cm long, almost round, with a heart-shaped base and abruptly pointed tip, the margins sharply toothed or with shallow toothed lobes and the surfaces somewhat hairy, especially the underside. They are usually in 2 rows. Flowers appear before the leaves in February or even earlier. The long pendulous pale yellow male catkins, "lambs'-tails", are 2–8 cm long, while the tiny red-tipped female spikes are 3–5 mm long. The male catkins soon fall but the female persist while the 1–4 nuts enlarge and ripen in deeply lobed green cups from which they fall when ripe in early autumn. Large birds, squirrels, and mice may drop or store nuts, thus aiding dispersal and germination. Hazel is native throughout the British Isles. (For introduced species see p. 154.)

SALLOWS (*Salix*); ill. p. 32. These are broad-leaved willows, sufficiently shade-tolerant to live under a woodland canopy and less restricted to wet places than most willows. They resemble other willows in having deciduous stipulate leaves and insect-pollinated flowers in catkins, with separate male and female catkins on different plants. The flowers have neither sepals nor petals, but have small nectaries that attract bees. The ripe fruits split open to release large numbers of tiny seeds with long silky hairs that make them readily wind-carried. Most willow seeds can germinate only within a few days of being shed.

The flowers of sallows are borne singly in the axils of crowded silky-hairy and black-tipped catkin-scales, and the catkins are short and held almost erect. The flowering shoots are the "pussy willows" or "palm" gathered for decorating homes and churches on Palm Sunday; they appear in March–April. We have two sallows that may grow as trees up to 10 m high or as shrubs, both with rather stout twigs and ascending branches.

2-3 Great Sallow or **Goat Willow** (*S. caprea*) (**2**) and **Common** or **Grey Sallow** (*S. cinerea*) (**3**). Both are common throughout the British Isles and both have ovate or elliptical leaves with margins often wavy but untoothed or scarcely toothed; their stipules usually fall early. Difficulties in distinguishing them sometimes arise from the not infrequent hybrids with intermediate characters. Moreover the grey sallow is very variable. The table below refers to the widespread form, but another form, lacking rusty hairs and soft to the touch on the underside of the leaf, is found locally—especially in the East Anglian fens.

	Great Sallow	Common Sallow
Twigs	Brown, hairless by autumn. Surface of wood beneath bark smoothly cylindrical	Blackish, remaining hairy. Surface of wood beneath bark distinctly ridged
Size and shape of leaves	5–10 cm long, broadly ovate or elliptical, not more than twice as long as broad; tip abruptly pointed and turned downwards	2·5–7 cm long, narrowly ovate to elliptical, usually more than twice as long as broad; tip blunt or pointed, not turned downwards
Underside of leaf	Softly and densely covered with short grey hairs; not blue-green	Rather thinly hairy, not soft to the touch and some or all of the hairs rust-coloured; blue-green

DOGWOOD and ELDER

4 Dogwood (*Cornus sanguinea*); ill. p. 32. This deciduous freely suckering shrub up to 4 m high often forms large thickets. Its twigs are conspicuously red, at least on the south-facing side. The leaves are opposite and decussate, 4–8 cm long, broadly elliptical but with a rounded base and long-pointed tip; they are thinly covered on both sides with prostrate hairs and have an untoothed margin. The main side veins curve up towards the leaf tip, and if the two ends of a leaf are carefully pulled apart, the halves remain connected by delicate threads from the vein. The leaves turn purple-red in autumn. The creamy-white flowers, which are bisexual and insect-pollinated, are borne in many-flowered corymbs in June–July. The 4 petals are 4–6 mm long, and the 4 stamens alternate with them. In September the fruit ripens: it is black, almost globular, 6–8 mm across, the 2-celled stone having a seed in each cell. Dogwood grows in woods and scrub, and sometimes in hedges, especially on calcareous soils. It is common in Southern England and Wales but is not native in Scotland; it is local in Ireland. (For introduced species see p. 151.)

5 Elder or **Bourtree** (*Sambucus nigra*); ill. p. 33. This is a deciduous shrub or small tree up to 10 m high, with deeply fissured, softly corky, grey-brown bark. Long branches arise from the base and later arch back towards the ground. The twigs are stout and soon become grey with prominent lenticels. The leaves are opposite and decussate, pinnate, with a terminal leaflet and usually 2–3 pairs of lateral leaflets, each 3–9 cm long, narrowly ovate to elliptical, long-pointed, toothed. The leaves and twigs have a characteristic and rather unpleasant smell. The small creamy-white bisexual flowers, 5 mm across, are massed in large corymbs, 10–20 cm across, in June–July. They are pollinated by small insects and the numerous purple-black fruits, ripening in August–September, are berry-like but with 1–3 single-seeded stones; they are used for making jam, jelly, and wine. Elder is found all over the British Isles, especially in woods, scrub, and hedges near human dwellings, where it behaves as a shrubby weed, thriving on disturbed and especially on dunged soil. Rabbits and domestic stock avoid eating it.

GUELDER ROSES (*Viburnum*); ill. p. 33. This large genus of woody plants, related to elder, extends over much of the northern hemisphere though chiefly in the temperate zone. Many species are cultivated for ornament (p. 143). The simple leaves are opposite and decussate. The usually small flowers are in umbels or corymbs, white or pink, with the 5 petals joined into a tube below and the stamens alternating with them. The fruit is berry-like but has one single-seeded stone. There are two native species, both deciduous shrubs.

Wayfaring Tree (*V. lantana*) (**6**) and **Guelder Rose** (*V. opulus*) (**7**). Wayfaring tree is a common component of scrub on chalk and limestone in Southern and South-eastern England (p. 59) and a few areas in Wales but is absent from the rest of the British Isles. Guelder rose occurs in woodlands, scrub, and hedges on fertile moist soils throughout the British Isles with a preference for valley-bottom alluvium and fen-peat (pp. 82–3). It can spread by layering. In its cultivated forms (the so-called snowball tree) the globular inflorescences are composed exclusively of large sterile flowers like the marginal flowers of the wild shrub.

Both wayfaring tree and guelder rose have flowers in corymbs 5–10 cm across but differ in several ways as shown in the table below.

	Wayfaring Tree	Guelder Rose
Twigs	Densely covered with scale-like stellate hairs	Hairless
Buds	Enclosed in unopened ordinary leaves, not bud-scales	Having specialized bud-scales
Stipules	None	Narrow and pointed
Size and shape of leaves	5–10 cm long, ovate, heart-shaped at base, often blunt-tipped; margin toothed	5–8 cm long, with 3(–5) long-pointed toothed lobes
Leaf surfaces	Densely stellate-hairy beneath	Smooth and hairless
Leaf-stalk	No glands	2 conspicuous glands close to the blade
Flowers	All cream-coloured and similar in size, 6 mm across; in May–June	Most cream-coloured and 6 mm across, but outer row white and much larger, 15–20 mm across and sterile; in June–July
Ripe fruits	Dull red to almost black, July–September	Pale transparent red, September–October

scale for trees 1, 2, 3, 4, 5, 6, & 7

m 7
6
5
4
3
2
1
0

1

2

3

3

3

(F)

(M)

(F)

4

1 STRAWBERRY TREE (*Arbutus unedo*)　2 HOLLY (*Ilex aquifolium*)　3 GORSE (*Ulex europaeus*)
7 COMMON PRIVET (*Ligustrum vulgare*).　(M) = male flowers; (F) = female flowers. Details of bark, leaves, flowers,

6

7

(M)

(F)

4 BROOM (*Cytisus scoparius*) 5 JUNIPER (*Juniperus communis*) 6 BOX (*Buxus sempervirens*)
and fruit × ⅔. Text pp. 38–9

NATIVE BRITISH SHRUBS AND TREES: Evergreen

1 **Strawberry Tree** (*Arbutus unedo*); ill. p. 36. Our largest member of the heather family is a shrub or small tree often reaching 8 m in height and occasionally 12 m. It has thin, reddish, irregularly peeling bark and the simple alternate laurel-like leaves are 4–10 cm long, elliptical, pointed at the tip and with a toothed margin; they are dark green and shining above, paler beneath. The flowers, opening in autumn and early winter, are in terminal panicles, 5 cm long, of 40–50 flowers. The petals are joined to form a flask-shaped white or pink-tinged corolla with 5 very small rounded and rolled-back teeth. The fruit is a warty red berry, 1·5–2 cm across, not unlike a strawberry; it ripens in September–December of the following year. Strawberry tree is native only in Western Ireland and especially near Killarney, where it grows in rocky places in scrub and developing woodland but does not survive the shade of mature oak-wood. The fruits are regarded by some as having a pleasant flavour; a few are taken by birds but many fall uneaten. It is often grown as an ornamental tree, as are other species of *Arbutus*.

2 **Holly** (*Ilex aquifolium*); ill. p. 36. This is a shrub or small tree up to 15 m high but occasionally much larger, with smooth grey bark which eventually becomes finely fissured. The twigs are green and hairless. The leaves are alternate, simple, 3–10 cm long, elliptical-oblong; they have a wavy and usually spiny margin, but on old or strongly shaded trees there is often only a terminal spine; they are dark glossy green above, paler beneath, and hairless. The leaves are short-stalked and have minute black stipules. The insect-pollinated flowers open in May–June: they are 6 mm across, their white petals joined below into a short tube, and grow in small axillary clusters. There are usually separate male and female flowers on different trees, the male with 4 stamens and a functionless ovary, the female with abortive stamens and one 4-celled ovary ripening in September–March to a scarlet berry-like fruit with 3 or 4 single-seeded stones. The seeds germinate only in the second or third spring after shedding, and the seed-leaves emerge from the seed. Holly is native over almost the whole of the British Isles in woodland, scrub, and hedges over a wide range of soil types, from calcareous to very poor and acid, and locally forming almost pure woods. It is more abundant on the west side of the country than the east. Holly may suffer frost damage in very severe winters like that of 1962–3. The wood is white, very dense, and even-grained, and was formerly used for carving engravers' blocks and for inlay work. The twigs yielded bird-lime. The most important use of holly was however as winter feed for sheep and other stock, and trees were pollarded for this purpose, especially in parts of the north and west. For holly as a hedge plant see pp. 98–9. Some hybrid hollies are described on p. 138.

3 **Gorse** or **Furze** (*Ulex europaeus*); ill. p. 36. This is a densely spiny shrub reaching 2 m or more in height, with narrow spine-tipped leaves and with most of the axillary branches appearing as rigid, deeply furrowed spines only 1·5–2·5 cm long but bearing a few leaves and further branch-spines. The seedling leaves are compound, comprising 3 leaflets. There are no stipules. The golden-yellow pea-like flowers appear in small numbers all through the year but the main flowering period is the spring. They are 1·5 cm long and are borne in the axils of leaves on the spines. Their 10 stamens are all the same length and the style does not coil up as strongly as in broom, though the flower explodes in much the same way when a bee alights. The ripe pod is blackish but only 1·5 cm long, and it opens with a crack audible some metres away. The seeds, like those of broom, have a "fat-body" and are ant-dispersed. Gorse is found all over the British Isles, especially on the lighter non-calcareous soils, but not in woods. It is a valuable winter feed for stock and seems to have been planted for this purpose in many areas.

Western Gorse (*U. gallii*) is usually rather smaller than common gorse, flowers only in early autumn, and differs further in having only faintly furrowed spines and less brown-furry sepals. Another clear distinction is that the 2 small bracteoles on the flower-stalk are narrower than the stalk, whereas in common gorse they are wider than the stalk. It is native in Western England and Wales and just across the border into Galloway; also near the coast of East Anglia and in Ireland. In these parts it is more characteristic of open moorland and heath remote from dwellings than is common gorse. In South-eastern England it is replaced by **Dwarf Gorse** (*U. minor*)—smaller, often prostrate, with weaker spines and shorter sepals (less than 9·5 mm compared with more than 9·5 mm in western gorse).

4 **Broom** (*Cytisus scoparius*); ill. p. 36. Gorse and broom are related shrubs of the pea family (Leguminosae) and both have root-nodules with nitrogen-fixing bacteria, but broom is not spiny like gorse. It is a "switch plant", a shrub up to about 2 m high with erect angular green twigs from which the leaves soon fall. These leaves are alternate and compound, each with 3 small hairy leaflets; they have no stipules. The large lemon-yellow pea-like flowers, 2 cm long, are borne in leafy racemes in May–June. Their stamens, 5 long and 5 short, are all joined below into a tube round the style which is like a stiff spring held almost straight until a heavy bee alights and releases it. Then the flower "explodes" irreversibly, the style coiling violently upwards and pollen being scattered over the insect (there is no nectar). The fruit ripens in summer: it is a black pod 2·5–4 cm long which splits suddenly and audibly, the separated halves curling up independently and flinging the seeds some distance. Ants, attracted by a fleshy and oily swelling at one end, carry the seeds away. Broom grows throughout the British Isles on non-calcareous and especially on light or sandy soils and is a very beautiful sight when in full flower. It was formerly used for making brooms. It is now much planted to stabilize steep road-banks and to increase the fertility of their soil.

5 **Juniper** or **Savin** (*Juniperus communis*); ill. p. 37. This is one of our native conifers, a shrub varying in form from wide-spreading to narrowly erect and sometimes reaching 10 m in height. The bark is reddish-brown. The evergreen sessile leaves are in whorls of 3 and are up to 2 cm long, very narrow and tapering to a spiny tip, white-banded above, green beneath. Male and female cones are borne on different plants, the male 8 mm long, cylindrical, with about 15 "stamens" in whorls of 3; the female about 2 mm long with 3 ovules, exposed until after pollination, then sealed in. After this the whole cone enlarges slowly until it ripens, in September–October of the second or third year, to a roughly globular "berry", blue-black with a whitish bloom. These are taken, and the seeds dispersed, by birds. Juniper is scattered over the British Isles but is concentrated on the chalk of Southern England and on well-drained, not very acid, fertile rocks and soils, including soils over limestone, in parts of Wales, Northern England, Scotland, and Western Ireland: it is a feature of outcrops of the Whin Sill in North-eastern England. It flourishes in scrub but is intolerant of deep shade (see p. 58). An almost prostrate form grows on some cliffs and mountains. "Savin charcoal" from the Lake District was valued for making gunpowder.
For introduced scale-leaved junipers see p. 134.

6 **Box** (*Buxus sempervirens*); ill. p. 37. This evergreen shrub or small tree, rarely up to 10 m high, has hairy angular twigs and small opposite and decussate leathery leaves, 1–2·5 cm long, oblong to elliptical, rounded or notched at the tip, untoothed, and short-stalked. Each axillary cluster of whitish-green flowers, which open in April–May, has a single terminal female flower and several lateral male flowers, all with sepals but no petals, secreting nectar and attracting pollinating flies. The male flower has 4 stamens, the female a 3-celled ovary and 3 styles. The fruit, which ripens in September, is dry and opens suddenly to project the seeds up to 3 m away. Box is known as a component of natural vegetation only from the well-known Box Hill in Surrey and two other localities in Southern England, but has been lost from two or three places. It is known from archaeological evidence to have been present in Neolithic times. The wood is yellow and very hard. It has been much used for carving, turnery, and inlay work. For the ecology of box see pp. 70–1.

7 **Common Privet** (*Ligustrum vulgare*); ill. p. 37. This is a straggling shrub up to 5 m, with long branches that arch over and root where they make contact with the soil so that large thickets are formed. The leaves are simple, opposite, 3–6 cm long, oblong-lanceolate, short-stalked, with an untoothed margin; they are not truly evergreen but varying numbers persist through the winter. Flowers appear in June–July. They are bisexual, white, 4–5 mm across, in terminal panicles 3–6 cm long. The petals are joined into a funnel-shaped tube, from which the 2 stamens project. Privet is pollinated by insects, attracted by the fragrance and nectar. The fruit, which appears in September–October, is a shining purple-black berry, 7–8 mm across, with 2–4 seeds. Common privet occurs in woods, scrub, and hedges, especially on calcareous soils, throughout England and Wales but is uncommon in Northern England and probably not native in Scotland, though widely planted; it is locally native in Ireland on rocks and cliffs.
The privet so commonly planted for garden hedges is the broader-leaved Japanese species *L. ovalifolium* (see p. 143).
Children have been fatally poisoned by eating the berries of privet.

Hazel coppice with oak standards (April). Canopy: PEDUNCULATE OAK (*Quercus robur*), with some EUROPEAN ASH (*Fraxinus excelsior*)—background, left. Shrub layer: recently coppiced HAZEL (*Corylus avellana*). Other trees include FIELD MAPLE (*Acer campestre*)—centre, and COMMON HAWTHORN (*Crataegus monogyna*)—right. Ground-cover: DOG'S MERCURY (*Mercurialis perennis*), PRIMROSE (*Primula vulgaris*), and WOOD ANEMONE (*Anemone nemorosa*). Text pp. 42–3

ornbeam coppice with oak standards (June). Canopy: SESSILE OAK (*Quercus petraea*). Shrub layer: HORNBEAM
arpinus betulus)—old coppice. Ground-cover (sparse): BLUEBELLS (*Endymion*). Text pp. 42–3

NATIVE BRITISH WOODLAND: Coppice with Oak Standards

About half of our native or extensively naturalized woody plants seem able to grow anywhere in lowland Britain where they are not excluded by unsuitable soils or too severe wind-exposure, and most of them can be found also in one or more of the distant island groups—Orkney, Shetland, and the Outer Hebrides. Amongst the remaining half, however, there are several species that seem to reach either northern or southern climatic limits within the country. Field maple, spindle tree, dogwood, and both purging and alder buckthorn are common in Southern England and present in Wales, but become much less frequent towards the north and finally peter out just short of or just beyond the Scottish border. Small-leaved lime and wild service tree, much more local in occurrence, similarly fail to extend north of the Scottish border. Midland hawthorn and wayfaring tree are still more restricted, extending northwards only to a line roughly from the Bristol Channel to the Humber. On the other hand some species, like bird cherry and bay willow, are common in Scotland and Northern England but fail to reach Southern England, neither extending further south than Wales and East Anglia. Little is known about the precise way in which climate limits the distribution of these and other species. Most can be grown in gardens in parts of the country where they are not found in natural vegetation, but many of them fail to set good seed outside their natural range or do so in very small amounts or only at long and irregular intervals.

Climate is not the only factor determining whether a given woody species can or cannot grow in a particular spot. Wayfaring tree, for instance, grows almost exclusively on calcareous soils and especially on the chalk of South-eastern England, and it grows much more commonly in scrub and hedges than under a continuous tree-canopy. Soil and light-intensity seem therefore to be additional factors operating here, and this will be seen to be true of many woody plants. Other factors are their different degrees of vulnerability to browsing animals, their capacity to send up new shoots from the base after being coppiced, and their resistance to fire. Apart from all this, the presence or absence of individual species may depend on man's deliberate or unintentional favouring of some at the expense of others.

Oaks are a major component of woodland all over the lowland counties and on the lower slopes of many hills in the north and west, and they are also amongst the most frequent trees in hedges. We know, from the pollen grains left in datable layers of peat, that birches were the first trees to invade the low-growing vegetation of Late Glacial times some 12 000 years ago, when our climate was growing warmer after the retreat of the ice. After a period when birch-woods covered much of the country, Scots pine and hazel spread from the south. Only later still did elm and oak, followed by alder and lime, complete their migration from more distant Ice Age refuges. These then formed mixed forests with oak predominating over wide areas, and by about 5000 B.C. they had largely replaced the former birch- and pine-hazel forests. They must have been "high forest" in structure, with their tree-crowns touching and the shade beneath them too great to allow a continuous shrub layer: there would have been a sparse mixture of shrubs with a good deal of hazel on the better soils. There is in fact no lowland forest that has not been exploited by man for centuries or even millennia and therefore modified to a largely unknown extent. The commonest types of oak-woods left in lowland England today are mainly run-down forms of what were for long valuable kinds of managed forest, and especially of "coppice with standards". The coppice was of shrubs or trees cut down to the ground at regular intervals to provide long straight poles for a great variety of purposes. The standards were large trees grown for timber—commonly oaks but sometimes mixed with or replaced by ash, elm, hornbeam, or lime. Oaks were favoured for the strength and durability of their wood and also because if they were widely spaced their heavy lower branches provided the curved timbers essential for shipbuilding. It was customary—and became a statutory requirement in Tudor and Stuart times—to leave twelve oak standards to the acre (thirty per hectare) as sources of branchy timber. The selection of oak against other kinds of tree almost certainly began in earlier times and caused a gradual conversion of much mixed forest into more or less pure oak forest. The wide spacing of standards had the further consequence that light now penetrated the gappy canopy to allow an almost continuous understorey, commonly of hazel. This was coppiced at regular intervals of not less than seven years to supply slender poles for hurdle-making and stakes for hedging. Split poles made spars for thatchers and thinner stems were bent into hoops for dry casks and barrels. Anything remaining was used as firewood. In the early years after coppicing the increased illumination of the woodland floor allowed primroses, bluebells, wood anemones, and dog-violets to flower profusely. Page 40 illustrates a wood with standards of pedunculate oak over hazel coppice, once a widespread type on the better soils throughout lowland England. Now that large ships are no longer made of oak and sheep no longer kept in hurdled enclosures, and now that coal has generally replaced firewood for domestic fires, few such woods are still managed in the traditional way. Many are derelict, the hazel left uncut and felled standards no longer replaced. Some have been converted into more profitable high forest, often of planted conifers.

Coppice with standards was not invariably of hazel under pedunculate oak. The coppiced underwood might be of any useful species that survives repeated cutting to ground level, and the standards might be of the same or a different species or there might be none at all. In South-eastern England, where hornbeam is a native tree, it was often coppiced, chiefly for firewood and charcoal, though the very hard wood was also used for pulleys, cog-wheels, and axle-bearings. It can grow on a wide range of soil types but better on moderately acid than on calcareous soils. The standards over it may be either pedunculate or sessile oaks, the former usually on heavier and less acid soils than those with sessile oaks. Page 41 shows a wood in Hertfordshire with sessile oak standards over hornbeam coppice. In Epping Forest, where for centuries commoners held rights of taking firewood, the most abundant trees in some parts are hornbeams which until recently were regularly pollarded (not coppiced) to yield large branches for firewood.

Another widespread type of coppice, and one still economically valuable, is of sweet chestnut, grown chiefly for making split-chestnut fencing. If standards are present they are commonly of oak and often of sessile oak, which grows well on the acid and not too heavy soils that favour chestnut.

I Southern oak-birch heath on sands: HEATH (*Calluna*) invaded by 1 PEDUNCULATE OAK (*Quercus robur*)
2 HAIRY BIRCH (*Betula pubescens*)   3 SCOTS PINE (*Pinus sylvestris*)   4 GORSE (*Ulex europaeus*)
5 WAVY HAIR-GRASS (*Deschampsia flexuosa*).   Text pp. 46–7

II Oak-birch-pine-wood on southern sands: for diagram identifying species see p. 47. Text pp. 46–7

IA Adjacent planted roadside oaks and the pine plantation act as "seed-parents" of invading trees. The shrub by the ditch in the foreground is alder buckthorn (*Frangula alnus*). Text pp. 46–7

NATIVE BRITISH WOODLAND: Oak-Birch-wood and the Succession to Oak-wood

The sandy and gravelly soils of England are of limited agricultural value. Large areas are covered either by open "heaths", with heather and heaths as the most conspicuous plants, or by woodland in which sessile or pedunculate oak, or both together, are commonly accompanied by birch, holly, and mountain ash and frequently also by beech and Scots pine. Elsewhere there is an intermediate type of vegetation of open heath with some scattered shrubs and trees. Illustration II, pp. 44–5, shows the kind of woodland found on such soils. The trees shown include pedunculate oak with hairy birch, mountain ash, and holly; and the shrubs are chiefly hawthorn, gorse, and broom. The sparse ground-cover is of bracken, wavy hair-grass, and the pale green cushions of the moss *Leucobryum glaucum*, so characteristic of woods on very acid soils. Apart from these plants that are native in the area there is also some Scots pine, no doubt originating from the plantation nearby (ill. IA).

Illustration I, p. 44, shows a common sight on these southern sands and gravels: heath being invaded by trees and shrubs. This raises the question of how it is that open heathland should anywhere persist. There are two main factors at work: grazing by animals that eat tree-seedlings and so prevent their growing large; and fire, fatal to most young trees. Fires are a common feature of heaths. Some are started deliberately because the burnt-back heather sends out tender young shoots which afford much better grazing than the old twiggy plants; but often fires are the result of mere careless-ness. If grazing and burning are discontinued for any reason then seedlings of the larger woody plants soon appear, the first to establish themselves on these light acid soils commonly being birches. Birches are typical "pioneer trees", well-equipped biologically to colonize suitable ground made newly available for trees. Almost every year they produce very large numbers of small, winged, and readily wind-borne fruits. Their seeds germinate easily and their seedlings soon develop a strong root-system. They are the fastest-growing of our native trees and, if widely spaced, begin to bear flowers and fruit when only 10–12 years old. Both species are notably frost-resistant even as seedlings—the hairy birch extends further north in Europe than any other kind of tree—and both are also drought-resistant, silver birch more so than hairy birch. They are therefore not dependent on the protection against extremes of frost and drought that the woodland climate affords, but can survive in the open. On the other hand they normally live for only about 100 years. Our two oaks, small-leaved lime, sycamore, and yew can live for more than 400 years; only mountain ash, aspen, field maple, and hornbeam have normal life-spans of less than 150 years, like the birches. Finally birches are much more light-demanding than our other native trees. Experiments carried out nearly fifty years ago on first-year tree-seedlings, artificially shaded, showed larch and birch to be the least shade-tolerant, followed by Scots pine and alder, then oak and lime, after which came hornbeam, beech, and ash in order of increasing tolerance. It must be noted, however, that ash becomes more light-demand-ing in later years.

Illustration I, p. 44, shows other trees, as well as birch, invading a heath near the south coast: Scots pine, which resembles birch in many ecological respects and can also be a pioneer tree in suitable circumstances, and oak, favoured by the proximity of seed-parents. Oak is often a much later arrival than either birch or Scots pine because its heavy acorns are less readily dispersed than the wind-borne birch and pine. Even where oaks have arrived at this early stage the much more rapid early growth of birch and pine will certainly lead to an initial woodland with these two trees more prominent than oak. But in time the first oaks will grow steadily and others will join them in due course. The birches and pines will be unable to establish their seedlings in the shade of the oaks and will moreover die much sooner than the oaks. It may confidently be expected that after a century or so the wood will begin to look like an oak-wood with some birch and pine present, and after another century it will be still more clearly an oak-wood. In this way a "succession" of vegetation types will have occupied the same ground: heath → heath with invading birch and pine → woodland chiefly of birch and pine → woodland chiefly of oak. In this succession the pioneer trees, birch and Scots pine, are eventually superseded by oak which, as a "successor tree", is usually later to arrive, less frost-resistant but more shade-tolerant, much slower-growing, and much longer-lived.

This picture illustrates a further point about the source of succession from low-growing vegetation to woodland: shrubs, in this instance gorse, commonly play an important part. It is a familiar fact that neglected pasture or abandoned arable land is soon invaded by shrubs, though the colonizing species vary with soil type and from one part of the country to another. Blackberries and wild roses usually appear early but are soon followed by such larger shrubs as hawthorn, elder, and sloe. On shallow soil over chalk in Southern England the main colonists are wayfaring tree, dogwood, and juniper, as well as hawthorn. Shrubs are usually earlier colonists than pioneer trees. They resemble them in many respects but have some additional features equipping them still better for their pioneering role (pp. 58–9).

Species shown in colour illustration **II**, pp. 44–5: Trees and shrubs—1 PEDUNCULATE OAK (*Quercus robur*) 1a OAK sapling   2 HAIRY BIRCH (*Betula pubescens*)   3 SCOTS PINE (*Pinus sylvestris*)   4 MOUNTAIN ASH (*Sorbus aucuparia*)   5 HOLLY (*Ilex aquifolium*)   6 COMMON HAWTHORN (*Crataegus monogyna*) 7 GORSE (*Ulex europaeus*)   8 BROOM (*Cytisus scoparius*). Ground-cover (sparse)—9 MOSS (*Leucobryum glaucum*)   10 BRACKEN (*Pteridium aquilinum*)   11 WAVY HAIR-GRASS (*Deschampsia flexuosa*)

48

I Lower slopes of northern valley-side mixed woodland: for diagram identifying species see p. 51. Text pp. 50–1

II Upper slopes of wood in illustration I: SESSILE OAKS (*Quercus petraea*), with sparse MOUNTAIN ASH (*Sorbus aucuparia*), HAIRY BIRCH (*Betula pubescens*), and HOLLY (*Ilex aquifolium*). Ground-cover: WAVY HAIR-GRASS (*Deschampsia flexuosa*). Text pp. 50–1

A Distant view of same wood. Text pp. 50–1

NATIVE BRITISH WOODLAND: Northern Valley-side Oak-woods

Coppice with oak standards (pp. 42–3) seems to date from early mediaeval times, presumably replacing a much less efficient use of open forest near villages when trees were felled, pollarded, or coppiced as required and farm animals browsed and rooted at will. The change became essential with increasing rural population during the twelfth and thirteenth centuries and a growing shortage of agricultural land. Some existing coppice with standards may go back to this period, but much is undoubtedly of later plantings from Tudor times onwards, as is the majority of oak-wood in high forest. Important areas of surviving woodland, like much of the New Forest and Sherwood Forest, are within former Royal Forests and private parks, originally reserved for hunting and once very extensive but much reduced in size during sub-sequent periods of acute land-shortage and now largely on soils too light or otherwise unsuitable for arable agriculture. They include areas of former coppice and pollards where villagers exercised their common rights, as well as of old high forest, but there has been much new planting. Finally there are some woods that are of special ecological interest because they are on slopes too steep for cultivation. Some valley-side woods in Southern England extend from a plateau with light, acid, and infertile soil down a slope where the soil becomes progressively heavier, less acid, and more fertile; there is a corresponding change from high forest of sessile oak with birch and holly at the top to pedunculate oak-wood with ash, field maple, and wych elm lower down. This relationship between the two oaks is frequent in old woodland in the English lowlands, though the distinction is far from clear-cut. In the north and west, however, and also in Ireland, sessile oak is much the more common in old woodland irrespective of soil type, being found even on shallow soils over limestone and on limestone scree.

The illustrations on pp. 48–9 illustrate a type of sessile oak-wood very characteristic of valley-sides over much of Northern England and especially of Pennine valleys cut in the Millstone Grit and Coal Measure Sandstones from Derbyshire northwards. Similar woods occur in other hilly districts of Northern England, including the Lake District. The soil on the upper slopes is typically thin, very acid, and infertile, but becomes deeper, less acid, and more fertile lower down. Where, as often, the valley has cut through a bed of hard rock into softer shales or clays below, the ecological contrast between upper and lower slopes will be particularly striking, but the general change from steeper to less steep slopes and from thin to much deeper soils is not dependent on a geological discontinuity. The changes are reflected in all layers of the wood. The trees increase in size down the slope and the number of tree species increases, the oaks being accompanied on the lower slopes by several species more dependent on a good moist deep soil—like ash, wych elm, sycamore and, more locally, the small-leaved lime. More shrubs appear towards the bottom and are likely to include hazel, hawthorn, sloe, and guelder rose, all rare or absent above. The ground flora, too, becomes much richer in species and more luxuriant. The valley-bottom usually has the deepest soils of all, a consequence of both the downwash of fine soil-particles from the valley-sides and the deposition of silt when the stream along the bottom is in flood. Here, with the water-table never very far below the surface and sometimes above it for longer or shorter periods, alder, sallows, and perhaps other willows become prominent amongst the woody plants, while those intolerant of water-logging are absent. The ground flora now includes such moisture-loving plants as ramsons, lesser celandine, marsh marigold, meadowsweet, and various sedges.

Illustration II, p. 49, shows the upper part of such a wood. The trees are rather poorly-grown sessile oaks with scattered mountain ash, hairy birch, and holly. There is virtually no shrub layer and the steeply sloping floor is almost completely carpeted with wavy hair-grass, so characteristic of grazed woods on poor acid soils. If grazing animals cannot get into the wood bilberry would become a prominent component of the ground flora, but it is quickly eliminated by grazing.

Illustration I, p. 48, shows the lower slopes of the same wood, which is close to the River Lune in Northern Lancashire (see ill. IA, p. 49, for a general view). Here ash, wych elm, small-leaved lime, and alder join the sessile oak in the tree layer, while mountain ash and holly remain as small trees beneath the main canopy and there is some hazel and guelder rose. Wavy hair-grass is largely replaced by wood soft-grass, patches of bracken, and great woodrush, with some bluebell, red campion. wood anemone, and other herbs.

Of special interest are the circular depressions which still mark sites where charcoal was made by the slow combustion of wood under conditions of limited access of air. Such charcoal pits are a common feature of these northern woods and especially of those close to sources of iron-ore for the smelting of which charcoal was essential until coke was found a satisfactory substitute. They are particularly conspicuous in the woods of High Furness, just south of the Lake District and conveniently close to the iron-ore of Furness on which the Lancashire iron industry was based.

Species shown in colour illustration **I**, p. 48: 1 SESSILE OAK (*Quercus petraea*)   2 SILVER BIRCH (*Betula pendula*)   3 MOUNTAIN ASH (*Sorbus aucuparia*)   4 HOLLY (*Ilex aquifolium*)   5 EUROPEAN ASH (*Fraxinus excelsior*)   6 WYCH ELM (*Ulmus glabra*)   7 ALDER (*Alnus glutinosa*)   8 SMALL-LEAVED LIME (*Tilia cordata*)   9 charcoal burner's pit   10 GREAT WOODRUSH (*Luzula sylvatica*)

I Interior of oak-wood under extreme conditions, at altitude 309–440 m: for diagram identifying species see p. 55. Text pp. 54–5

II North-east boundary of wood in illustration I: young PEDUNCULATE OAKS (*Quercus robur*) and a MOUNTAIN ASH (*Sorbus aucuparia*), with BRACKEN (*Pteridium*) and BILBERRY (*Vaccinium myrtillus*), are colonizing the moss- and lichen-covered boulders. Text pp. 54–5

III Distant view of wood on steep mountain ridge. The stunted sessile oaks (*Quercus petraea*) at the top of the wood are on scree at an altitude of 450 m; the lower edge of the wood is at an altitude of 300 m. Text pp. 54–5

⁄ Interior of wood in illustration III. Stunted, formerly coppiced sessile oaks. Ground flora of grasses, mosses, and lberry (*Vaccinium myrtillus*). Text pp. 54–5

NATIVE BRITISH WOODLAND: High-level Oak-woods

Remains of trees preserved in hill-peat and the solitary trees or small groups to be seen, well above any continuous woodland, on cliff-ledges and elsewhere where they are inaccessible to sheep, cattle, and deer, are reasons for believing that woods once extended to appreciably greater altitudes on our hills and mountains than they do today, and that grazing animals are largely responsible for the change. There are certainly many more such animals than there were formerly and they destroy tree-seedlings and so prevent woods from maintaining themselves when older trees die, the more so because conditions for regeneration by seed are in any case hazardous towards the upper limit of woodland. There is now little extensive woodland above 300 m (about 1000 feet), so that fragments of oak-wood at greater heights than this on Dartmoor and in the Lake District are of particular interest to ecologists.

On Dartmoor there are two small oak-woods lying between 309 and 440 m above sea-level and three others whose upper limits reach or exceed 300 m. The two highest, Wistman's Wood and Black Tor Copse, are both on granite block-scree and the oaks are all pedunculate, despite the fact that climate and substratum might seem to favour sessile oak (see p. 14). Illustrations I and II, p. 52, are of Wistman's Wood and show some of the small twisted oaks, most of them no more than 4·5 m high though a few have erect stems up to 8 m high. Occasional trees of mountain ash, holly, and common sallow fill gaps in the oak canopy and there is some ivy and honeysuckle. Bilberry, wood soft-grass, and great woodrush are the chief higher plants upon and between the granite boulders, but mosses, liverworts, and lichens drape the boulders as well as the trunks and main branches of the trees. Of special interest, too, and doubtless relatable to the high atmospheric humidity, is the abundance of higher plants growing as epiphytes on the trees. These include ferns (common polypody and broad buckler fern) and also great woodrush, bilberry, and wood sorrel.

Illustrations III and IV, p. 53, show a similarly high-level oak-wood, called the Keskadale Oaks, in the Newlands Valley between Derwentwater and Crummock Water in the Lake District. These, like the nearby Birkrigg Oaks, are on fairly steep stabilized scree and differ from Wistman's Wood in being of sessile and not pedunculate oaks. They extend from about 300 m to 450 m above sea-level and are mostly many-stemmed and about 5 m high near the bottom of the wood but up to 10 m towards the top where they are protected from strong winds by much steeper ground above them. The only other trees are a few mountain ashes, and there are no large shrubs, though both bilberry and heather are components of the ground layer together with bracken, wavy hair-grass and other grasses, wood sorrel, heath bedstraw, tormentil, and others. The many-stemmed form of the oaks was caused by former coppicing—discontinued more than a century ago—for tanbark. No oak seedlings seem now to survive the grazing by large numbers of sheep, so that the wood is not likely to maintain itself in present conditions.

Wistman's Wood and the Keskadale Oaks raise the question of why they should have survived to the present day when surrounding woodland seems to have disappeared long ago. Wistman's Wood, with its great granite blocks, must always have proved difficult of access for grazing animals and this may have been sufficient to enable the necessary few seedlings to establish themselves, perhaps in narrow spaces between large boulders. The Keskadale Oaks are on scree of much smaller boulders and their origin might go back to some accidental absence of grazing animals for enough time to enable oak seedlings to colonize the area. During the period of regular coppicing for tanbark they were probably fenced, at least for some time after each cutting, but they might maintain themselves by shoots from the old stools for a very long time even with some sheep constantly present. Alternatively, and this applies also to Wistman's Wood and others on Dartmoor, they might have been planted—as seems true of some other high-level woods in the Lake District.

There are many oak-woods on the lower slopes of hills in Devon and Cornwall, Wales, Northern England including the Lake District, and the Highlands of Scotland, which resemble the Keskadale Oaks in being of coppiced sessile oaks and in some of which the trees are similarly dwarfed and misshapen. They are mostly on soils and in situations unfavourable for growing good timber and have therefore been cut more or less regularly for tanbark, charcoal, or pitprops, all providing a modest cash return. They have also served as sources of firewood and as browse and shelter for sheep. Bark from old stems is of little value for tanning and the best material came from coppice, commonly cut on about a 24-year rotation. Coppice-oak was also favoured for charcoal and pitprops. The chief use to which the produce of any particular wood was put depended on its accessibility to potential purchasers. Charcoal for smelting was in special demand in High Furness, and pitprops near coal-mining areas; in low-land England the largest demand for charcoal for the iron industry was in the Forest of Dean, the Weald of Kent, and Sussex. Now that these old coppiced woodlands are no longer economic many of them have been replaced by coniferous plantations or have been abandoned to the sheep, cattle, and deer on the hills. In these circumstances they will be unable to replace dead stools and will gradually disappear.

In England and Wales no woods extend higher up the hills than these scrubby oak-woods. In the west and north of Scotland, however, birch-woods are often found above oak-wood and in some places pine-woods occupy an intermediate belt (pp. 78–9).

Species shown (in colour illustration **I**, p. 52: 1 MOUNTAIN ASH (*Sorbus aucuparia*)   2 BILBERRY (*Vaccinium myrtillus*)   3 WHITE CLIMBING FUMITORY (*Corydalis claviculata*)   4 WOOD SORREL (*Oxalis acetosella*)   5 GREAT WOODRUSH (*Luzula sylvatica*)   6 WAVY HAIR-GRASS (*Deschampsia flexuosa*)   7 BROAD BUCKLER FERN (*Dryopteris dilatata*)   8 HARD FERN (*Blechnum spicant*)   9 COMMON POLYPODY (*Polypodium vulgare*) 10 MOSSES, LIVERWORTS, and LICHEN

I Juniper scrub (August): for diagram identifying species see p. 59. Text p. 58

III Hawthorn scrub (May): for diagram identifying species see p. 59. Text pp. 58–9

II COMMON WHITEBEAM (*Sorbus aria*)—foreground; YEW (*Taxus baccata*)—background

IV Oak-ash-wood (June): PEDUNCULATE OAK (*Quercus robur*) and EUROPEAN·ASH (*Fraxinus excelsior*). COMMON HAWTHORNS (*Crataegus monogyna*) and other shrubs persist on the borders of the wood. Text pp. 58–9

NATIVE BRITISH WOODLAND: The Scrub Stage in Succession to Woodland

On pp. 46–7 we considered the different characteristics and roles of "pioneer" and "successor" trees in the woodland succession from heath to oak-wood and referred briefly to the part played by shrubs at a still earlier stage. Pages 44–5 and 56 illustrate two different examples of woodland successions with well-marked scrub stages. The shrubs that figure prominently in such successions have a number of features that fit them for this ecological role. All have efficiently dispersed seeds: some, like those of sallows, are dispersed by wind; those of gorse and broom are flung violently from their pods; and most of the remainder have fleshy fruits which are eaten by birds so that the seeds are dropped at some distance from the parent plants. This ensures that seedlings of suitable shrubs can be established very quickly after colonization becomes possible. Many of the shrubs soon spread into large thickets, either because they form suckers on their roots, as do dog rose, sloe, and dogwood, or because long shoots arch over and root where they touch the ground, as in blackberries, guelder rose, and privet. And they all begin to flower and fruit when quite young, so that second-generation seedlings soon appear in spaces between the initial colonists. All these are features that favour a rapid colonization of any suitable ground made available as the result of the abandonment of cultivated ground or grassland, the felling or burning of woodland, or the stabilization of blown sand, landslides, or scree. A further characteristic is that most of these shrubs are thorny or prickly so that grazing animals find them unattractive. Even those that are not spiny are for the most part avoided, presumably because, like elder and wayfaring tree, they are of unpleasant taste or texture. The really important consequence of this is that other woody plants, which grazing animals would eat if they were readily accessible, can become safely established within the thickets of spiny or unpalatable shrubs. Hazel is a shrub that often benefits in this way, as do young trees of birch, ash, or oak and, on chalk or limestone, of whitebeam, yew, and beech. Protected against casual grazing, the young trees eventually overtop their nurses and later, with further increase in their size and numbers, they close over the pioneer shrubs. Many of these are intolerant of heavy shade so that their growth is checked and they eventually die.

It is seen, then, that scrub is an essentially transient type of vegetation, establishing itself quickly when changed circumstances allow woody seedlings to survive, and being replaced in due course by woodland. It is a stage in the sequence or succession of vegetation in neglected pasture or abandoned cultivation from the initial communities of grasses or weeds to the final woodland.

Illustration I, p. 56, shows juniper scrub which has invaded grassland on the Chiltern escarpment south-east of Oxford at a time when the pressure of grazing by sheep and rabbits was sufficiently relaxed to allow juniper seedlings to survive their vulnerable early years. Over very large areas of chalk grassland in Southern England the death of rabbits through myxomatosis resulted in widespread invasion by scrub, but the advance of juniper on the Chiltern scarp began much earlier and seems to have been due to changes in farming practice. The juniper is accompanied by other shrubs, in particular by wayfaring tree, purging buckthorn, and dogwood, all very typical of scrub on shallow chalky soils. Whitebeam and yew have also been able to establish themselves because of the protection afforded by the prickly juniper. Page 57 shows a later stage of the succession when whitebeam and yew have formed more or less closed woodland. In many such places on the Chiltern Hills or elsewhere dead or dying junipers serve as reminders of the preceding stage (see ill. III, p. 61) and young beeches show what is yet to come.

Illustration III, p. 56, shows corresponding stages in the succession to mixed woodland of oak and ash on deeper soil over chalk in Wiltshire. Here the main components of the scrub are hawthorn, dog rose, sloe, and purging buckthorn—all spiny, with wayfaring tree, dogwood, and privet. On these deeper soils it is young pedunculate oaks and ashes, rather than whitebeam and yew, that can establish themselves in dense clumps of spiny shrubs and in time close over to form a mixed oak-ash-wood. Illustration IV, p. 57, shows this later stage and shows also how the shrubs may persist as a kind of hedge along the woodland margin where light is better than in the interior.

Species shown in colour illustration **I**, p. 56: 1 JUNIPER (*Juniperus communis*)   2 DOG ROSE (*Rosa canina*) 3 YEW (*Taxus baccata*)   4 COMMON WHITEBEAM (*Sorbus aria*)   5 PURGING BUCKTHORN (*Rhamnus catharticus*)   6 WAYFARING TREE (*Viburnum lantana*) 7 DOGWOOD (*Cornus sanguinea*).

Species shown in colour illustration **III**, p. 56: 1 COMMON HAWTHORN (*Crataegus monogyna*)   2 PURGING BUCKTHORN (*Rhamnus catharticus*)   3 SLOE (*Prunus spinosa*)   4 COMMON PRIVET (*Ligustrum vulgare*)   5 WAYFARING TREE (*Viburnum lantana*)   6 DOGWOOD (*Cornus sanguinea*)   7 DOG ROSE (*Rosa canina*) 8 PEDUNCULATE OAK (*Quercus robur*)   9 EUROPEAN ASH (*Fraxinus excelsior*)

I Open scrub of juniper (*Juniperus communis*) in foreground, with two areas of dense scrub near the top of the hill, invaded by trees from the wood. Text pp. 62–3

II Dense scrub of juniper (*Juniperus communis*) invaded by 1 EUROPEAN BEECH (*Fagus sylvatica*) from the wood above, 2 young COMMON WHITEBEAM (*Sorbus aria*), 3 YEW (*Taxus baccata*), and 4 an older BEECH supporting 5 TRAVELLERS' JOY (*Clematis vitalba*). Text pp. 62–3

IA Open mixed scrub on lower slopes: COMMON HAWTHORN (*Crataegus monogyna*) and DOGWOOD (*Cornus sanguinea*) replacing JUNIPER (*Juniperus communis*). On the distant hill, centre, cultivation prevents scrub formation. Text pp. 62–3

II Interior of young beech-wood, showing the dead shrubs of the preceding juniper. Text pp. 62–3

NATIVE BRITISH WOODLAND: Succession to Beech-wood from Juniper Scrub

Pages 60–1 provide further illustrations of the woody succession on the west-facing slopes of the Chiltern Hills from grassland on shallow soils over chalk through juniper scrub to developing beech-wood. Illustration I, p. 60, shows that it is only on the steeper slopes that juniper is the main component of the scrub invading the chalk grassland when grazing is relaxed. On more gently sloping ground (ill. IA, p. 61), where the soil tends to be deeper and to dry out less readily, hawthorn replaces juniper as the most prominent shrub, as was described for the Wiltshire chalk on p. 59. This is because hawthorn establishes itself more readily and grows more rapidly than juniper on these deeper and moister soils, the reverse being true of the dry and shallow soils.

On the steeper slopes juniper scrub may be invaded directly by beech (ill. II, p. 60), but if there are no fruiting beeches close at hand the first trees to appear may often be whitebeam and yew, the grey foliage of the former contrasting strikingly with the deep green of yew. Both have bird-dispersed seeds and are therefore less dependent than beech on the close proximity of seed-parents, and they may colonize the scrub quickly enough to form a mixed whitebeam-yew-wood for a period before the less rapidly invading beeches are sufficiently numerous and tall enough to overtop them in a developing beech-wood. Illustration III, p. 61, shows dead juniper bushes beneath young beech and provides clear evidence of the earlier stage in the succession. It should be added that scrub is not essential for the entry of beech into chalk grassland. If grazing animals are very few or quite absent, then beech seedlings can dispense with the protection of prickly shrubs, as can whitebeam and yew.

Just as whitebeam and yew—or yew alone—can form a transient woodland stage on steeper slopes, so ash can invade hawthorn scrub on gentler slopes and may lead to an ash-wood stage in the succession. And on the still deeper and more or less acid soils of the Chiltern plateau oak also appears as an invader of hawthorn-blackthorn scrub and then an oak-ash-wood may precede beech-wood. Ash may in fact be found in the juniper scrub of steep slopes but seems unable to invade in sufficient numbers to become an important component of the developing wood, probably because it cannot thrive in dry soil.

Beech as a Native British Tree

Beech is confined, as an undoubtedly native tree, to the Chiltern Hills, the North and South Downs, and very locally on sands of the Weald, the Cotswold Hills, and, further west, the Wye Valley and one or two localities in South Wales. Elsewhere beech may be widely grown, and it may regenerate from seed as far west as Cornwall and parts of Ireland and as far north as Aberdeen, but all the woods appear to have been planted or to be derived from earlier planting.

The study of pollen grains preserved in datable layers of peat suggests that beech may have reached Southern England, after the final retreat of the ice, as long ago as about 5000 B.C. Much of the country must then have been covered by mixed oak forest, and beech appears to have been unable to displace the already established oak, elm, and lime. It was only much later, in Iron Age times from about 500 B.C. onwards, that beech seems, from the increasing abundance of its pollen, to have begun a more rapid spread. There is some evidence that this may have taken it further than its present range as a clearly native tree—perhaps as far as the western coast of Wales and northwards to Yorkshire. Two questions are raised by this. Why did beech begin its real advance from the south in Iron Age times, and why did it lose ground subsequently, if it is true that it once extended as far north as Yorkshire? Professor Godwin has suggested that the introduction of the heavy iron plough was the critical factor. It now became possible to plough the heavy lowland soils, with the result that populations tended to leave the thin soils over the chalk and limestone of Southern England, long since cleared of their forest, and move to the more fertile lowlands. The Chiltern Hills, the North and South Downs, and the Cotswolds thus became available for recolonization by trees, and in these circumstances beech was able to maintain itself in competition with oak and other trees of the mixed oak forest. It seems likely that it became an additional component—rather than the principal tree—of this mixed forest, except perhaps on the steeper chalk slopes. But its special value as firewood for the domestic user in London and later, when coal replaced wood as the chief domestic fuel, for making furniture, led to its being preferred to oak and other trees and so to the origin, by selection and by planting, of pure beech-woods. Elsewhere in the country these were less important considerations and beech was less valuable than oak so that deliberate or unintentional selection had the reverse effect. A further possible reason for the disappearance of native beech from west and north of its present native area may have been its incapacity to survive regular coppicing. Oak was commonly coppiced for charcoal-making and for tanbark, and woods coppiced for these purposes would soon lose all their beech.

The Declining Abundance of Juniper

A careful study of evidence from place-names, old local floras, and herbarium specimens has confirmed the suspicion that there has been a decrease in the amount of juniper in southern counties of England during the past two centuries or so, and that it has become extinct in several of its former localities. The chief reason for the decline has undoubtedly been the increasing amount of land put under the plough during that period, and this has included much of the flatter land on good soils, chalky or otherwise, that was formerly unimproved grassland. What remains is chiefly chalk grassland on steep slopes, but here also juniper seems to be diminishing in amount. Juniper is on the one hand vulnerable to heavy grazing as well as to mowing and burning, and on the other hand it is too intolerant of shade to survive in closed woodland, though it can persist in open woodland, on woodland margins, and in clearings. Its more general survival depends on a rather special set of conditions—in particular grassland on suitable soil and with a fluctuating intensity of grazing so that there are always some areas open to invasion by woody plants and not yet at the advanced stage of invasion when juniper is outshaded by trees. If grazing is maintained at a high intensity for a long period, or if the whole area becomes either woodland or arable land, then there will no longer be a place for juniper, and this is presumably what has happened in many of its former sites.

64

I WOOD OF EUROPEAN BEECH (*Fagus sylvatica*) on loam—chalk plateau type: well-grown mature trees and a group of young beech. Text pp. 66–7

II Wood of EUROPEAN BEECH (*Fagus sylvatica*) on chalk escarpment in autumn. Text pp. 66–7

IA A group of young EUROPEAN ASH (*Fraxinus excelsior*) colonize a gap in the EUROPEAN BEECH (*Fagus sylvatica*) trees on the right. Text pp. 66–7

III Twisted and stunted EUROPEAN BEECH (*Fagus sylvatica*), with a few HAIRY BIRCH (*Betula pubescens*) and HOLLY (*Ilex aquifolium*) on sand and gravel (podsol). Hummocks of MOSS (*Leucobryum glaucum*) in beech litter on the ground. Text pp. 66–7

NATIVE BRITISH WOODLAND: Types of Beech-wood

The illustrations on pp. 64–5 show three of the different kinds of beech-wood to be seen on the Chiltern Hills and elsewhere in Southern England within the native range of beech. Illustration I is of a wood on deep and moderately acid but fertile soil on the Chiltern Plateau. It is in such woods that the tallest and straightest naturally-growing beech can be found. At their best the trees reach heights of 25–30 m on the Chilterns and there are records of even greater heights in woods further south in Hampshire and Sussex. The fine beech-woods on the South Downs near Goodwood have now been largely felled. Most of the trees in these plateau woods are of beech but pedunculate oaks are frequent and there are some ash, wild cherry, and also syca-more. There is no real shrub layer but only scattered individuals of elder, hawthorn, sallow, and a few other species, and there are suppressed trees of beech, yew, holly, and sycamore. The ground flora is largely of blackberry, with some patches of woodland grasses and bracken and of herbs such as yellow archangel, wild arum, sweet woodruff, bluebell, enchanter's nightshade, and wood sorrel.

When a gap is opened up by the death or felling of one or more large trees, it is ash seedlings that usually appear first (see ill. IA). They grow rapidly in the better light and, if the gap is large enough not to be closed again by the spread of branches from the adjoining trees, a group of ash saplings comes to occupy it, forming what is termed a "regeneration core". The ashes may be shaded out by neighbouring beeches before they attain maturity, but if the gap is really wide some will reach the canopy. In this way ash can maintain itself as a component of the mature wood, provided it is uneven-aged so that gaps develop from time to time; and it maintains itself because its abun-dant and readily wind-carried fruits and the rapid growth of young plants enable it to colonize gaps much more quickly than beech. In this behaviour, as in its capacity to invade grassland or scrub with similar speed, ash is a counterpart of birch on lighter and more acid soils and it provides a further example of a pioneer tree (p. 46).

Illustrations II and III show examples of beech-woods on less favourable soils. Illustra-tion II is of a beech-wood on a steep chalk slope where the soil is shallow and tends to become very dry in summer. The trees are only about 20 m high and poorer in form than on the good plateau soils. There is no continuous shrub layer but dogwood and wayfaring tree are occasional. A few ashes and some whitebeam and wild cherry may reach the canopy and yew and holly survive as scattered individuals or groups beneath the main canopy. The ground flora varies greatly in density, sometimes being very sparse with much open ground exposed, sometimes forming extensive patches of wood sanicle, ivy, and dog's mercury, with wood violet, hairy violet, wild strawberry, yellow archangel, and many others. Specially characteristic of these steep chalk woods are orchids, including several kinds of helleborine, fly orchid, and the colourless bird's nest orchid, which, having no chlorophyll, derives all its food from humus in the soil. It is sometimes thought that the low light-intensity beneath a beech canopy is wholly res-ponsible for the poor development of the ground flora in many of these woods on steep chalk slopes. If, however, all the beech roots are severed in trenches surrounding an area of woodland floor, so that no living roots penetrate the area, then the ground flora usually improves markedly in cover, vigour, and diversity: this suggests that competition for water with the tree roots is an important part of the reason for the bareness of the ground.

Burnham Beeches (see ill. III) is a very different kind of beech-wood on coarse gravelly sand, poor and acid, to the north of Slough. In this wood the growth of beech is even poorer than it is on the steep dry slopes of the chalk escarpment, poorer in form as well as in height, with slender bent or twisted stems. Accompanying trees are oak and birch with some mountain ash and whitebeam. Holly occurs as a small tree not reaching the canopy, and the chief species of the sparse shrub layer are alder buckthorn and sallow, with a little juniper. The soil surface, with its covering of leaf litter over raw humus, is bare over large areas but there are patches of wavy hair-grass and wood soft-grass with some cow-wheat and wood-sage and poorly-grown bracken. The illustration shows very clearly the pale cushions of the moss *Leucobryum glaucum*—so characteristic of woods on these very acid soils. It is of interest that gaps in these woods are colonized by birch instead of by ash as on the fertile soils of the Chiltern Plateau.

It will be seen that the term "beech-wood" covers a wide range of woodland types which have little in common except that most of the trees are beeches. The associated trees, shrubs, and herbs, as well as the mosses and toadstools, and the course of succession from abandoned ploughland or pasture, all vary considerably from one site to another and the beech itself differs in rate of growth, straightness, and final height. The chief factors determining these differences appear to be the depth, texture, and fertility of the soil and whether it is either strongly calcareous or highly acid. Beech can tolerate this wide range of conditions and withstand competition from other trees so that within its native range it can form more or less pure woods wherever the soil is neither too dry, too frequently waterlogged, nor too infertile for its successful growth. The deep shade beneath it prevents the development of a shrub layer and the growth of certain light-demanding woodland herbs, but in other respects the various types of beech-wood are so different as to constitute distinct ecological systems.

I Yew-wood (*Taxus baccata*) on chalk hill-top. Old pioneer trees form the core of the wood. Text pp. 70–1

II Box-wood on oolitic limestone. The trees have frequently been coppiced and there is little or no ground-cover. For diagram identifying species see p. 71. Text pp. 70–1

IA An opening in the wood, where yew seedlings and young trees grow with grasses, gladdon (*Iris foetidissima*), and common privet (*Ligustrum vulgare*). Text pp. 70–1

IIA An opening in the wood, showing young box trees with nettles, brambles, and elder (*Sambucus nigra*). There is an old common hawthorn (*Crataegus monogyna*) on the edge of the clearing. Text pp. 70–1

NATIVE BRITISH WOODLAND: Woods of Yew and Box

Pages 68–9 show two rather unusual types of wood. Illustration I is of a yew-wood on chalk in Dorset. Yew is a frequent plant of limestone cliffs and rocky knolls in the west and north, and old yews along a cliff-top may here and there be sufficiently numerous and contiguous to form a narrow strip of woodland. But it is only in certain localities on the chalk in Southern England that really extensive yew-woods are to be found, and it must be inferred that they depend for their origin on certain special circumstances. For yew commonly plays a part in the succession from open chalk grassland through juniper scrub to developing beech-wood. The juniper protects it in early stages from casual grazing by sheep, and the future course of events depends on the relative build-up in numbers of the chief tree-invaders of the scrub. Yew is slow-growing compared with whitebeam, ash, and beech and is soon overtopped by them if they are all of about the same age. However, yew casts a very deep shade in which seedlings of the other trees cannot establish themselves successfully. All depends, therefore, on whether yews can invade the scrub fast enough and become sufficiently abundant to form closed woodland before whitebeam, ash, and beech can overtop them. Normally they fail to do this and so persist only as a more or less sparse under-storey in a developing beech-wood or at best join with whitebeam and perhaps ash in a mixed wood preceding the final beech-wood. Professor A. S. Watt, who nearly fifty years ago made a careful study of yew-woods in Southern England, pointed out that they occur chiefly round the heads and along the steep sides of dry valleys or "coombes" in the chalk of the North and South Downs and on steep chalk slopes further west, and especially in areas where there was or clearly had previously been severe rabbit-infestation. Juniper scrub grows well on these steep slopes with very shallow soil and is also little eaten by rabbits; it is the typical scrub in the areas where yew-woods are found. If rabbits are very numerous only woody plants that can establish seedlings in the heart of a juniper bush have much chance of survival, and yew is so outstandingly shade-tolerant that it can take full advantage of the protection afforded by the juniper and soon outnumbers all other invaders. Yew is also like juniper in tolerating shallow soils in which hawthorn and ash cannot thrive and even beech is at a disadvantage. It is in these special circumstances that yew can outstrip all its normal competitors and form first yew scrub and then a more or less pure yew-wood in the shade of which the junipers soon die. Yews are long-lived trees and cast so heavy a shade that beech seedlings cannot grow up beneath them. Consequently a yew-wood, once established, cannot be replaced by beech-wood until, after many centuries, gaps begin to appear through deaths of old yews and allow beech to gain a foothold from which ultimately it can close over the surviving yews. The yew-wood on Hambledon Hill, Dorset (ill. I and IA, pp. 68–9) has old pioneer yews branching at a low level and with the heavily-shaded ground beneath them bare except for ivy, dog violets, male fern, and scattered seedlings of yew. Beneath an opening to the right of the picture the ground is grass-covered, with better-grown young plants of yew and patches of the gladdon or stinking iris (*Iris foetidissima*).

Illustrations II and IIA, pp. 68–9, show an ancient wood of box on oolitic limestone in Gloucestershire. Box is almost certainly a native tree in Southern England but is confined to a very small number of localities on chalk and limestone. Of these by far the best known is Box Hill in Surrey, where, on the steep slope, nearly 120 m high, which is being actively cut back by the River Mole, there is a mixed wood of box and yew. The steepness of the slope, almost 40°, and the constant river-erosion of its base, makes the surface unstable and devoid of soil. In these extreme conditions only box, with some yew and whitebeam, seem able to maintain themselves; beech, common in the woods nearby, is absent from the steepest parts of the slope. There is clearly a similar situation to that which enables yew to form pure woods in a few places on the chalk. Box is like yew in its capacity to thrive on these steep slopes, in being evergreen, and in casting a very dense shade so that seedlings of other woody plants cannot readily establish themselves beneath it. But only where they are favoured by slopes too steep for their competitors or, certainly for yew if not also for box, by rabbits so numerous as to allow only very shade-tolerant seedlings to survive in the heart of juniper bushes, is beech excluded so that it can succeed in forming woods of its own. The box-wood shown in illustration II was mentioned in Domesday. It is on a limestone slope and is one of the largest areas of pure box in the country. The trees have been coppiced, presumably for their valuable timber, which is yellow in colour and very hard and heavy and used in particular for turning and carving and as wood for woodcuts and wood engravings. There is no continuous ground flora but some patches of dog's mercury and stinging nettle.

Species shown in illustration **II**, p. 68: 1 BOX (*Buxus sempervirens*)   1A young regenerating BOX
2 COMMON HAWTHORN (*Crataegus monogyna*)   3 ELDER (*Sambucus nigra*)   4 STINGING NETTLES (*Urtica dioica*)   5 DOG'S MERCURY (*Mercurialis perennis*)

I Northern ash-wood on carboniferous limestone scar with ash-wood below: for diagram identifying species see p. 75. Details × ⅔: 1 CLIFF WHITEBEAM (*Sorbus rupicola*)   2 LANCASHIRE WHITEBEAM (*S. lancastriensis*). Text pp. 74–5

IA Top of the scar: for diagram identifying species see p. 75

Northern valley-side ash-wood. Almost pure EUROPEAN ASH (*Fraxinus excelsior*) at lower levels. Sparse ground-cover WILD STRAWBERRY (*Fragaria*) and SLENDER FALSE-BROME GRASS (*Brachypodium sylvaticum*), with some BRAMBLE *ubus*), COMMON HAWTHORN (*Crataegus monogyna*), and PURGING BUCKTHORN (*Rhamnus catharticus*). Text pp. 74–5

NATIVE BRITISH WOODLAND: Northern Ash-woods

Ash plays an important part in lowland Britain in the vegetational succession to oak-wood (p. 59), and more locally to beech-wood (p. 62), on good moist soils that are not highly acid. In view of its soil preferences ash is commonly a colonist of scrub in which hawthorn is a major component. A wood of ash, or of mixed oak and ash, may then develop as a temporary stage before the slower-growing oak or beech can finally re-place most of the ash. Some ash remains in the final woodland because it can colonize large gaps more quickly than oak or beech and single trees or small groups often survive to reach the canopy (p. 66).

There can be little doubt that the former natural woodland on good lowland soils usually contained wych elm, small-leaved lime, field maple, wild cherry, and others, as well as ash, accompanying the more numerous oaks. With the extensive clearance of forest from good agricultural land, and the favouring of oak in what was left, this kind of mixed woodland almost disappeared. Only locally, as on the lower slopes of steep-sided valleys and on clays too heavy for arable agriculture, may examples still be found, and in these woods ash is very often a prominent component. It is, however, in the hill-lands of the west and north—particularly in limestone areas—that ash and more or less pure ash-woods are a conspicuous feature of the landscape.

On the carboniferous limestone in Derbyshire natural woodland can now be seen only here and there on the steeply sloping and otherwise grassy dale-sides. Here ash is often the only tree in the canopy, though in some places it is mixed with other trees. These ash-woods, including the famous Dovedale Woods, were at one time regarded as the final stage of woodland succession on limestone slopes outside the natural range of beech and in sites where oak is at some ecological disadvantage. Against this view are facts to which Professor C. D. Pigott and others have recently drawn attention— that most of the dale-side ash-woods are even-aged and date only from the nineteenth century, and that they seem to have arisen through the colonization of former pasture by hawthorn and ash. The question raised is what the composition of the dale-side woodland would have been had there been no intensive grazing by cattle, sheep, and rabbits during past centuries. The oldest of the even-aged ash-woods usually have some wych elm and field maple and a good deal of the introduced sycamore in the canopy. There are, moreover, fragments of what appears to be much older woodland still present in some of the dales, and in these the individual trees are of widely different ages. Ash is always present, as are wych elm and field maple, while sycamore is found in some but not all of them. But there are also the two native limes and both native oaks, and there are several kinds of shrubs and herbs never or rarely seen in the even-aged ash-woods. The conclusion must be that the original woodland of the dale-sides, which could return if they were left ungrazed, had a mixture of trees and was not entirely or even mainly of ash. This is supported by studies of pollen grains in peat samples from near limestone in Northern England, which show that ash became prominent only after a period of widespread destruction of forest. It seems likely that ash-woods on the Mendip Hills and elsewhere in South-western England and in Wales are also of recent origin.

Ill. II, p. 73, shows an almost pure and apparently even-aged ash-wood on a steep scree-slope in Littondale in the Craven Pennines, below a cliff on which yew and cliff white-beam (*Sorbus rupicola* (see ill. I)) are growing. Here again ash may be supposed to have invaded the slope during a period of reduced grazing-pressure—perhaps round the turn of the century.

Ill. I shows the top of a limestone cliff near the western edge of the Lake District, where the woody plants include hazel, hawthorn, purging buckthorn, juniper, yew, mountain ash, and the local variant of cliff whitebeam called *S. lancastriensis*, which differs from *S. rupicola* in having leaf-teeth that are symmetrical and point outwards, instead of curving towards the leaf-tip, and also in having large lenticels confined to the base of the darker red fruits. Mixed woodland, with ash present throughout, extends from the cliff down to the side of a small lake. Oak, wych elm, small-leaved lime, and alder are also present in this wood, which must retain many features of the former natural woodland.

Ash is prominent in narrow limestone "gills" and on limestone pavement in several localities in Northern England, but suitable conditions for it are by no means confined to limestone areas. In the Lake District ash is the main colonist of scree-slopes and quarry-waste on a variety of nutrient-rich rocks that weather easily, including many beds of the Borrowdale volcanic rocks as well as certain slates and shales. Where natural woodland remains it is commonly of sessile oak with wych elm and small-leaved lime as well as much ash.

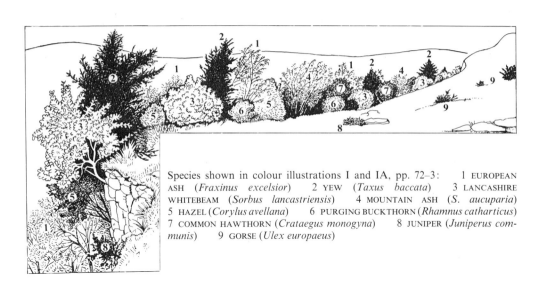

Species shown in colour illustrations I and IA, pp. 72–3: 1 EUROPEAN ASH (*Fraxinus excelsior*) 2 YEW (*Taxus baccata*) 3 LANCASHIRE WHITEBEAM (*Sorbus lancastriensis*) 4 MOUNTAIN ASH (*S. aucuparia*) 5 HAZEL (*Corylus avellana*) 6 PURGING BUCKTHORN (*Rhamnus catharticus*) 7 COMMON HAWTHORN (*Crataegus monogyna*) 8 JUNIPER (*Juniperus communis*) 9 GORSE (*Ulex europaeus*)

I Scottish pine-wood: SCOTS PINE (*Pinus sylvestris*), with HAIRY BIRCH (*Betula pubescens*), JUNIPER (*Juniperus communis*), and HEATHER (*Calluna*) in foreground. Text pp. 78–9

II SCOTS PINE (*Pinus sylvestris*) at high altitude, with some JUNIPER (*Juniperus communis*). Wood of HAIRY BIRCH (*Betula pubescens*) below. Text pp. 78–9

III Scottish birch-wood: SILVER BIRCH (*Betula pendula*) and JUNIPER (*Juniperus communis*). Text pp. 78–9

IV Scottish birch-wood in the far north: heavily grazed HAIRY BIRCH (*Betula pubescens*) in foreground. Text pp. 78–9

NATIVE BRITISH WOODLAND: Pine and Birch in Scotland

Many centuries of forest clearance for agricultural and other purposes have left only scattered remnants of the former natural woodland in Scotland, most of them in sparsely populated areas where access is difficult—especially in the Highlands. These remnants fall into three main categories. First there are those with oak as an important component and then those with either Scots pine or birch as the chief trees. There are also some alder-woods by streams, a few ash-woods on limestone in the west, and some small patches of almost pure mountain ash or rowan. The oak-woods are on the deepest and most fertile soils, chiefly in valley-bottoms and on the lower slopes of hills. They commonly have some ash and wych elm in them, with alder in wetter areas; and in some steep-sided valleys on calcareous rocks oak may be no more abundant than these other kinds of trees. Birch is also generally present and all gradations can be seen between oak-woods with a little birch and woods predominantly of birch. Birch is no doubt more and more at an advantage over oak the poorer the soil, but in many instances the large amount of birch is due not to soil type but to the selective removal of oak or to grazing animals preventing the survival of oak seedlings.

Locally, and particularly on well-drained morainic sands and gravels over a wide area of the Highlands, there are woods of native Scots pine, surviving fragments of what must once have been extensive pine-forests. The best-known are in Deeside, including Ballochbuie Forest on the royal estate of Braemar; Speyside, with Rothiemurchus Forest; the famous Black Wood of Rannoch in Perthshire; woods in and near the Great Glen and in Glen Affric; and, further west, the wood on the north side of Loch Maree. The woods are of two main types. There are those where the pines are close together, with little birch or mountain ash in the canopy and few tall shrubs beneath it; and those with more widely spaced pines and often with quite large amounts of birch and with juniper conspicuous in a well-developed shrub layer. Both have a ground-cover of heather, bilberry, and cowberry, with many and luxuriant mosses. Ill. I, p. 76, shows the former type in a locality in Deeside but with some juniper and much heather in the clearing in the foreground. This illustration also shows how the native Scots pine tends to retain its fairly narrow and round-topped crown for much longer than some of the continental races used in many plantings in Southern England, which soon become broad and flat-topped. Ill. II, p. 76, shows pines becoming more and more dwarfed and more widely spaced with increasing altitude until they peter out completely. On the western flanks of Creag Fhiaclach in the Cairngorms the tree limit is at 640 m above sea-level and is of Scots pine with some birch. This is perhaps close to the natural limit of tree growth in the area, but more usually trees extend only to about 500 m or lower, as in the locality illustrated. This is because grazing animals, and the practice of burning moorland so as to ensure earlier and better feed for sheep, prevent the survival of a sufficient number of tree-seedlings to maintain the woodland. The illustration also shows birch-wood below the pine-wood on heavier soils of the lower slopes, where oak would probably be found if the area had not been affected by man's activities.

Page 77 illustrates birch-woods in Northern Scotland, representative of large numbers all over the Highlands and extending from sea-level to the upper limit of tree growth. Both birches are found in these woods but silver birch (*Betula pendula*) is abundant only on the drier eastern side of the country and the most widespread is the northern sub-species of hairy birch (*B. pubescens* ssp. *odorata*, perhaps the same as the Scandinavian ssp. *tortuosa*), which has young twigs that are hairless or nearly so, with sticky brown warts. Ill. III shows a birch-wood in Inverness-shire where most of the birch is in fact silver birch and where there is a great deal of juniper present. The soil is sandy and the site is one that might well carry pine-wood. It seems, indeed, that most birch-woods occupy sites that could have—and at one time probably did have—either oak-wood or pine-wood, and it is questionable whether there are circumstances in which vegetational succession in Scotland necessarily terminates in a birch-wood. As has already been stated (p. 46) birch is a typical pioneer tree, quick to occupy available sites on a wide range of soil types and in a wide range of climates. It will colonize gaps in an oak-wood and, if the gaps are large enough, some individuals will survive to reach the canopy so that there will always be a mixture of oak and birch unless the latter is deliberately removed to favour the more valuable species. And if oak-wood or pine-wood is felled and not immediately replanted then recolonization will in general be by birch so that eventually a birch-wood will replace the former kind of wood until the oak or pine can re-establish themselves. There can be little doubt that most birch-woods are secondary in this sense. Even on mountains where birch-woods lie above woods of pine or oak the factors at work do not seem to be directly climatic; more usually it is the poorer soil and the greater difficulties of seedling establishment because of grazing and moor-burning that favour birch against pine and oak. There is nevertheless some evidence that there might be a fringing belt of dwarfed birch and mountain ash with juniper beyond the uppermost true forest if there were fewer grazing animals on the hills. Ill. IV shows birch-wood in Sutherland and brings out the contrast between the closed wood of tall trees on the lower slope of a hill and the open scrub of dwarfed trees further up the hill-side. This is an area of heavy grazing-pressure and there are no young birches, so that it is only a matter of time before the surviving trees, already diseased and dying, have all succumbed and the tree limit will have been further depressed.

I Colonizing woody plants

II Woody plants compete for light

III Canopy closed—purging buckthorn dominant

1 ALDER BUCKTHORN (*Frangula alnus*)   2 COMMON SALLOW (*Salix cinerea*)
6 COMMON HAWTHORN (*Crataegus monogyna*)   7 young EUROPEAN ASH (*Fraxinus excelsior*). Text pp. 82–3

81

IV Colonizing woody plants

V Woody plants compete for light

VI Canopy closed—alder dominant

3 PURGING BUCKTHORN (*Rhamnus catharticus*)   4 ALDER (*Alnus glutinosa*)   5 GUELDER ROSE (*Viburnum opulus*)

NATIVE BRITISH WOODLAND: Alder-wood and the Fen Succession

Examination of the natural vegetation in an undisturbed site where there is a gradual shallowing from deep water to ground only occasionally submerged, as at the edge of a lake or large pond, will usually show clearly marked zones of different vegetation. In deep water, if not too deep for sufficient light to reach the bottom, there will be wholly submerged plants; then waterlilies and other plants having leaves floating on the water surface but none at higher levels; and next, closest to the water's edge, tall plants—bulrushes, reeds, and sedges—with leafy shoots held well above the water. These form not only a series of zones in progressively shallowing water but also, if the general conditions remain unaltered, a time-sequence or "succession" at any one point where the water is becoming steadily shallower because of the deposition of silt round the rooted plant, the accumulation of their dead and waterlogged remains or, as often, for both reasons. Lengthy studies at Wicken Fen near Cambridge (ill. I–III, p. 80) have shown that woody plants can establish themselves only where the ground surface is above the water for most of the year and where winter flooding rarely persists for more than a few weeks at a time (see ill. I, p. 80). This stage is reached at Wicken when saw-sedge (*Cladium mariscus*) has replaced the common reed (*Phragmites australis*) of deeper water. In the Broads of the Bure Valley in Norfolk (see ill. IV, p. 81) common reed is followed by saw-sedge only where little or no silt is being brought in by streams: other sedges succeed it in more rapidly silting areas. One of these is the tussock-sedge (*Carex paniculata*) which forms tall tussocks eventually rising above even the normal winter water-level and so affording sites for the establishment of woody seedlings at a stage when the general surface is still much too wet for them. The first to appear in these Broadland fens are common sallow and alder, followed by guelder rose, alder buckthorn, and purging buckthorn (see ill. V, p. 81). Alder soon outstrips the others which then become the shrub layer in a developing alder-wood (see ill. VI, p. 81). At this stage, and especially when alders were established on plants of tussock-sedge, there is still some open water on the floor of the fen-wood and also patches of the more shade-tolerant herbs that can live in very wet places, such as certain sedges, hemp agrimony, meadowsweet, and marsh fern. Later, when the ground has become somewhat drier, other woody plants may enter and ash, birch, hawthorn, holly, and even oak take their place in a mixed fen-wood. This nevertheless remains quite damp unless its drainage is improved by accident or design: the ground level cannot continue to rise when dead plant-remains decay quickly because they are no longer permanently waterlogged and when silt deposition has ceased more or less completely.

There are good grounds for believing that in this country, as over much of North-western Europe, "fens", which developed under the influence of river water and ground water at least fairly rich in dissolved substances and especially in lime (calcium), normally passed through the successional stages described above but then became "bogs". This must have followed the entry of bog-mosses of the genus *Sphagnum* as soon as the fen surface was no longer permanently wet with the lime-rich water which they cannot tolerate. In a sufficiently moist climate these mosses grow rapidly and accumulate bog-peat which remains saturated to the surface because the compacted peat prevents rain-water from draining down to the water-table in the surrounding area, often many metres below the rising bog surface. The bog-peat being not only water-logged but also very infertile, very few other plants can grow with the mosses. Cores taken through the peat show that in some places woody plants entered before the bog-mosses but could not survive or reproduce themselves once the floor was covered by moss, so that the fen-wood stage was a transient one. Elsewhere no fen-wood developed at all, bog-mosses entering at an earlier stage. In the course of time most of the open water must have disappeared and been replaced by great areas of bog, alder-woods being restricted to the immediate vicinity of streams. The widespread drainage of wet-lands during recent centuries makes it difficult to appreciate the former extent of bogs in lowland Britain.

The fenlands have for long supplied a number of man's needs from their plant products as well as their fish and wildfowl. Apart from the extraction of peat, reed and sedge were harvested for thatching and large areas were regularly mown for hay and farm-yard litter, while drier parts were used as summer grazings. No colonization by woody plants could take place in these circumstances. At Wicken Fen an area in which cutting of saw-sedge and purple moor-grass (*Molinia caerulea*) had been discontinued was purchased by A. G. Tansley in 1923 so that the vegetational succession could proceed undisturbed. It has been mapped at intervals, and this has been the source of much of our information. The first colonists were seedlings of alder buckthorn and purging buckthorn (ill. I, p. 80), the former much the more numerous, and also of common sallow, guelder rose, hawthorn, and a few others (ill. II, p. 80). When the crowns of neigh-bouring bushes meet, the saw-sedge and moor-grass die out and are replaced by shade-tolerant species of the open fen with a few newcomers. Common sallow and guelder rose do not long survive the closure of the canopy and the taller and larger-crowned purging buckthorn slowly shades out the alder buckthorn (ill. III, p. 80).

A question that arises is why alder does not play the same pioneer role at Wicken as in the Broadland Fens. The reason must be sought in the different history of the two areas. Amongst the most important products of these wet-lands has undoubtedly been the peat itself, and especially bog-peat which leaves far less ash than fen-peat. It is now clear that the Norfolk Broads are not natural lakes but enormous mediaeval peat-cuttings which seem to have been abandoned because of flooding before the end of the fourteenth century. They thus provided large new expanses of open water in which the vegetational succession started all over again and eventually reached the stage of alder-woods or mixed fen-woods: alders still lining the many streams of the area would have provided the initial supply of seed. There was almost certainly cutting of peat (probably bog-peat) for fuel in the Wicken area too, but on a smaller scale and without giving rise to large areas of open water connected with alder-lined streams. It is of interest that buckthorns rather than alder invade abandoned mowing-fen in Broadland if it is at some distance from any mature alder-wood, and also that alders are now beginning to spread at Wicken from a few planted trees.

1 4 1 2 5 1 4 1 4 1

7 12 9 5 8 10

I Mature fen carr

3 6 6 4 6 5

6 11 6 6 4 12 13 6

II Pondside woodland

1 ALDER (*Alnus glutinosa*)   2 PEDUNCULATE OAK (*Quercus robur*)   3 SESSILE OAK (*Q. petraea*)
7 COMMON HAWTHORN (*Crataegus monogyna*)   8 PURGING BUCKTHORN (*Rhamnus catharticus*)
young tree   12 COMMON SALLOW (*Salix cinerea*)   13 WHITE WILLOW (*S. alba*)—young tree
17 GUELDER ROSE (*Viburnum opulus*)   18 HOLLY (*Ilex aquifolium*)   19 MOUNTAIN ASH (*Sorbus aucuparia*)

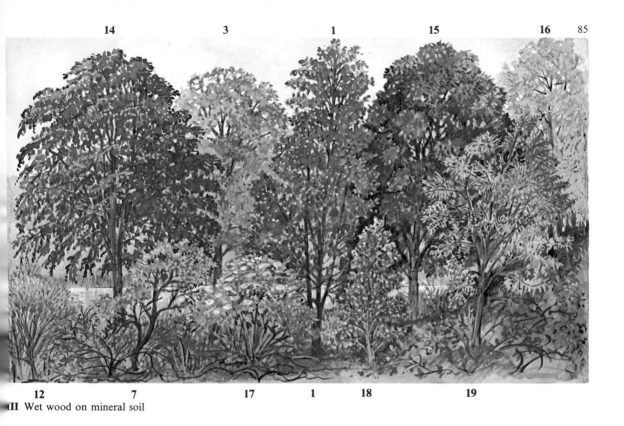

14   3   1   15   16

12   7   17   1   18   19

III Wet wood on mineral soil

20   1   1   20

1 21   1   12 12   1

V Riverside trees

HAIRY BIRCH (*Betula pubescens*)   5 EUROPEAN ASH (*Fraxinus excelsior*)   6 ASPEN (*Populus tremula*)
ALDER BUCKTHORN (*Frangula alnus*)   10 COMMON PRIVET (*Ligustrum vulgare*)   11 FIELD MAPLE (*Acer campestre*)—
4 WYCH ELM (*Ulmus glabra*)   15 SYCAMORE (*Acer pseudoplatanus*)   36 SMALL-LEAVED LIME (*Tilia cordata*)
0 CRACK WILLOW (*Salix fragilis*)   21 COMMON OSIER (*S. viminalis*). Text pp. 86–7

TREES OF WET PLACES

Places may be wet for different reasons and in different ways. The flood-plain of a river may be fairly dry for much of the year but be submerged for longer or shorter periods when the river is in flood. A depression or basin in which water collects during heavy rain will also be wet at some times but not at others—but here the water-table may fall to quite low levels in dry periods, whereas beneath the flood-plain it will be close to river-level throughout the year. How quickly and how far the water-table falls will depend also on the ease with which water can travel below the ground surface. It will fall quickly and far in a light, sandy or gravelly soil a long way from a river or any other permanent body of water, but slowly and less far in a heavy clay or an impermeable peat. At the other extreme there are areas where the water-table is always high, ranging perhaps from 30 cm above to 30 cm below the ground surface. This is true of certain basins fed by permanent springs but also of the ever-decreasing areas of still undrained fenland, like parts of the Somerset Levels, the Norfolk Broadland, and the fens of Cambridgeshire and Lincolnshire described on pp. 82–3. These great fenlands were formed as a consequence of rising sea-level since the last retreat of the ice: they are drowned estuaries and river valleys which have been filled with marine silts and clays, and to some extent with peat, but are still so little above sea-level that their rivers cannot act as efficient drainage channels. Large-scale drainage schemes carried out during recent centuries have lowered the water-table over what are now important areas of arable agriculture, but there is still some residual fen, like Wicken Fen near Cambridge. Finally there are the true bogs, fed by rain water that cannot get away because of the low permeability of bog-peat.

The trees that grow naturally in these various kinds of wet places will differ from one another in their tolerance of reigning conditions. No native trees can flourish where the ground surface is permanently covered with water, though established alders can survive better than any others. But even alders require an uppermost layer that is well-aerated for most of the growing-season if they are to thrive and, for the successful germination of their seeds, they must have a soil surface that is in contact with the air. On the other hand alder seeds fail to germinate successfully unless the ground surface remains continuously moist for about a month, and this is likely only if there is a maintained high water-table. Willows, too, seem to require a high water-table for healthy growth because they readily suffer from water-shortage and lose their leaves. They are however less dependent than alders on the successful germination of their seeds because they can regenerate so easily by the rooting of twigs and branches that have been carried by streams and deposited on the bank.

Alder and willows, then, and also black and grey poplars (pp. 94–5), can tolerate permanently damp though not completely water-logged conditions and seem, moreover, to require continuously moist ground. Several other trees can thrive in sites that are permanently moist up to the ground surface provided the water-table is above or close below the surface for no more than brief periods during the growing season. These include hairy birch, ash, wych elm, and pedunculate oak—none of which is as dependent as alder on the maintenance of damp conditions, though ash is very sensitive to drought. Aspen is also able to thrive in quite wet places. Beech and sycamore are examples of trees that are readily killed by periods of water-logging or flooding that would not seriously affect ash and wych elm. The factors operating here may be the reduced supply of oxygen to the root-system, the presence of high concentrations of ferrous iron or other toxic ions favoured by lack of oxygen, or both.

It is not merely the height and seasonal variation of the water-table that determine what trees will be found growing in particular wet places. A great deal also depends on the supply of plant nutrients. Flood-plains and river banks rank high in this respect, both because the deep layers of river-deposits are usually rich in nutrients but also because the fertility of the uppermost layers is frequently renewed by further silting during periods of flood. Silty fen-peat comes next, then fen-peat from areas where there is no silting, and finally bog-peat, which is poorest of all in plant nutrients.

There can be little doubt that the flood-plains of rivers were once more or less densely wooded, but few such woods remain today because of the great value of these moist and fertile areas for meadows and pastures or, after drainage, for arable agriculture. The surviving fragments have alder as the chief tree in the lower-lying parts, accompanied by the large crack willows and white willow and the smaller osiers (pp. 90–1) and sallows (p. 34), especially on the river bank where they are less likely to be shaded out by alder and where they are a little higher above the water-table. Ash is frequently present and also pedunculate oak, while black and grey poplars (pp. 94–5) occur much more locally. All persist as riverside trees, the last remains of our alluvial woodland, and also in fringing belts round ponds and lakes. On somewhat higher and drier ground elms, sycamore, and, more locally, field maple and small-leaved lime are found, especially where a wooded slope extends down to a stream or lake. Ill. II, III, and IV on pp. 84–5 show examples of trees on the sides of rivers, ponds, and lakes.

In woodland on fen-peat alder (p. 19) is still the chief tree, but the large willows and osiers are normally absent. They seem to demand the high level of nutrients that is ensured by periodic silting. It is of interest in this connection that round Esthwaite Water, in the Lake District, purple osier and a form of crack willow are concentrated round the entrance of the Black Beck, on the silts deposited by the Beck when in flood. Elsewhere the only abundant willow is the common or grey sallow (*Salix cinerea*).

Ill. I on p. 84 shows alder-wood on deep fen-peat in Cambridgeshire, with ash, aspen, oak, birch, and a variety of shrubs as accompanying woody plants. Common sallow is present but no other willows, and the birch is hairy birch, much more tolerant of a high water-table than is silver birch. Amongst the shrubs guelder rose and the two buckthorns are particularly prominent.

Lowland bogs with bog-mosses as the chief peat-formers are of two main kinds: valley bogs, with a stream through the centre, and raised bogs, dome-shaped with only peripheral drainage. Where bogs have remained undrained trees are unable to colonize the very wet and nutrient-poor bog-peat, and raised bogs are therefore treeless, though hairy birch spreads rapidly over them after drainage. In valley bogs, like the well-known Denny Bog in the New Forest, grey sallows, and often alders, too, are restricted to narrow strips along the streams.

scale for trees 1, 2, & 3

m 12
10
5
4
3
2
1
0

1 WHITE WILLOW (*Salix alba*)　　2 CRACK WILLOW (*S. fragilis*)　　3 BAY WILLOW (*S. pentandra*)
(M) = male catkin; (F) = female catkin. Details of catkins, leaves, and winter twigs × $\frac{2}{3}$. Text pp. 90–1

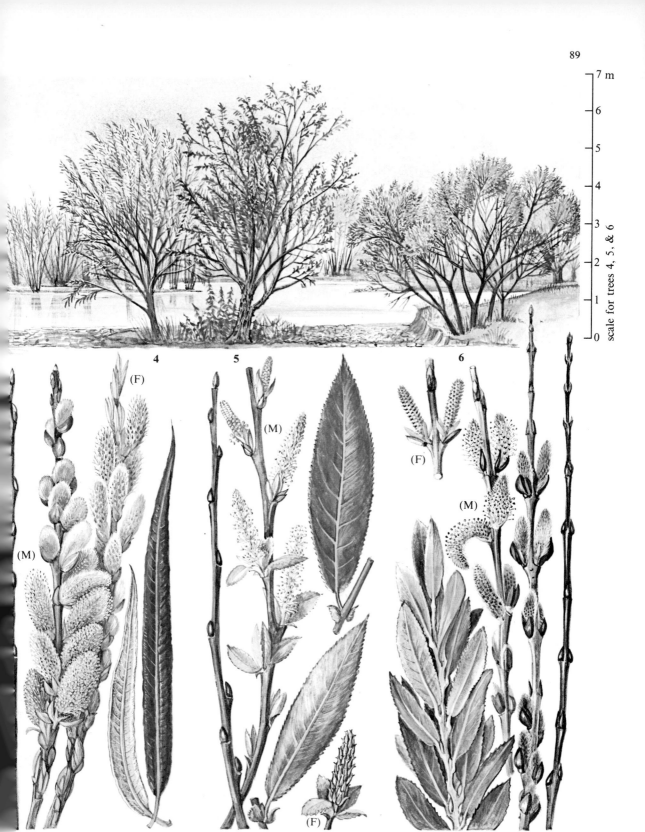

scale for trees 4, 5, & 6

4 COMMON OSIER (*S. viminalis*)   5 ALMOND WILLOW (*S. triandra*)   6 PURPLE OSIER (*S. purpurea*).

TREES OF WET PLACES

WILLOWS and OSIERS (*Salix*); ill. pp. 88–9. A brief general description of the genus is given on p. 34, preceding accounts of the broad-leaved species known as sallows.

WILLOWS. Those described here are all plants of wet places and especially of streamsides. All are widespread in lowland Britain except for bay willow which is native only northwards from North Wales and Derbyshire, and all except bay willow have been extensively utilized by man. The table below shows points of difference between our two really large tree-willows and bay willow. All three have catkins with uniformly yellow-green scales. White willow and crack willow grow in marshes and fens as well as by lowland streams and rivers. They have long been pollarded every four or five years for the crop of straight poles suitable for hurdle-making and other purposes, and old pollard willows are a very familiar feature of the riverside landscape. All three are native in the British Isles. (Introduced willows are described on pp. 166–7.)

	White Willow	Crack Willow	Bay Willow
Crown	Narrow, tower-shaped	Broad and rounded	Spreading
Branches	Ascending	Spreading	Widely spreading
Young twigs	Olive-brown, with silky white hairs	Olive-brown, hairless or slightly downy	Olive, hairless, shining as if varnished
Leaf length	5–8 cm; more than 4 times width	6–15 cm, more than 4 times width	5–12 cm, less than 4 times width
Leaf-margin	Finely toothed	Coarsely toothed	Finely toothed
Leaf-surfaces	Silky-hairy on both sides, more densely beneath	Hairless, shining above, blue-white bloom beneath	Hairless, glossy above, paler beneath
Leaf-stalk	No glands at top	2 glands at top	Several glands at top
Catkins open	April–May	April	May–June
Stamens	2 per flower	2 per flower	5 per flower

1 **White Willow** (*S. alba*) is a deciduous tree that can reach a height of 25 m. Its narrow crown is silvery-grey, especially when the undersides of the leaves are up-turned by wind. In winter it may be distinguished from crack willow by the less deeply fissured bark with shallow ridges forming a closed network and also by the whitish colour of the rootlets sent into water. The twigs and small branches are much less fragile than those of crack willow.

2 **Crack Willow** (*S. fragilis*) also reaches about 25 m in height. It is a deciduous tree whose broadly rounded crown appears green, not silvery-grey as in white willow, and the bark is more deeply fissured with the ridges not in a closed network. The rootlets that can be seen in water beneath the tree are red. The name of the tree is derived from the fragility of its twigs and branches which break off readily at the joins with main branches and make a distinct snap as they separate.

3 **Bay Willow** (*S. pentandra*) is a deciduous shrub or small tree with grey, shallowly fissured bark. It can reach a height of 10 m. Old trees tend to have their lowest branches spreading close to or touching the ground: these may root at intervals and send up vertical shoots. The leafy shoots are striking because of the varnished appearance of the stems and the glossy dark green of the upper sides of the broadly elliptic leaves, which are sticky and fragrant when young. The catkins may reach 6 cm in length. The male catkins, held obliquely erect, are especially attractive because of the large number of golden-yellow stamens. This beautiful tree is restricted to the sides of streams and lakes and other wet places in the hill-lands of the north and is less well known and cultivated than it deserves.

OSIERS. The remaining species are deciduous willows of the group called "osiers", formerly grown on a large scale in periodically flooded "osier-beds" and cut to the ground annually to yield the "rods" used in basket-making. They still exist in parts of the wet lowlands, but on a much smaller scale than in earlier times. Three species were used in this way and selection for the required qualities of length, straightness, pliancy, and colour led to large numbers of locally named varieties. Many osiers, moreover, were products of hybridization between pairs of species, so that precise identification may be quite difficult. The table below shows the main differences between the three native British species, all of which can grow as small trees and are common plants of streamsides and marshes.

	Common Osier	Almond Willow	Purple Osier
Bark	Grey-brown, short vertical fissures into orange underbark	Grey-brown, peels in patches exposing orange underbark	Dark grey, smooth; has lenticels, but not scaling nor fissured
Young twigs	Densely downy	Hairless, olive or reddish-brown	Hairless or nearly so; shining red-purple
Leaf position	Alternate	Alternate	Some in opposite or near-opposite pairs
Leaf length	10–25 cm, more than 7 times width	5–10 cm, less than 7 times width	4–10 cm, length/width ratio very variable
Leaf shape	Linear	Oblong-lanceolate	Oblanceolate
Leaf-margin	Untoothed	Toothed	Finely toothed
Leaf-surfaces	White with silky hairs beneath	Both sides hairless	Both sides hairless
Catkins open	Before leaves, April–May	With leaves, March or April	Before leaves, March or April
Catkin-scales	Black-tipped	Uniformly yellow-green	Black-tipped
Catkin stamens	2, separate, yellow	3, separate, yellow	2, joined, red-purple

Common Osier (*S. viminalis*) may be a tree up to 10 m high, but is often a shrub or treated as an osier. It is unmistakable owing to its long and very narrow leaves, dark green above and glistening white beneath, the margin untoothed, wavy, and more or less curled under. The hybrid with purple osier (*S.* x *rubra*) has the stamens joined only for part of their length and its narrowly oblanceolate leaves, 7–15 cm long, are almost hairless. It is grown as an osier.

Almond Willow (*S. triandra*) is usually a shrub but can be a tree up to 10 m high. This tree and its hybrids are distinct in their peeling bark. The hybrid with common osier, which has leaves of intermediate size and shape but becoming hairless, is grown for basket-making.

6 **Purple Osier** (*S. purpurea*) grows as a tree, up to about 4 m high, with shining dark grey bark; but it is usually a shrub and is much grown as an osier. The leaves vary greatly in width but are normally widest above the middle, and some of the winter-buds, shaped like wheat-grains standing erect, are often in opposite pairs. Purple osier has the 2 stamens of its male flowers joined throughout so as to appear a single structure.
Weeping Purple Osier is described on p. 167.

1 GREY POPLAR (*Populus canescens*)   2 BLACK POPLAR (*P. nigra* var. *betulifolia*)
(M)=male catkin; (F)=female catkin: a=top of sucker; b=summer leaves; c=spring leaves; d=autumn leaves;

4   2e   5   5b   5d   4c   2b   6   4b   6b

3 BLACK ITALIAN POPLAR (*P.* 'Serotina')   4 *P.* 'Robusta'   5 *P.* 'Regenerata'   6 *P.* 'Gelrica'.
e=young tree. Details × $\frac{2}{3}$. Text pp. 94–5

TREES OF WET PLACES

POPLARS (*Populus*); are closely related to willows (*Salix*), resembling them in having alternate deciduous leaves, catkins of male and female flowers on different individuals, and numerous small seeds surrounded by long silky hairs so that they are readily wind-carried. They differ from willows in the broader leaves, the long drooping catkins with toothed or deeply cut catkin-scales, and the oblique cup round the base of the stamens or ovary of the individual flower; and there are usually many more stamens than in willows.

NATIVE BRITISH POPLARS; ill. p. 92. One of our native poplars, the aspen, is described on p. 19 (ill. pp. 13, 17). Those dealt with here are the remaining native species.

1 **Grey Poplar** (*P. canescens*) is a large, freely suckering tree, sometimes reaching 35 m in height, with smooth grey bark patterned with rows of black rhomboidal lenticels and with somewhat downy twigs and buds. Catkins of male trees are reddish-purple in March. The early-opening leaves on short-shoots are usually almost circular, like those of aspen, but are broadest below the middle. They have 4–6 large blunt triangular teeth on each side and are dark green above but have whitish down beneath, lost later in the season. The larger ovate summer-opening leaves of the long-shoots and those on suckers are persistently downy beneath. The leaf-stalk is not or little flattened, and the catkin-scales are deeply cut. Grey poplar is regarded as native in wet woods in Southern and Eastern England and northwards to Derby and Shropshire, but has been planted elsewhere. Trees commonly occur in groups because of suckering. The grey poplar is in many respects intermediate between aspen and white poplar (p. 170): it differs from aspen in the retention of grey-white down on the undersides of late-opening leaves and in the scarcely flattened leaf-stalks; and from white poplar in the absence of definite lobing of the leaves and in the deeply cut catkin-scales (merely toothed in white poplar). It is native in much of Europe, south of a line from central France to Southern Russia and the Caucasus.

2 **Black Poplar** (*P. nigra*) is native in much of central and Southern Europe and extends into Western Asia. It is a large tree, up to 30 m high, with black deeply fissured bark, and it usually has many large bosses or burrs on the rather short trunk and larger branches. The main branches spread widely and arch downwards to form an unevenly rounded crown. The twigs are smoothly cylindrical and change from orange-yellow to grey before the third year. The leaves are 5–10 cm long, rhombic-ovate, with a broadly wedge-shaped or straight-cut base, and tapering to a long narrow-pointed tip. The margin is narrowly translucent and has many small blunt teeth. There are no glands at the junction of blade with stalk as there are on at least some of the leaves of all hybrid black poplars (see p. 95), nor are there forwardly-curved hairs on the actual leaf-margin as in the hybrid poplars. The leaf-stalk is 3–6 cm long and strongly flattened. Male catkins are reddish-purple in late March. The native form of the black poplar is var. *betulifolia*, found also in Western France and differing from the widespread continental tree in having the young twigs and leaf-stalks distinctly hairy or downy. It is now quite an uncommon tree of wet woods and streamsides in Eastern and central England, but it has been planted elsewhere and especially in parks in the Manchester area where it was found to withstand industrial pollution. Whereas the wild tree may be either male or female, the "Manchester poplar" is exclusively male, suggesting propagation by cuttings from a male parent. The continental form with hairless twigs and leaf-stalks (var. *nigra*) has also been planted here occasionally. The much more commonly grown black Italian poplar, described on p. 95, is quite different in crown shape, in the coppery colour of the very late-opening young leaves, and in other details of the leaves. It is also exclusively male.

HYBRID BLACK POPLARS; ill. pp. 92–3. These hybrids arose from crosses between the European black poplar (*P. nigra*) and either eastern cottonwood (*P. deltoides*, p. 170) of the Eastern U.S.A. or the related *P. angulata* (p. 170), but include also backcrosses to one or other parent and some hybrids with other species. They are fast-growing and their whitish easily-worked timber is both tough and light in weight. It is especially valuable for making matches, match-boxes, chip-baskets, and plywood, but its good qualities ensure a much wider range of uses. There are very many named forms in cultivation and only a few can be mentioned here. As a matter of nomenclatural convenience they are often treated as cultivars of *P.* x *canadensis* or *P.* x *euramericana*, so that the first of those described below may be cited as *P.* x *canadensis* 'Serotina', *P.* x *euramericana* 'Serotina', or merely as *P.* 'Serotina'. Their trunks lack the burrs so characteristic of our native black poplar, and in all of them at least some of the leaves have one or more glands at the junction of stalk with blade. The leaf-margin is translucent, as in all black poplars; but, as in the American parent, is ciliate with forwardly-curved hairs—sometimes not clearly visible without the help of a hand-lens—which are not present in our native black poplar. In most of the cultivars the young leaves are red or coppery in colour and the leaf-base is wide and truncate or even slightly heart-shaped, not often wedge-shaped as it commonly is in *P. nigra*.

The hybrid black poplars differ from each other chiefly in crown shape and rate of growth. Some are exclusively male, others female. They grow best in a moist site with the water-table between about 60 cm and 150 cm below the surface for most of the year, and for their most rapid growth require a good fertile soil and warm summers. They are therefore most successful in lowland Southern England but can grow further north if the soil is sufficiently fertile to compensate for cooler summers.

Black Italian Poplar (*P.* 'Serotina') is the oldest of the hybrids, dating from before 1755 and the one to which the name "black Italian poplar" was first applied, though it is now often used loosely for the whole complex of hybrids. 'Serotina' is a tree to 40 m high with grey fissured bark and with the main branches curving upwards to form a wide fan-shaped crown by which mature trees can be recognized from a great distance. The leaves on long-shoots are up to 20 cm long, deltoid, abruptly pointed at the tip, and truncate or slightly rounded to shallowly heart-shaped at the base, the margin having curved teeth. Those on short-shoots are smaller and are often broadly wedge-shaped at the base. The flattened leaf-stalk, 2–6 cm long, is hairless and often reddish. The top of the leaf-stalk usually has 1–2 glands but some leaves, especially those on short-shoots, have none. The Latin word *serotina* means late or backward and refers to the time of opening of the leaves—variable from year to year but often not until late May, later than in any other of the hybrid poplars and about a fortnight later than in 'Regenerata'. The leaves are copper-coloured when young. All trees are male, the bright red catkins elongating and opening in April. This is by far the commonest poplar in cultivation in this country, planted for screens and shelter-belts and as roadside trees as well as for its timber.

P. 'Robusta' is a tree with ascending branches forming a narrower crown than in 'Serotina', columnar and pointed at the top. The twigs and leaf-stalks are sparsely covered with short erect hairs when young, a feature distinguishing 'Robusta' from most other hybrids. The young leaves are bright orange-brown and are amongst the earliest to appear, as much as three weeks earlier than 'Serotina'. 'Robusta' arose as a hybrid between *P. nigra* and *P. angulata* (p. 170), the latter perhaps merely a mutant form of *P. deltoides*. It is exclusively male and very fast-growing and has been much planted in recent years.

5 *P.* 'Regenerata' is probably a backcross between 'Serotina' and *P. nigra* and is difficult to distinguish from 'Serotina' when young though its leaves open about a fortnight earlier and soon turn green. When older it develops a less deeply fissured grey bark than in 'Serotina' and a narrower crown, the branches ascending at a narrower angle but then arching outwards with slender branchlets hanging down from their ends. 'Regenerata' is widely planted for screens and shelterbelts and Mr. Alan Mitchell recommends the name "railway poplar" because of its abundance near main lines into cities. It is female only—with green catkins in late April, becoming white-woolly in ripe fruit.

6 *P.* 'Gelrica' arose as a hybrid between two hybrid parents and is very fast-growing and increasingly planted. The ascending branches arch outwards and the trunk becomes whitish rather than grey. The young twigs are grey (rather than brownish as in 'Serotina' and 'Regenerata') and the leaves are coppery, opening earlier than in 'Serotina'. The trees are exclusively male. There are not yet many large trees in this country.

Other hybrid black poplars that may be seen are the male **'Eugenei'**, which resulted from a cross between 'Regenerata' and Lombardy poplar and is columnar with dense ascending branches and pendulous branchlets; and **'Marilandica'**, female, with a wide-spreading and almost globular crown and upturned branchlets.

1	2	3	4	5	6	4	7	8

I Old northern mixed hedgerow (June). The shrubs and trees show signs of having been pollarded and/or laid in the past.

12	2	13	14 15	13 16	8	10	12

IA Southern mixed hedgerow (December). Travellers' joy, climbing over privet, dogwood, and spindle tree, are useful indicators of chalk soil

III Straight hawthorn hedge, indicating an area of land enclosed in the late eighteenth or early nineteenth century

1 GUELDER ROSE (*Viburnum opulus*)   2 COMMON HAWTHORN (*Crataegus monogyna*)   3 HAZEL (*Corylus avellana*)
7 ALDER (*Alnus glutinosa*)   8 ELDER (*Sambucus nigra*)   9 BIRD CHERRY (*Prunus padus*)
13 DOGWOOD (*Cornus sanguinea*)   14 COMMON PRIVET (*Ligustrum vulgare*)   15 TRAVELLERS' JOY (*Clematis vitalba*)

9   4   3   9   10   11   10

II Trees are sometimes left to mature by the hedge trimmers: holly is the most frequent tree in hedgerows; wych elm is plentiful in the north

10   8   17   18   2   13 18   17   17   17   18 17

IIA Beech, yew, and holly are the trees most often left in roadside hedges on chalk. Beech hedges retain their leaves in winter

V English elm (*Ulmus procera*), the commonest hedgerow tree in Southern England

4 SLOE (*Prunus spinosa*)   5 COMMON SALLOW (*Salix cinerea*)   6 MOUNTAIN ASH (*Sorbus aucuparia*)
10 HOLLY (*Ilex aquifolium*)   11 WYCH ELM (*Ulmus glabra*)   12 FIELD MAPLE (*Acer campestre*)
16 SPINDLE TREE (*Euonymus europaeus*)   17 EUROPEAN BEECH (*Fagus sylvatica*)   18 YEW (*Taxus baccata*).   Text pp. 98–9

HEDGES

Hedges (ill. pp. 96–7) are a conspicuous feature of the general landscape only in those parts of Europe, mainly in the west and north-west, where intensive grazing by farm animals is possible because of the high quality and productivity of the pastures. They are living stock-proof fences by means of which sheep or cattle can be kept in enclosures of modest extent without need of herdsmen. In tundra, moorland, or semi-arid country grazing animals must travel considerable distances each day in order to find enough food, and herdsmen are necessary to keep them together, to protect them against predators and thieves, and to prevent competition with animals belonging to different owners. The quality of the grazing in lowland Britain was in general high enough for the animals not to have to walk long distances, even on the shallow soils of the chalk and limestone hills or the sands and gravels of Southern England and East Anglia, where considerable numbers of sheep seem to have been kept as early as Saxon times. Barriers were needed, however, to keep animals out of the cultivated "open fields" (though some were no doubt tethered on the fallow and stubble) and to prevent them from straying into adjoining parishes or estates. These may in the first instance have been deep ditches, walls of earth or stone, or wooden palisades, but it must have been discovered early that a living fence, especially of thorny shrubs, had a great deal to commend it as a durable obstacle to stock. Some undoubtedly ancient parish boundaries seem to have originated as double ditches with the mounds, thrown up on either side, planted at some stage with hedges to ensure that the barrier was stock-proof. Hedges continued to be planted to mark new boundaries following the progressive enclosure, over many centuries, of former forest or "waste", either to increase the area of cultivated land or to provide enclosed pasture. Some of this hedging can be shown from old maps and records to date from before Tudor times and probably from as far back as the thirteenth century or earlier. In some villages this seems to have been true of the hedging of parts of the open fields themselves, as when a farmer had been able to collect a number of adjacent strips and enclose them for permanent pasture. Even in those Midland counties where the open-field system flourished until a later period and where large-scale enclosure dates from Tudor or subsequent periods, many existing hedges are shown on Tudor maps and presumably mark earlier enclosures.

Hawthorn was probably found from the first to be especially suitable for hedges, being easy to establish and tolerant of the cutting and laying necessary to ensure that a hedge neither becomes too large nor develops gaps at ground level. In fact hedges where hawthorn is clearly the most abundant component predominate over most of central and Northern England and lowland Scotland and are a common type everywhere. In Southern and Eastern England almost pure sloe hedges are found locally, and others of the non-thorny beech and elm. Holly and, very locally near coasts, sea buckthorn were sometimes planted. But after the more or less pure hawthorn hedge the next commonest type is that with a mixture of three or more different shrubs (see ill. I and II, p. 96). These mixed hedges seem sometimes to have been planted as such, but there are two other ways in which they appear to have arisen more commonly: from woodland shrubs along the edge of a forest clearing, and by the colonization of a once pure hawthorn hedge from seeds carried by wind or birds. There seems no doubt that mixed hedges have in fact come about in both these ways. In the country round Peterborough and Huntingdon, where careful studies have recently been made with the help of old maps, hedges identified as being of the woodland margin type are very mixed in composition and include some species either absent from planted hawthorn hedges or much less common in them—like hazel, Midland hawthorn, and wild service tree. Common woodland herbs are a feature of such hedgerows, though by no means confined to them. As for the invasion of hawthorn hedges by other shrub species, Dr. Max Hooper has shown not only that this has taken place but that it is progressive, the hedge becoming more and more mixed as time proceeds. He claims, as a general working rule, that the average number of woody species in a 30-metre length of hedge increases by about one for each century since planting. Thus a pure hawthorn hedge planted after parliamentary enclosures some 200 years ago would have on average two additional species in a 30-metre length; a hedge dating from Tudor enclosures four centuries ago would have four additional species; and if ten additional species are found the hedge must have been planted 1000 years ago—although it might have been from a mixed planting or be an old woodland margin. The most frequent additions are the wind-carried ash, sallow, and sycamore and the bird-dispersed elder, sloe, guelder rose, privet, dogwood, purging buckthorn, and, in the north, bird cherry, as well as the ubiquitous dog rose and blackberry. This explains why the straight hedges dating from the widespread parliamentary enclosures of the period 1750–1850 are still largely of hawthorn with only one or two additional species along an average 30-metre length (see ill. III, p. 96).

Hedges have served other purposes than merely to bar the movement of farm stock and mark boundaries. They yield, during the annual cutting and trimming, a valuable supply of firewood as well as blackberries and other fruits. Moreover, in most parts of the country it has been customary to allow a few well-spaced trees to grow up undisturbed, and the oaks, elms, ashes, sycamores, and, more locally, beeches of our hedgerows have provided most of the timber requirements of the small farmer (see ill. p. 97). Such trees also provide shade and shelter for stock and in the past have been an important source of food for both cattle and sheep, especially in the northern and western uplands. Ash and elm were commonly pollarded to yield leafy branches for stock, and holly has been especially valuable in this way because it remains green and nutritious throughout the winter. This probably explains why holly, common in hedges in many western counties, is so often allowed to grow up into a tree. It is still pollarded to feed stock in parts of the Lake District, but more generally it has now become merely a source of Christmas decoration.

Recent changes from grassland to arable farming and the use of large modern farm machinery have made many hedges useless or even a serious nuisance. The consequent reduction in total length has meant a considerable and, as many would feel, regrettable change in the appearance of our countryside.

1a × 1

1b × 1

3 × ⅔

1 × ⅔

2 × ⅔
(F)

2a
× 1

2b × 1

1a × 1

1b × 1

4 × ⅔
(F)

4b × 1

4a × 1

7
× ⅔

5 × ⅔
(F)

6 × ⅔
(F)

7 (F

1 NOBLE FIR (*Abies procera*)   2 NORWAY SPRUCE (*Picea abies*)   3 WESTERN HEMLOCK (*Tsuga heterophylla*)
7 CORSICAN PINE (*Pinus nigra* ssp. *laricio*)   8 CALIFORNIAN REDWOOD (*Sequoia sempervirens*)
11 SWAMP CYPRESS (*Taxodium distichum*)   12 JAPANESE UMBRELLA-PINE (*Sciadopitys verticillata*)
b = leaves from below; c = young shoot; d = young cone. Sprays and cones × ⅔; other details × 1. Text pp. 102–3, 106–7

4 DOUGLAS FIR (*Pseudotsuga menziesii*)   5 EUROPEAN LARCH (*Larix decidua*)   6 CEDAR OF LEBANON (*Cedrus libani*)
9 CALIFORNIAN BIG-TREE (*Sequoiadendron giganteum*)   10 DAWN REDWOOD (*Metasequoia glyptostroboides*)
13 JAPANESE CEDAR (*Cryptomeria japonica*). (M)=male cone; (F)=female cone; a=leaves from above;

INTRODUCED CONIFERS: Identification of Main Families

The conifers, with the unique maiden-hair tree, are the only trees hardy in the British Isles that reproduce by seed but do not have true flowers. They are divided into several families whose botanical characteristics are summarized below.

GINKGOALES

Ginkgoaceae (Maiden-hair Tree family). The maiden-hair tree of China is the sole survivor of a once large group of trees. It is readily recognizable by its fan-shaped deciduous leaves which are more or less deeply lobed and have repeatedly forking veins which do not form a closed network as in leaves of flowering plants. Stamens and ovules are borne on different trees—the stamens in drooping catkins, the ovules in long-stalked pairs, each ovule with a small fleshy collar round its base, only one of a pair usually ripening to a fleshy-walled seed looking rather like a small green plum. Most trees grown in the British Isles are male and do not often produce catkins.

CONIFERALES

The conifers differ from maiden-hair tree in a number of technical features and notably in lacking male sexual cells (sperms) capable of swimming, such as are found in mosses, ferns and, amongst seed-plants, in the palm-like cycads as well as in the maiden-hair tree. Further, no conifer has deciduous fan-shaped leaves. Conifers are so called because their ovules, which become seeds after fertilization of the egg, are usually borne on scales aggregated into compact "cones", woody when ripe. There are exceptions to this, such as juniper and yew, but it is true of the majority of conifers.

Pinaceae (Pine family). The leaves are alternate or clustered, flat and linear or needle-like, evergreen or deciduous. The twigs become brown and woody by the end of the first year. Male and female cones are borne on the same tree, both with spirally arranged scales. The female appear in spring as small erect crimson "flowers" which enlarge after pollination and become brown and woody when ripe. The scales of the female cone consist of 2 more or less separated parts, the lower "bract-scale" often projecting beyond the broader "cone-scale" which bears 2 broadly winged seeds on its upper side. The family includes the genera *Abies, Cedrus, Larix, Picea, Pinus, Pseudolarix, Pseudotsuga, Tsuga*, and a few others, and is confined to the northern hemisphere.

Taxodiaceae (Big-tree family). The leaves are usually alternate but in opposite pairs in dawn redwood (*Metasequoia*) and in distant crowded whorls in Japanese umbrella-pine (*Sciadopitys*). They are of various shapes and sizes, single-veined, evergreen or deciduous. Twigs usually remain green through the second year. Male and female cones are borne on the same tree, both with spirally arranged scales except in the dawn redwood where they are in opposite pairs. The female cones, woody when ripe, have cone-scales that consist of 2 parts but are visibly compound only at their ends, which have a groove or ridge across the middle or separate free tips to both top and bottom halves. Each scale has 2–7 narrowly winged seeds on its upper side. The family includes the genera *Athrotaxis, Cryptomeria, Cunninghamia, Metasequoia, Sciadopitys, Sequoia, Sequoiadendron, Taxodium*, and a few others, and is almost confined to the northern hemisphere.

Araucariaceae (Monkey-puzzle family). The leaves are alternate, often quite broad and with forking veins but sometimes small and narrow. They are always evergreen. The twigs remain green during the second year. Male and female cones are on different trees, both with spirally arranged scales. The male cones are much larger than in other families, those of the monkey-puzzle up to 15 cm long. The female cones become woody when ripe. They are very large and are held erect, fragmenting while still attached to the tree, the scales breaking off from above downwards. The single seed either remains fused to the scale (in *Araucaria*) or becomes detached with a thin piece of the scale which acts as a wing (in *Agathis*). Only species of *Araucaria* can be grown in the open in the British Isles, the kauri pines (*Agathis*) being too tender. Both genera are native mainly in the southern hemisphere.

Cupressaceae (Cypress family). Here the leaves are in opposite pairs or whorls of 3 and are usually small and scale-like but are sometimes short spine-tipped needles as in many junipers. They are always evergreen, and the twigs remain green through the second season. Male and female cones are on the same or different plants, their scales in opposite pairs or whorls of 3. The male cones are very tiny and the female much smaller than in typical members of the preceding families. Female cones either become woody or remain soft and berry-like as in junipers, each apparently simple scale bearing 1–20 small narrowly winged seeds. The family includes the genera *Calocedrus*, *Chamaecyparis*, *Cupressus*, *Fitzroya*, *Juniperus*, *Thuja*, and *Thujopsis* and has a world-wide distribution.

Podocarpaceae (Podocarp family). The leaves are alternate and evergreen; they are of varying size and shape but the hardy species commonly seen in the British Isles have linear or narrowly lanceolate leaves. Male and female cones are on different plants, with their scales spirally arranged. Female cones have one or a few fertile scales, each bearing a single ovule which at maturity is more or less enclosed in fleshy structures of various kinds and colours, making it attractive to birds. The family includes the genera *Podocarpus*, *Saxegothaea*, and some others, native mainly in the southern hemisphere.

Cephalotaxaceae (Cow's-tail Pine family). These are shrubs or small bushy trees with alternate evergreen leaves resembling those of yew but longer. The twigs remain green for 3 years. Male and female cones are on different plants, the male borne along the underside of young shoots. The female cones have several pairs of scales each bearing 2 ovules, but usually only one ripens to a seed resembling an olive, with the outer layer of its wall fleshy, the inner stony. This small family includes the genus *Cephalotaxus* and is confined to Eastern Asia.

Taxaceae (Yew family). The leaves are alternate (rarely opposite), linear, flat, and evergreen, and the twigs remain green through the second year, though reddish twigs may develop in *Torreya*. The male cones are small and their stamens are exceptional amongst conifers in having expanded heads to which 5–9 pollen-sacs are attached all round the stalk. The female cones consist of a few sterile basal scales and a single terminal ovule which ripens to a large seed more or less enclosed in a fleshy cup or "aril", variously coloured when ripe (bright red in our native yew). Members of this small family, comprising the true yews (*Taxus*), the nutmeg-yews (*Torreya*), and one or two other genera, are scattered throughout the northern hemisphere.

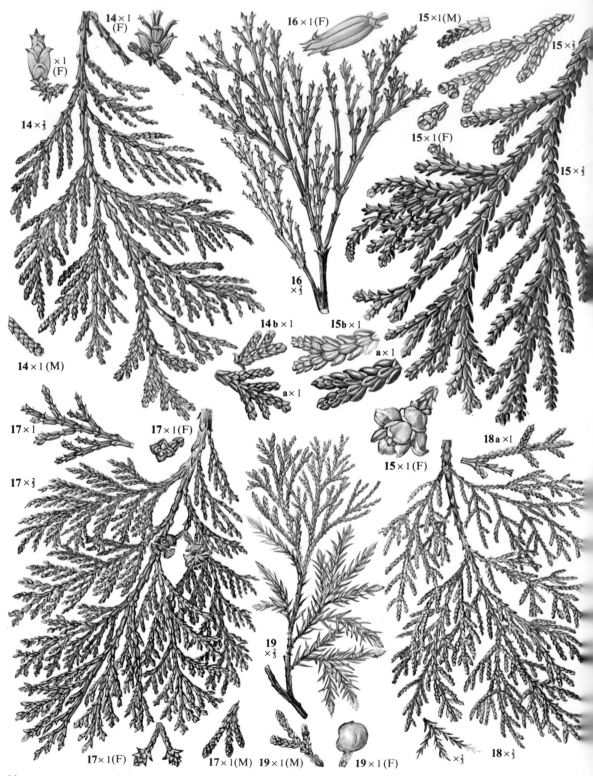

14 × 1 (F)

× 1 (F)

14 × ⅔

14 × 1 (M)

16 × 1 (F)

15 × 1 (M)

15 × ⅔

15 × 1 (F)

15 × ⅔

16 × ⅔

14b × 1

a × 1

15b × 1

a × 1

17 × 1

17 × 1 (F)

17 × ⅔

18a × 1

15 × 1 (F)

19 × ⅔

17 × 1 (F)

17 × 1 (M)

19 × 1 (M)

19 × 1 (F)

× ⅔

18 × ⅔

14 WESTERN RED CEDAR (*Thuja plicata*)   15 HIBA (*Thujopsis dolabrata*)   16 INCENSE CEDAR (*Calocedrus decurrens*)
19 CHINESE JUNIPER (*Juniperus chinensis*)   20 MONKEY-PUZZLE TREE (*Araucaria araucana*)
23 CALIFORNIAN NUTMEG (*Torreya californica*)   24 MAIDEN-HAIR TREE (*Ginkgo biloba*). (M) = male cone;

$20 \times \frac{1}{16}(\text{F})$

$20 \times \frac{2}{3}$

$21 \times \frac{2}{3}$

22

$22\,\text{a} \times 1$

$\text{b} \times 1$

$23 \times \frac{2}{3}$

$23\,\text{a} \times 1$

$\text{b} \times 1$

$24 \times \frac{2}{3}$

17 LAWSON'S CYPRESS (*Chamaecyparis lawsoniana*)   18 MONTEREY CYPRESS (*Cupressus macrocarpa*)
21 IRISH YEW (*Taxus baccata* 'Fastigiata')   22 PLUM-FRUITED YEW (*Podocarpus andinus*)
(F) = female cone; a = leaves from above; b = leaves from below. Text pp. 102–3, 106–7

INTRODUCED CONIFERS: Key to Main Genera (ill. pp. 100–1, 104–5)

1   Leaves deciduous ⇨ 2
    Leaves evergreen ⇨ 6

2   Leaves fan-shaped, more or less deeply 2-lobed, with forking veins = Maiden-hair Tree (*Gingko biloba*) (ill. 24)
    Leaves linear (narrow and more or less parallel-sided), 1-veined ⇨ 3

3   Leaves densely clustered at ends of woody short-shoots or "spurs" ⇨ 4
    Leaves in 2 rows on deciduous branchlets ⇨ 5

4   Spurs becoming long and curved; leaves with pale edges; cones fragmenting when ripe = Golden Larch
        (*Pseudolarix*)
    Spurs short and straight; leaves not pale-edged; cones remaining intact when ripe = Larches (*Larix*) (ill. 5)

5   Leaves in opposite pairs = Dawn Redwood (*Metasequoia*) (ill. 10)
    Leaves alternate = Swamp Cypress (*Taxodium*) (ill. 11)

6   Leaves ovate, 2·5–4 cm long and at least 2 cm wide, spine-tipped and very rigid, with forking veins = Monkey-
        puzzle (*Araucaria*) (ill. 20)
    Leaves of varying shape and size but less than 2 cm wide ⇨ 7

7   Green leaves 10–15 cm long, 3–4 mm wide, in distant whorls of 10–30, with brown scales forming bumps on
        stem between whorls = Umbrella-pine (*Sciadopitys*) (ill. 12)
    Green leaves not in distant whorls ⇨ 8

8   Leaves more or less regularly spaced along shoots ⇨ 10
    Most leaves in bundles of 2–5 or in dense clusters at ends of woody "spurs" ⇨ 9

9   Leaves in bundles of 2–5 = Pines (*Pinus*) (ill. 7)
    Leaves in dense clusters on woody spurs = Cedars (*Cedrus*) (ill. 6)

10 Leaves alternate ⇨ 11
    Leaves in opposite pairs or whorls of 3 ⇨ 26

11 Leaves of 2 kinds—those on main and fertile stems only 6–8 mm long, scale-like, sharp-pointed, those on side
        branches linear, 6–20 mm long, shortest at two ends of a season's growth, longest round the middle; bark
        orange to dark red, spongy = Californian Redwood (*Sequoia*) (ill. 8).
    Leaves not of 2 kinds ⇨ 12

12 Leaves narrowly lanceolate, 3–7 cm long, up to 5 mm across just above base—tapering steadily to a long fine
        point, with 2 broad whitish bands beneath = Chinese Fir (*Cunninghamia*)
    Leaves linear, or overlapping and scale-like so as to conceal stem more or less completely ⇨ 13

13 Twigs already brown and woody at end of first year's growth ⇨ 14
    Twigs still entirely or partly green during second year of growth ⇨ 17

14 Scars of fallen or detached leaves circular and almost flat; cones erect and breaking up at maturity = Silver Firs
        (*Abies*) (ill. 1)
    Leaf-scars raised above surface of stem on persistent peg-like bases; cones pendulous, remaining intact at
        maturity and after falling ⇨ 15

15 Leaves with distinct green stalk pressed close to stem; cones only 2–3·5 cm long, bract-scales not visible at
        surface = Hemlock Spruces (*Tsuga*) (ill. 3)
    Leaves with indistinct or very short green stalks; cones usually at least 5 cm long ⇨ 16

16 Persistent leaf-bases prominently raised so that leafless stem is very rough; bract-scales not visible at cone surface
        = Spruce Firs (*Picea*) (ill. 2)
    Persistent leaf-bases not very prominent; bract-scales 3-pointed, projecting well beyond cone-scales = Douglas
        Firs (*Pseudotsuga*) (ill. 4)

17 Leaves linear and flattened (like those of yew) ⇨ 18
    Leaves not linear and flattened ⇨ 23

18 Leaves with 2 conspicuous whitish bands on lower side ⇨ 19
    Leaves uniformly green beneath, without whitish bands ⇨ 22

19 Most leaves less than 2·5 cm long ⇨ 20
    Most leaves more than 2·5 cm long ⇨ 21

20 Stem ridged below each leaf; branchlets pendulous = Prince Albert's Yew (*Saxegothaea conspicua*)
    Stem not ridged; branchlets not pendulous = Plum-fruited Yew (*Podocarpus andinus*) (ill. 22)

21 White bands beneath leaf narrow and sunken; leaf stiff and spine-tipped = Californian Nutmegs (*Torreya*) (ill. 23)
    White bands beneath leaf broad, not sunken; leaf pointed but not spiny = Cow's-tail Pine (*Cephalotaxus*)

22 Leaves 5–12 cm long, curving; stem not ridged = Willow Podocarp (*Podocarpus salignus*)
    Leaves 2–4 cm long, straight; stem ridged below each leaf = Yew (*Taxus*) (ill. 21)

23 Leaves scale-like, entirely pressed against stem or curving outwards but with tip incurved ⇨ 24
    Leaves not scale-like and pressed to stem ⇨ 25

24 Leaves less than 3 mm long = Tasmanian Cedars (*Athrotaxis*)
    Leaves more than 3 mm long = Big-tree (*Sequoiadendron*) (ill. 9)

25 Leaves rounded in section, tapering from base to non-spiny tip and curving forward, no white band beneath =
    Japanese Cedar (*Cryptomeria*) (ill. 13)
    Leaves flattened, tapering from base to a spiny tip and with 2 broad white bands beneath = King William Pine
    (*Athrotaxis selaginoides*)

26 Some or all leaves more or less broadly scale-like and pressed close to stem or with only tip raised ⇨ 29
    All leaves spreading ⇨ 27

27 Leaves mostly in opposite pairs, soft, often variegated = False Cypresses (*Chamaecyparis*) with permanently
    juvenile foliage
    Leaves in whorls of 3, usually stiff ⇨ 28

28 Leaves 2–4 mm long, oblong with rounded but short-pointed tip, dark blue-green with white bands above and
    below = Patagonian Cypress (*Fitzroya cupressoides*)
    Leaves more than 5 mm long, slender, finely pointed = Junipers (*Juniperus*) (ill. 19)

29 Scale-like and spreading leaves borne on same shoot ⇨ 30
    All leaves scale-like ⇨ 31

30 Spreading leaves in opposite pairs or whorls of 3, stiff and sharp-pointed = Junipers (*Juniperus*) (ill. 19)
    Spreading leaves usually in opposite pairs, slender and soft = False Cypresses (*Chamaecyparis*) retaining juvenile
    foliage (ill. 17)

31 Leafy shoots with their branching confined to single plane to give flat sprays of foliage held horizontally, vertically,
    or obliquely ⇨ 32
    Leafy shoots with branchlets in all directions, not in extensive flat sprays = True Cypresses (*Cupressus*) (ill. 18)
    and Hybrid Cypresses (x *Cupressocyparis*)

32 Individual shoots strongly flattened, up to 5 mm wide; exposed faces of leaves on underside of shoot white except
    for narrow green margin = Hiba (*Thujopsis*) (ill. 15)
    Individual shoots flattened or not, less than 5 mm wide ⇨ 33

33 Female cones up to about 1 cm long, almost globular, ends of scales angular and touching along their edges—
    not overlapping = False Cypresses (*Chamaecyparis*) (ill. 17) and Hybrid Cypresses (x *Cupressocyparis*)
    Female cones 1–2 cm or more long, at first ovoid but becoming cylindrical or flask-shaped when overlapping scales
    curve outwards in open cone ⇨ 34

34 Lateral leaves almost hiding much smaller top-and-bottom leaves, their tips reaching beyond them = Chilean
    Incense Cedar (*Austrocedrus chilensis*)
    Tips of lateral leaves falling short of or about equalling those of next pair of top-and-bottom leaves ⇨ 35

35 Tree narrowly columnar; leaves appearing to be in rather distant whorls of 4; cones cylindrical = Incense Cedar
    (*Calocedrus*) (ill. 16)
    Trees and shrubs with conical crowns; leaves appearing crowded; cones narrowly or broadly flask-shaped =
    Thuyas (*Thuja*) (ill. 14)

m 45

40

35

30

25

20

15

10

5

0

scale for trees 1, 2, 3, 4, 5, 6, & 7

1

2

3

$1 \times \frac{2}{3}$ (F)

$1c \times \frac{2}{3}$

$1 \times \frac{2}{3}$ (M)

$1 \times \frac{2}{3}$ (M)

$2 \times \frac{2}{3}$ (F)

3

2

$2a \times 1$

$2b \times 1$

1 NOBLE FIR (*Abies procera*)   2 GRAND FIR (*A. grandis*)   3 NORWAY SPRUCE (*Picea abies*)
7 DOUGLAS FIR (*Pseudotsuga menziesii*). (M)=male cone; (F)=female cone;
Text pp. 110–11

4 SITKA SPRUCE (*P. sitchensis*)   5 SERBIAN SPRUCE (*P. omorika*)   6 WESTERN HEMLOCK (*Tsuga heterophylla*)
a=leaf from above; b=leaf from below; c=individual mature female cone-scales with bracts and ripe seeds.

INTRODUCED CONIFERS: Commercially Planted

SILVER FIRS (*Abies*), which belong to the family Pinaceae (p. 102), have evergreen linear leaves regularly spaced along the stems and leaving very distinctive flat circular scars when they fall or are removed. The female cones mature in a single season. In some species, but not in all, the bract-scales project beyond the cone-scales. The cones are held erect and their scales eventually fall off from above downwards, releasing the pairs of broadly winged seeds but leaving the slender cone-axis on the tree. For a key to all species of silver firs commonly grown in this country see p. 202; species commonly grown in parks and gardens are described on p. 118. Two silver firs have been planted extensively for commercial purposes.

1 **Noble Fir** (*A. procera*, formerly *A. nobilis*); ill. p. 108. This tree may reach 80 m in height in western North America where it is native. It is at first narrowly conical but may broaden later and become flat-topped. The young stems are orange-brown and finely downy but turn dark purple-brown; and the winter-buds are small, rounded, and dark purplish. The leaves are 1–3·5 cm long, those above the stem crowded, pointing forwards at their base and then curving upwards and almost concealing the stem; those below the stem are parted to left and right and upturned. They are bluish-green, flat, grooved on top, and with 2 whitish bands beneath. The tip is simply rounded, not notched. The mature cones are 15–25 cm long with projecting down-curved bract-scales. Noble fir is much planted for ornament and may become commercially valuable in western upland areas.

2 **Grand Fir** (*A. grandis*); ill. p. 108. This tree—reaching 80 m in height in western North America where it is native and, so far, 54 m in the British Isles—is narrowly conical but becoming broader. Young stems are pale brownish-green, and the winter-buds are only 2 mm long, purplish and resinous. The leaves, 1–5 cm long, are all spread horizontally to left and right of the stem in overlapping layers with the shortest on top. They are dark glossy green, grooved on top and with 2 white bands beneath: the leaf-tip is rounded and usually notched. Mature cones are red-brown, 6–10 cm long, with the bract-scales not visible. Grand fir is very promising as a fast-growing timber tree for good sites in areas of fairly high rainfall.

Low's White Fir (*A. concolor* var. *lowiana*), also from the western part of North America, differs from grand fir only in its rather longer leaves—2–7 cm long, with some rows of white dots on top as well as white bands beneath. Low's fir has shown promise in experimental planting.

SPRUCE FIRS (*Picea*). This genus belongs to the family Pinaceae (p. 102). Spruce Firs have linear evergreen leaves which, when they fall or are removed, leave strongly projecting woody pegs, making the bared stem very rough. The leaves are either flat or 4-sided and their tips are not notched. The female cones ripen in a single season. They are pendulous and the very small bract-scales cannot be seen at the cone surface. The cone remains intact, the scales gaping apart to release the winged seeds. For a key to commonly grown spruce firs, see p. 203. Species commonly grown in parks and gardens are described on p. 119.

3 **Norway Spruce** (*P. abies*, formerly *P. excelsa*); ill. p. 108. This tree, native in central and Northern Europe, has reached over 40 m high in favourable sites in the British Isles. It is narrowly conical with the whorled main branches spreading and the lower ones drooping, the branchlets more or less pendulous. The reddish-brown young stem is hairless or has small scattered hairs, and the dark brown winter-buds are about 5 mm long. The leaves, mostly 1–2 cm long, are widely parted below and spread to left and right of the stem, but those on the upper side point forwards and overlap. They are stiff and horny-pointed, with 4 sides all dark yellow-green and all with a few rows of faint white dots. The ripe cones are 12–18 cm long, pale brown. Norway spruce is much planted for timber and for Christmas trees.

4 **Sitka** or **Silver Spruce** (*P. sitchensis*); ill. p. 109. Native and up to 80 m high in western North America, this is at first narrowly conical but broadens later. Young stems are hairless and become orange-brown, and the buds are pale brown and resinous. The leaves spread horizontally sideways beneath the stem but point forwards on the upper side. They are 1–2·5 cm long, slender, flat, very sharp-pointed, blue-green above, and with 2 distinct white bands beneath. The ripe cones are 5–10 cm long, very pale brown and with toothed and wavy ends to the scales, and they are curiously soft but springy to handle. Sitka spruce thrives in wetter parts of the British Isles on all but the poorest soils and peats but suffers from late spring frosts. This is our most widely planted exotic tree and the tallest already exceed 50 m.

Serbian Spruce (*P. omorika*); ill. p. 109. This is native on limestone in Yugoslavia and has a narrow conical crown. The young stems are hairy and the leaves, 1–2 cm long, are flat, dark shining blue-green above and with 2 broad white bands beneath. The tip is rounded with or without an abrupt short point. The ripe cones are 3–6 cm long. Serbian spruce has reached 28 m in the British Isles and promises to be commercially useful, but is not yet widely planted.

HEMLOCKS or **HEMLOCK SPRUCES** (*Tsuga*) belong to the family Pinaceae (p. 102). They have evergreen linear leaves spaced regularly along the stems. Hemlocks differ from silver firs in the raised bumps left when leaves fall, and from spruce firs and Douglas firs in having very distinct leaf-stalks, which lie close-pressed to the stem. The cones are small and pendulous; they remain intact when ripe and have bract-scales too short to be visible at the cone surface. (Other introduced species are described on p. 122.)

Western Hemlock (*T. heterophylla*); ill. p. 109. This narrowly conical tree, native in western North America, reaches 40–50 m in height in the British Isles. The leading shoot arches widely over so that its tip points downwards. Young stems are covered with coarse wavy pale hairs. The leaves are well parted both above and below the stem, the lower and longer spreading horizontally at right angles to the stem, the short upper leaves pointing forwards and often inclining upwards. They vary in length from less than 5 mm to about 18 mm, tapering slightly to a rounded tip, and are eventually shining dark green above, with 2 broad white bands beneath. The rounded bumps to which the leaf-stalks are attached, and which remain when the leaves fall, are shining orange-brown. The ripe cones are 2–3 cm long. Western hemlock has been much planted for timber and has proved useful in the rehabilitation of run-down deciduous woodland because of its shade-tolerance.

DOUGLAS FIRS (*Pseudotsuga*) belong to the family Pinaceae (p. 102). They have linear evergreen leaves spaced along the stem. These are narrowed into the base but not as distinctly stalked as in hemlocks. The oval scars left when they fall are slightly raised above the surface of the stem, and so are intermediate between those of silver firs and spruce firs. The female cones are pendulous; they ripen in a single season and remain intact. The 3-pointed bract-scales project beyond the cone-scales. Only one species is likely to be seen in the British Isles.

Douglas Fir (*P. menziesii*); ill. p. 109. This very tall broadly conical tree up to 100 m in height in western North America where it is native, reaches over 50 m in the British Isles. The young stems are yellowish-green, minutely downy; the winter-buds are glossy brown and pointed. The leaves are 2–3 cm or more long, at first dull green but becoming dark and glossy above, with 2 white bands beneath and a blunt unnotched tip. They spread obliquely to left and right of the stem but with some curving forwards and upwards on the upper side and often with a few directed forwards on the lower side as well. Douglas fir extends from British Columbia to Mexico, and the northern forms, often called Oregon Douglas, have the old leaves dark green and mostly parted to form a V-shaped trough on the upper side of the stem, and the cones are 7–10 cm long with the bract-scales lying forwards close to the cone surface. The southern forms, called Colorado Douglas, have blue-green leaves, less clearly parted on the upper side, and the cones are only 5–7·5 cm long with the bract-scales curved back towards the stalk. There are intermediates between the extreme types. Douglas fir has been much planted for commercial purposes and does well except on the poorest and most wind-exposed sites but it may suffer from drought in Eastern England and also from late frosts. The wood is called "Oregon pine".

m 40

35

30

25

20

15

10

5

0

scale for trees 1, 2, 4, 5, 6, 7, 8, & 9

1   2   4   5

(F)   (M)   (F)   (F)   (F)   (F)   (M)   (F)   (F)   1   2   3   4

1 EUROPEAN LARCH (*Larix decidua*)   2 JAPANESE LARCH (*L. kaempferi*)
5 MONTEREY PINE (*P. radiata*)—see also p. 121   6 COASTAL LODGEPOLE PINE (*P. contorta* var. *contorta*)
9 LAWSON'S CYPRESS (*Chamaecyparis lawsoniana*). (M) = male cones; (F) = female cones. Details × ⅔. Text pp. 114–15

113

3 DUNKELD LARCH (*L.* x *eurolepis*)—cone details only   4 CORSICAN PINE (*Pinus nigra* ssp. *laricio*)
7 INLAND LODGEPOLE PINE (*P. contorta* var. *latifolia*)—young tree   8 WESTERN RED CEDAR (*Thuja plicata*)

INTRODUCED CONIFERS: Commercially Planted

LARCHES (*Larix*) belong to the family Pinaceae (p. 102). Their leaves are clustered at the ends of woody short-shoots, except for the few that are regularly spaced along first-year long-shoots. The leaves on short-shoots are deciduous. The female cones become woody and ripen within a single season. They are usually held erect and remain intact when ripe. The bract-scales in some species are not visible or barely visible at the cone surface, but in others they project well beyond the cone-scales. The three larches commonly grown in the British Isles are described below. See also the table on p. 203.

1 **European Larch** (*L. decidua*); ill. p. 112. This is an alpine tree of central Europe. It can exceed 40 m in height and is much grown in the British Isles for the strength of its timber and is often planted in mixture with other trees because even early thinnings are valuable as poles. It is hardy but suffers from late frosts and salt spray. It is also much grown as an ornamental tree for the beauty of its fresh-green foliage in spring and its autumn colouring. The young female cones are bright red in April.

2 **Japanese Larch** (*L. kaempferi*, formerly *L. leptolepis*); ill. p. 112. Japanese larch is native in mountain areas of Japan and grows up to 35 m in height. It has become one of the most important of our introduced conifers, largely because it is much less susceptible to a fungal disease, larch canker, that causes serious damage to European larch.

3 **Dunkeld Larch** (*L. x eurolepis = L. decidua* x *L. kaempferi*); ill. p. 112. This larch is also resistant to larch canker and grows somewhat faster than either parent on the best soils. In the British Isles it has already exceeded 30 m in height. The first-generation hybrid is intermediate between the parents, but trees grown from seed derived from hybrid trees show great variation.

PINES (*Pinus*) belong to the family Pinaceae (p. 102). They are readily distinguishable from all other conifers because most of their leaves are in groups, usually of 2–5, on short spurs. There are about 100 species of pines varying greatly in size and ranging all over the northern hemisphere. Young trees are usually conical and have regular whorls of lateral branches, but they may become rounded or flat-topped with age. Each leaf-bearing spur arises in the axil of a scale-leaf and has a basal sheath of papery scales and a terminal group of 2–5 needle-like green leaves. After two or three years the whole spur is shed with its needles. The young female cones are tiny erect crimson "flowers" which enlarge after pollination and turn downwards, becoming first green and finally brown and woody. They normally take two seasons to reach their final size and the end of the cone-scale shows a small lozenge-shaped area (the umbo) which was the whole of the scale-end after one season's growth but is later surrounded, or nearly so, by the additional growth of the second season. Pines with 2 or 3 needles on each spur have the umbo central on the scale-end, but 5-needle pines have it at the tip. Cones normally open and shed their seeds during dry periods of the late winter and early spring almost two years after the appearance of the "flowers", but three years or more elapse before seed-shedding in some species.

Apart from the native Scots pine (*P. sylvestris*, p. 27), the following three species have been extensively planted for commercial purposes. A key to these species and other commonly planted pines is given on p. 204. See also p. 123.

4 **Corsican Pine** (*P. nigra* ssp. *laricio*); ill. p. 112. Native in Corsica, this pine reaches up to 35 m in the British Isles. It is conical at first but old trees may become flat-topped. The bark becomes dark grey and fissured. Young stems are red-brown and hairless and the winter-buds are up to 2 cm long, light brown and resin-covered. The leaves are in pairs, 10–16 cm long, light or greyish green, slender, and tending to be twisted and untidy in appearance.

The ripe cones are 6–8 cm long, yellow-brown, with the ends of the scales horizontally ridged and with a short prickle. Corsican pine requires a warm summer and has been extensively planted only in Eastern and Southern Britain and especially in sands and gravels: there are some plantations on sand-dunes in Wales and Scotland.

5 Monterey Pine (*P. radiata*); ill. p. 112. Native only in a small area of coastal hills and islands of Monterey Bay, California, this is a fast-growing tree with dark grey-brown and deeply fissured bark. Its conical crown broadens later and is bounded below by ascending living or dead branches. Young stems are hairless and the winter-buds are 1–2 cm long, abruptly pointed, brown, and resinous. The leaves are in threes, 10–15 cm long, bright green, slender, and straight. The broadly ovoid ripe cones are 7–15 cm long, very short-stalked and strongly asymmetrical at the base, with the ends of the cone-scales rounded and glossy brown (see ill. p. 121). They are mostly borne in whorls of up to 5 or more and may remain on the tree for many years. Monterey pine is not completely frost-hardy and requires a warm summer, and commercial plantings here have been restricted to South-western England, with a few up the western coastal belt as far as the north of Scotland.

6–7 Coastal Lodgepole Pine or **Shore Pine** (*P. contorta* var. *contorta*) (**6**) and **Inland Lodgepole Pine** (*P. contorta* var. *latifolia* (**7**); ill. p. 113. Lodgepole pine in the broad sense is a wide-ranging tree of western North America from lower California to Alaska and inland to the Rocky Mountains. It varies from one part to another: the description given here is of the coastal form (**6**) now planted extensively in this country, but there are no clear-cut distinctions between this and the taller inland forms (**7**). Coastal lodgepole pine reaches 10–25 m in height and in general form resembles Scots pine. The branches are short and twisted and the crown often becomes flat-topped with age. The bark is brownish-black with a pattern of small square plates. Young stems are brownish-green and hairless, later orange-brown, and the winter-buds are dark chestnut-brown and resinous. The leaves are in pairs 3–5 cm long, rigid but often twisted and densely covering the stem.

The ripe cones are 2–6 cm long, scarcely stalked, with the ends of the scales pale shining brown and with a longish prickle that may fall off early. They are in whorls of 2–5 and may remain on the tree for many years. Coastal lodgepole has been found valuable for the poorest upland soils of the north and west and is used either alone, as a pioneer tree to prepare the site for other species to be planted later, or as a shelter for more exacting species planted at the same time. It has the further advantage of being able to suppress luxuriant heather. The timber is useful for pit-props, box-wood, and wood-pulp.

THUYAS (*Thuja*) **and FALSE CYPRESSES** (*Chamaecyparis*). These two genera belong to the family Cupressaceae (p. 103). They are similar in having opposite pairs of small scale-like leaves, close-pressed to the stem except near their tips, and in having the higher orders of branching restricted to a single plane—giving flat green sprays held at various angles. They differ in their mature female cones: in thuyas these are at first ovoid but widen above when the overlapping scales gape apart to open the cone; in false cypresses they are nearly spherical, with the angular ends of the scales touching only along their edges until they part to release the seeds. (See also table p. 205.)

Western Red Cedar (*Thuja plicata*); ill. p. 113. Western red cedar is native in western North America from Alaska to California. It is a tall narrowly conical tree which has already reached 40 m in height in the British Isles. Its bark is at first cinnamon-red but later turns greyish. The leading shoot is straight and erect or nearly so. The leaves on small branchlets are about 3 mm long: the bright yellow-green glossy upper side may have an indistinct central translucent dot or "gland"; the lower side is paler and white-streaked. The unopen cones are erect, narrowly ovoid-oblong, and about 1 cm long. In the British Isles western red cedar thrives best in the west and north, in sheltered sites on deep moist soils.
For a description of other introduced species, see p. 130.

9 Lawson's Cypress (*Chamaecyparis lawsoniana*); ill. p. 113. This tree, also from western North America, is similar in form though denser than western cedar but is readily distinguishable by its drooping leading shoot and its smaller blue-green leaves, only 2–3 mm long on smaller branchlets. Those on the upper side have a central translucent gland, and those beneath are paler and indistinctly white-streaked. The spherical cones are only up to 8 mm across. This cypress is grown everywhere as an ornamental tree in innumerable horticultural varieties and has been planted commercially on a small scale. It may have a limited value as a pioneer tree on very poor sites.
For a description of other introduced species, see p. 131.

m 40

30

20

10

5

0

scale for trees 1, 2, 3, 4, 5, 7, 9, & 10

1 EUROPEAN SILVER FIR (*Abies alba*) 2 FORREST'S FIR (*A. delavayi* var. *forrestii*) 3 KOREAN FIR (*A. koreana*)
7 BLUE SPRUCE (*Picea pungens* 'Glauca') 8 ORIENTAL SPRUCE (*P. orientalis*)—details only
a = individual female cone-scales. Details × ⅔. Text pp. 118–19

4 CAUCASIAN FIR (*A. nordmanniana*)   5 SPANISH FIR (*A. pinsapo*)   6 VEITCH'S SILVER FIR (*A. veitchii*)—details only
9 WEST HIMALAYAN SPRUCE (*P. smithiana*)   10 SARGENT'S SPRUCE (*P. brachytyla*). (M)=male cone; (F)=female cone;

INTRODUCED CONIFERS: Parks and Gardens

SILVER FIRS (*Abies*) belong to the family Pinaceae (p. 102). A general account of the genus is given on p. 110 and a key to commonly cultivated species on p. 202. There are about 40 species, most of them shapely trees with attractive foliage, and many are at least occasionally planted here. It has been possible to illustrate in this book only those most commonly grown.

1 **European Silver Fir** or **Common Silver Fir** (*A. alba*); ill. p. 116. This forest-forming tree of the mountains of central Europe has initially a narrowly conical crown with regular whorls of horizontal branches upturned near their ends, but older trees become irregular in shape. In sheltered sites on moist fertile soils it can reach greater heights than any other European tree, not infrequently up to 55 m and occasionally to 70 m. The bark is dark grey, at first smooth but later developing a pattern of small square plates. The young stem is buff-coloured and covered with short dark hairs, and the winter-buds are ovoid, red-brown, and not or only slightly resinous. The linear leaves, mostly 1–2·5 cm long, are well parted above and below the stem so that most of them lie more or less in a single horizontal plane in overlapping layers with the longest leaves below, but the short upper leaves may be inclined upwards. Each leaf is dark glossy green above and has 2 narrow white bands beneath. The ripe female cones are 10–15 cm long, with strongly down-curved bract-scales. This fine fir, the Tannenbaum of German-speaking peoples, is no longer being planted in the British Isles because of damage by various insect and fungal diseases, but old trees may often be seen, especially in the west and north.

2 **Forrest's Fir** (*A. delavayi* var. *forrestii*); ill. p. 116. Native in China, this tall conical tree reaches 20 m high in the British Isles, with smooth grey bark. Young stems are rusty-red, hairless or nearly so, and the large winter-buds are broadly ovoid, up to 6 mm long, and very resinous. The leaves, 2–4 cm long, are usually parted into a narrow V-shaped trough above the stem where they are crowded and inclined forwards, while those beneath the stem tend to spread sideways. They are dark green and grooved above, with 2 shining white bands beneath. The leaf-tip is truncate and notched. The ripe female cones are about 9 cm long with the narrow tips of the bract-scales projecting.

3 **Korean Fir** (*A. koreana*); ill. p. 116. This is known in the British Isles only as a bush or small tree up to 10 m, of broadly conical shape and with smooth dark olive-brown bark becoming rough later. Young stems are pale and slightly downy, and the almost spherical winter-buds are brown and resinous. The leaves are mostly 1–2 cm long and distinctly broadest close to the notched tip. They are crowded above the stem, pointing forwards and upwards or even curving backwards, those beneath also for the most part directed forwards. All are dark green above and have 2 very broad white bands beneath. The ripe female cones are 5–7 cm long, with only the tips of the bract-scales showing.

4 **Caucasian Fir** (*A. nordmanniana*); ill. p. 116. Native in the Caucasus and Northern Anatolia, this tall conical tree reaches 70 m high, commonly with a stout trunk and smooth grey bark. The young stem is brownish-green and more or less downy, and the winter-buds are pale brown and not resinous. The leaves, 1·5–3·5 cm long, are well parted beneath to spread obliquely forwards, but the shorter leaves above the stem point forwards close over it. All are dark glossy green and grooved above with 2 white bands beneath, and are notched at the rounded tip. The ripe female cones are 5–7 cm long with only the tips of the bract-scales showing.

5 **Spanish Fir** (*A. pinsapo*); ill. p. 116. This is native in South-western Spain and reaches up to 30 m. It is conical at first and has a stout trunk with dark bark at first smooth but later cracked into lifting plates. The short thick leaves, 1–2 cm long, stand stiffly perpendicular to the stem and equally so all round it. They are bluish-green, usually with lines of white dots above and distinct white bands beneath, and the tip is blunt or short-pointed, unnotched. The ripe female cones are 10–15 cm long, with the bract-scales not visible.

The only other fir with leaves arranged strictly radially all round the stem is the **Greek Fir** (*A. cephalonica*) differing in its longer leaves, 1·5–3 cm long, which end in a sharp point and have no white dots on the upper side. In **Nikko Fir** (*A. homolepis*, formerly *A. brachyphylla*) the rigid leaves part to form a V-shaped trough above and spread horizontally beneath, and they have blunt notched tips. They are up to 2·5 cm long.

6 **Veitch's Silver Fir** (*A. veitchii*); ill. p. 116. Native in Japan, this is a broadly conical tree, about 25 m high, with the lower branches often markedly upturned. The bark is dark grey and smooth. Young stems are pale brownish and more or less downy, and the winter-buds are small and rounded, 2–3 mm long, dark purplish, and resinous. The leaves are 1–2·5 cm long, spreading horizontally to left and right of the stem beneath, but the shorter leaves above point forwards and conceal the stem though they are not closely pressed to it as in Caucasian fir. They are glossy dark green above and with 2 broad and conspicuously white bands beneath, and the tip is truncate and notched. This silver fir is quite widely planted.

SPRUCE FIRS (*Picea*) belong to the family Pinaceae (p. 102). A general account of the genus is given on p. 110 and a key to commonly cultivated species on p. 203. There are about 40 species in the northern hemisphere, but no more than 10 are at all commonly planted. Some species have 4-sided leaves with faint lines of white dots about equally numerous on all the sides; others are flattened, with lines of white dots or more distinct white bands only on the downwardly-directed side, which may be either the true underside or be turned downwards by twisting of the leaf-stalk.

7   **Blue Spruce** (*P. pungens* 'Glauca'); ill. p. 117. This culti-vated variety of the Colorado spruce of the South-western U.S.A. is a narrowly conical tree already over 23 m high in the British Isles, with purplish-grey or brown bark. The young stem is pale yellowish and hairless and the winter-buds are broadly ovoid, up to 4 mm long, blunt-ended, pale yellowish-brown, and non-resinous. The leaves are 1·5–2·5 cm long, rigid and spine-tipped, spreading outwards all round the stem but more crowd-ed above. They are of varying shades of blue-green and of similar colour on all 4 sides. The ripe female cones are 6–10 cm long. Blue spruce is very much planted all over the British Isles in parks and gardens.

8   **Oriental Spruce** (*P. orientalis*); ill. p. 117. Native in the Caucasus, Armenia, and Anatolia, this narrowly conical and densely branched tree reaches 40 m or more in height and has brown scaling bark. The young shoots are pale brown and densely hairy, and the winter-buds are conical, sharp-pointed, red-brown, and non-resinous. The leaves are mostly less than 1 cm long, parted and spreading below the stem but overlapping and pointing forwards so as to conceal the upper side of the stem. They are 4-sided, similarly dark green on all 4 sides and they end in a blunt tip. The ripe female cones are 6–9 cm long and distinctly tapered to both ends. Oriental spruce is quite commonly grown all over the British Isles.

West Himalayan Spruce (*P. smithiana*, formerly *P. morinda*); ill. p. 117. Native in the Himalayas, this is a broadly conical tree with dark purplish bark. It reaches 50 m or more in height and has horizontally-spreading branches and pendulous branchlets. The young stems are pale and hairless and the ovoid winter-buds are up to 8 mm long, dark purple-brown, and resinous. The slender 4-sided leaves, 2–4 cm long, spread stiffly all round the stem and point obliquely forwards. They are dark green and end in a fine horny point. The ripe female cones are 12–18 cm long. This fine and handsome tree is planted only occasionally.

10   **Sargent's Spruce** (*P. brachytyla*); ill. p. 117. Native in China, this is a conical tree up to 25 m high, with pendu-lous branchlets from the upturned ends of the main branches. The bark is pale grey, cracking into small roundish plates. The young stem is white to pale buff, hairless, and shining, and the winter-buds are pale red-dish-brown and glistening with resin. The flat leaves are 1–1·7 cm long, those on the upper side directed forwards and pressed close to or below the stem and those beneath parted to form a V-shaped trough. They are slightly ridged on both sides and end in a short horny tip, either blunt or spiny. They are light green above and the conspicuously broad blue-white bands beneath often merge and hide the midrib. The ripe female cones are about 10 cm long, tapering to both ends and slightly curved.

Brewer's Weeping Spruce (*P. brewerana*) is also some-times seen in gardens. Native in the mountains of Oregon and California, it is a broadly conical tree up to 38 m. It has spreading branches and very slender pendulous branchlets up to 2·5 m or even more in length. The slender flattened leaves are 2–3 cm long, spreading obliquely forwards all round the stem, with some curving outwards. They are dark green above and have 2 broad white bands on the underside, and the tip is usually blunt. This is a very striking tree be-cause of the long-drooping and very dark green branchlets, and it is being increasingly planted.

Hondo Spruce (*P. jezoensis* var. *hondoensis*), native in Japan, is narrowly conical and up to 30 m high, and its horizontal lower branches are downturned at their ends. The young stems are shining white to pale buff and hairless. The flat leaves, 1–2 cm long, are parted beneath the stem and spread to left and right, turning upwards round the sides; those above the stem point forwards close to its surface. They are stiff and short-pointed, glossy dark green above and with 2 broad silvery-white bands beneath.

m 30

20

10

5

0

scale for trees 1, 2, 3, 4, 5, 6, 7, 8, 9, 10, & 11

6 × ⅙ (

1 EASTERN HEMLOCK (*Tsuga canadensis*)   2 MOUNTAIN HEMLOCK (*T. mertensiana*)
6 AROLLA PINE (*Pinus cembra*)   7 BHUTAN PINE (*P. wallichiana*)—young tree   8 WEYMOUTH PINE (*P. strobus*)
12 MONTEREY PINE (*P. radiata*)—cone only, other details p. 112.   (M) = male cone; (F) = female cone.

3 ATLANTIC CEDAR (*Cedrus atlantica*)   4 DEODAR (*C. deodara*)   5 CEDAR OF LEBANON (*C. libani*)
9 MARITIME PINE (*P. pinaster*)   10 AUSTRIAN PINE (*P. nigra* ssp. *nigra*)   11 STONE PINE (*P. pinea*)
Leaf and shoot details × ⅔. Text pp. 122–3

INTRODUCED CONIFERS: Parks and Gardens

HEMLOCK SPRUCES or **HEMLOCKS** (*Tsuga*) belong to the family Pinaceae. (p. 102). There is a general account of the genus on p. 111.

1 **Eastern Hemlock** or **Canadian Hemlock** (*T. canadensis*); ill. p. 120. Eastern hemlock is native in eastern North America. It only rarely reaches 30 m in height and often less than 20 m, and it develops a broad and dense conical crown with the drooping lower branches commonly touching the ground. The young stems are pale brown and covered with long wavy reddish hairs, and the winter-buds, only 1–2 mm long, are ovoid. The leaves are well parted to left and right of the stem except for some that point forwards along the middle of the upper side. They are dark shining green above and have 2 broad white bands beneath, but the forwardly-directed leaves above the stem are turned to expose the white under-side. The leaves differ from those of the two other species commonly grown in the British Isles in being usually less than 1·5 cm long and in tapering very distinct-ly from near the base to the rounded tip. The cones, too, are only 1·3–2 cm long.

2 **Mountain Hemlock** (*T. mertensiana*); ill. p. 120. Native in mountains of western North America, this varies from a narrowly conical tree up to 30 m high to a small or even prostrate shrub at the tree limit. In the British Isles it reaches 20 m or higher, with a very narrow crown and drooping leading shoot, the somewhat downwardly-directed main branches ending in clusters of pendulous branchlets. The blue-grey leaves, 1·5–2 cm long, are not parted above the stem as in the western and eastern hemlocks but point forwards all round the stem, and the cones, 2–8 cm long, can be much longer than in the other two species. Mountain hemlock may occasionally be seen in gardens, especially in central Scotland.

CEDARS (*Cedrus*) belong to the family Pinaceae (p. 102). True cedars are unique amongst conifers in that most of their 3–5-sided evergreen leaves are borne in dense clusters on long-lived woody short-shoots. Cedars are also unusual in having male and female cones that open in autumn. The barrel-shaped female cones take two seasons to mature, and their bract-scales do not reach the cone surface. They are held erect and fall to pieces on the tree—releasing the pairs of winged seeds.

3 **Atlantic Cedar** or **Atlas Cedar** (*C. atlantica*); ill. p. 120. This cedar is native in the mountains of Algeria and Morocco, and can reach 40 m high in the British Isles. It has an erect leading shoot, ascending branches, and a crown broadly conical at first but broadening with age though usually retaining a narrowish and rounded top, neither as broad nor as flat as in cedar of Lebanon. In mature trees the older main branches ascend from their base and level out in the leaf-bearing part, commonly with their tips pointing obliquely upwards, but they do not form the very large horizontal tables of foliage characteristic of cedar of Lebanon. The bark is dark grey, at first smooth but later fissured and scaly. Young stems are downy with dark curly hairs and the buds are 2–3 mm long, ovoid, pale brown with dark-tipped scales. The leaves on short-shoots are 1·5–2 cm long and taper to a non-green translucent spiny tip. The ripe female cones are 5–8 cm long and are more often hollowed at the top end than in other cedars. The form most commonly grown is 'Glauca', with pale blue-grey leaves.

4 **Deodar** or **Himalayan Cedar** (*C. deodara*); ill. p. 120. Deodar, which is native in the Western Himalayas, is readily distinguished from other cedars by its retention of a conical shape to an advanced age, its markedly drooping leading shoot and branch-tips, and its longer leaves. Young trees are narrowly conical and, although they broaden with age and may develop multiple trunks, they retain one or more pointed tops. The bark is dark grey-brown, smooth at first then cracking into vertical plates. Branches are horizontal or somewhat drooping and their tips curve downwards. Young stems are densely downy for at least two years, and the pointed buds are only 1 mm long, orange-coloured with pale-tipped scales. The leaves on short-shoots are 3–3·5 cm long, dark to bluish green and tapering to a translucent tip. The ripe female cones are 8–13 cm long, dark brown. Deodar has been much planted for its ornamental value and has reached a height of 36 m in the British Isles.

5 **Cedar of Lebanon** (*C. libani*); ill. p. 120. This tree is native in the mountains of Lebanon, Syria, and Southern Anatolia. It is our most familiar cedar, reaching 40 m high in the British Isles and recognizable by its broadly rounded or flat-topped crown and its massive horizon-tally-extended plates of foliage. The leading shoot is erect or somewhat leaning and the tips of the horizontal branches tend to droop on old trees though held level on younger trees. Young stems have a rather sparse or incomplete covering of pale brown hairs and become hairless by the second year, and the buds are 2–3 mm long with dark-tipped scales. The leaves on short-shoots are 2–3 cm long and taper to a spine which is non-green and translucent only close to its tip. They are usually dark green but can vary to blue-green or pale blue-grey. The ripe female cones are 7–10 cm long and taper up-wards more markedly than in other species (ill. p. 100). Atlantic cedar, apart from the difference in general form, has more densely hairy young stems and shorter leaves with a longer translucent tip.

Cyprus Cedar (*C. brevifolia*) is in many ways intermediate between *C. atlantica* and *C. libani* but is a smaller tree than either, more narrowly conical and so far reaching only 18 m high in the British Isles. The leaves on short-shoots are only about 1 cm long, much shorter than in other species. It is native only in Cyprus and is rarely cultivated.

PINES (*Pinus*) belong to the family Pinaceae (p. 102). There is a general description of the genus on p. 114 and a key to commonly cultivated species on p. 204. Trees **6**, **7**, and **8** below are 5-needle pines (table p. 204). The rhombic umbo of first-year growth is at the tip of the cone-scale, not central as in 2 and 3-needle pines. The wood of 5-needle pines is also softer and they alone are susceptible to the serious fungal disease called blister-rust.

Arolla Pine (*P. cembra*); ill. p. 120. This alpine and sub-arctic tree is up to 25 m high, narrowly columnar, clothed to the base with short upturned branches. The needles are glossy dark green on the outer side but blue-white on the flat inner sides. The small ovoid reddish ripe cones do not open but are gnawed apart on the ground by squirrels and mice for the large and almost wingless seeds.

Bhutan Pine (*P. wallichiana*, formerly *P. excelsa*); ill. p. 121. Native in the Himalayas, this is a tree up to 50 m in height, becoming broadly conical, with long drooping branches. The needles are markedly slender, flexible and drooping, and the long slightly curving cones usually have the umbo projecting tooth-like beyond the broad and grooved second-year growth. Bhutan pine is quite commonly grown in parks and gardens for its very attractive foliage.

Weymouth Pine (*P. strobus*); ill. p. 121. Weymouth pine is native in eastern North America. It reaches 30 m in height and is narrowly conical at first but later becomes irregular in shape and finally flat-topped. The needles are bunched and directed forwards, and the slightly curving cones have the umbo usually not projecting beyond the narrow and ungrooved second-year growth. Weymouth pine is much less commonly grown than Bhutan pine.

Other 5-needle pines occasionally seen are **Macedonian Pine** (*P. peuce*), like Bhutan pine but with shorter more rigid needles; **Japanese White Pine** (*P. parviflora*), usually a short wide-spreading tree with short, twisted, blue-green leaves, 2–8 cm long; and, more rarely, **Montezuma Pine** (*P. montezumae*), with very slender blue-grey leaves 25–30 cm long or even longer.

Besides the Monterey pine (*P. radiata* p. 115) two other North American 3-needle pines are often seen in gardens: **Western Yellow Pine** (*P. ponderosa*), with resinous buds, leaves 10–25 cm long, and cones 8–15 cm long, each scale with a stout persistent prickle; and **Jeffrey's Pine** (*P. jeffreyi*), like yellow pine but with non-resinous buds, stiffer and pale blue-green leaves, and bigger cones, 15–25 cm long.

Maritime Pine (*P. pinaster*); ill. p. 121. Native in South-western Europe, this is a tree reaching 40 m in height, with deeply fissured red-brown bark and widely-spaced whorls of branches. The young stems are hairless and the winter-buds bright reddish-brown. The long stout leaves, borne in pairs, are pale greyish-green, 10–25 cm long.

The ripe cones, 8–20 cm long, are glossy pale brown with the umbos projecting and prickly. Maritime pine grows best on sandy soils and there are enormous plantations of it in South-western France, where it is tapped for resin from which turpentine is obtained. It is commonly grown in Southern England, as at Bournemouth.

10 **Austrian Pine** (*P. nigra* ssp. *nigra*); ill. p. 121. Native in South-eastern Europe and often on limestone, this is a 2-needle pine closely related to Corsican pine (p. 114) but has a more spreading crown and rarely exceeds 30 m in height in the British Isles. Old trees commonly have 2 or more trunks and very irregular crowns. The bark is very dark grey or blackish-brown and markedly scaly. Young stems are brownish, shining and hairless, and distinctly ridged, and the buds are about 1 cm long, broadly ovoid and sharp-pointed and with loose whitish papery scales. The leaves are 8–10 cm long, very dark green. They are straighter and more rigid than in Corsican pine and tend to be bunched at the ends of branches. The ovoid cones are 5–10 cm long. Austrian pine is commonly planted, especially for wind-breaks and screens, particularly near coasts and on calcareous soils.

11 **Stone Pine** or **Umbrella Pine** (*P. pinea*); ill. p. 121. Stone pine, native in the western Mediterranean region, is readily recognized by its very wide-spreading and rounded or flat-topped crown which gives it the alternative names "umbrella pine" and "pin parasol". The bark is orange-red and deeply fissured into large vertical plates. Young stems are pale and hairless and the buds are 1 cm long, ovoid, with bright red-brown white-fringed scales. The dark green leaves, 10–15 cm long, are stout and often twisted and are borne in pairs. The large broadly ovoid cones, 8–15 cm long, take three years to mature and the three stages of growth of the scale-ends can be easily seen. The scales break off to release the very large wingless seeds, which are the "pine-kernels" of cookery. Stone pine is occasionally planted in Southern England where it reaches a height of about 20 m.

Mountain Pine (*P. uncinata*), native in the Alps and Pyrenees, is a tree up to 20 m high with pinkish-grey bark cracking into small squares. Its stiffly twisted dark green leaves, 4–7 cm long, are borne in pairs and its irregularly ovoid cones, about 5 cm long, have the basal scales prolonged and curving down towards the stalk. Mountain pine is planted occasionally as shelter for upland forest-plots, as is the closely related but shrubby *P. mugo*, which reaches the tree limit in the Alps.

1 COAST REDWOOD (*Sequoia sempervirens*)   2 CALIFORNIAN BIG-TREE (*Sequoiadendron giganteum*)
5 DAWN REDWOOD (*Metasequoia glyptostroboides*)   6 JAPANESE UMBRELLA-PINE (*Sciadopitys verticillata*).

4

5

6

25 m

20

15

10

5

0

(F)

6

(M)

5a

(F)

scale for trees 4, 5, & 6

3 JAPANESE CEDAR (*Cryptomeria japonica*)   4 SWAMP CYPRESS (*Taxodium distichum*)
(M) = male cone; (F) = female cone; a = autumn colour. Details × $\frac{2}{3}$. See also pp. 100–1; text pp. 126–7

INTRODUCED CONIFERS: Parks and Gardens

The conifers illustrated on pp. 124–5 all belong to the big-tree family, Taxodiaceae (p. 102). They vary greatly in the form and arrangement of their leaves and in the appearance of their cones, but they all have female cones with scales visibly compound only at the ends. Details of all the genera are illustrated on p. 101.

REDWOOD

1 **Coast Redwood or Californian Redwood** (*Sequoia sempervirens*), native in Oregon and California, is a magnificent broadly columnar tree reaching a height of 112 m, rivalled only by the biggest of the Australian eucalypts. The bark is thick and spongy and scales off to expose a red underbark. Redwood is unusual amongst conifers in sprouting freely from a stump. Young shoots are green and hairless and the winter-buds small and scaly. The alternate evergreen leaves are of two different kinds. Those on main branches are borne all round the stem and are scale-like, 6–8 mm long, pressed to the stem except for the raised and incurved pointed tip. Those on smaller branchlets are linear, shortly stalked and in 2 rows to left and right of the stem. They vary in length from 6 to 20 mm, the shortest being at the two ends of the season's growth and the longest round the middle, so that the season's growth is elliptic in outline. They are dark green above and have 2 distinct white bands beneath. The female cones ripen in a single season and are only 2–2·5 cm long, broadly oblong-ovoid, each scale-end with a narrow transverse ridge across it. There are 3–5 narrowly winged seeds on each fertile scale. Redwood has been frequently planted as a specimen tree in parks and gardens and the tallest in the British Isles are now over 40 m high.

BIG-TREE

2 **Californian Big-tree** or **Wellingtonia** (*Sequoiadendron giganteum*) is native only on the Pacific slope of the Sierra Nevada in California where it is a gigantic narrowly conical tree, pointed at the top, with long downwardly-inclined branches turning upwards near their ends. The tallest surviving tree is 83 m in height. The bark is much like that of redwood—thick, spongy, deeply furrowed, and reddish in colour—and the base of the tree is often much enlarged and buttressed. The first-year stems are pale green and hairless and the winter-buds are naked, having no protective bud-scales. The alternate evergreen leaves are all of one kind, up to 1 cm long, scale-like, pressed to the stem but with the long-pointed tip usually raised above it, becoming dark green, with 2 bands of white dots on the concave upper side. The female cones ripen in the second year and are 5–8 cm long, the scale-ends wrinkled, transversely grooved, and with a slender erect spine when young. The big-tree, under the name of Wellingtonia, was much planted in the British Isles after its introduction in the middle of the nineteenth century and can be seen everywhere, often in long avenues. The surviving trees in California are conserved in a number of separate groves. They are remarkable not merely for their height but also for their great girth and bulk and for their longevity. The largest individuals have been named: "General Grant", "Grizzly Giant", and many others. Individuals now dead have reached 100 m in height and 27 m in circumference of the trunk, and ring-counts have revealed an age of almost 3500 years. The tallest specimen in the British Isles is 50 m high.

JAPANESE CEDAR

3 **Japanese Cedar** (*Cryptomeria japonica*), native in China and Japan, somewhat resembles the big-tree but reaches only about 50 m in height. It is narrowly conical with the lower branches upturned near their ends. The bark is cinnamon-red and peels off in long shreds. The young stems are green and hairless, ridged below the leaves. The alternate evergreen leaves are 6–12 mm long, arranged in 5 vertical rows spaced round the stem. They are bright yellowish-green, rounded in section and tapering to a point, directed forwards and with the tip incurved. The female cones ripen in the first year. They are almost spherical, 2–3 cm across, with the scale-ends narrowed downwards with a sharp-pointed triangular flap projecting downwards from the centre and above this a wider upper half with 3–5 sharp rigid teeth standing erect along its upper edge. Japanese cedar is commonly planted in the British Isles, especially in the west where it thrives best, and it has reached heights exceeding 35 m. In Japan, taking natural forests and plantations together, it occupies a much greater area than any other kind of tree and gives a special character to the landscape. Japanese cedar differs from big-tree in its much less rigid and spiny branchlets as well as in the very different female cones.

SWAMP CYPRESS

4 **Swamp Cypress** (*Taxodium distichum*) is native in a broad coastal belt of Eastern U.S.A. from Virginia round to Texas and up the Mississippi to Kentucky and the extreme south of Illinois. It is a medium-sized tree which can occasionally reach 50 m in height, and is broadly conical when young but broadens and becomes round-topped with age. The trunk is strongly fluted or buttressed at the base and the bark is pale red-brown weathering to grey, fibrous, and tending to peel in short vertical strips. Special features of the trees, which grow naturally in swamps, are the curious "knees" — stout round-topped branch-roots emerging up into the air and believed to facilitate the aeration of the submerged parts of the root system. The young stems are green, soon turning brown, and the winter-buds are rounded and scaly. The alternate deciduous linear leaves, 1–1·5 cm long and initially a fresh pale green but later darkening, are borne all round the persistent long-shoots but are arranged in 2 rows to right and left of the short side-shoots which are shed with the leaves at the end of each season. These deciduous side-shoots are about 10 cm long, each with up to 100 leaves. The female cones, almost spherical and 1·5–3 cm across, ripen in the first year. The scale-ends are wrinkled but usually have no central prickle. Swamp cypress has been much planted in Southern England, where it forms "knees" in suitably swampy conditions, but it is rarely seen further north. The tallest trees are about 35 m high.

DAWN REDWOOD

5 **Dawn Redwood** (*Metasequoia glyptostroboides*) belongs to a genus of fascinating interest: it was known as a fossil shortly before a living species was discovered in 1941 in the province of Szechuan in South-western China. Since that time many seeds have been distributed all over the world, many cuttings have been rooted, and the young trees have become a familiar sight. They have a conical shape, with ascending branches. The bark is orange- to reddish-brown. The young shoot is hairless and winter-buds are ovoid, 2–3 mm long, pale red-brown. Dawn redwood is like swamp cypress in having deciduous leaves borne on lateral branchlets that are themselves deciduous, but differs in that leaves and side-shoots are borne in opposite pairs. The leaves are linear and flat, 2 cm or more long, fresh green above but darkening later, greyish-green beneath. The female cones have only occasionally been seen in the British Isles. They are 1·5–2·5 cm long, with grooved scale-ends. An interesting peculiarity of the dawn redwood is that the small lateral buds are borne, singly or sometimes in groups, *below* the points where branchlets join their parent shoots, that is, not axillary but *infra-axillary*.

UMBRELLA-PINE

6 **Japanese Umbrella-pine** (*Sciadopitys verticillata*), which occurs wild only in mountain areas of Japan, is a tree reaching 40 m in height and has a conical shape with short spreading branches upturned at the ends. The greyish bark peels in long strips. Young shoots are green and hairless. Leaves are of two kinds: small triangular scale-leaves, at first green below the tip but becoming entirely brown by the end of the first year; and stout green "double needles", 10–15 cm long, grooved on both sides and slightly notched at the tip, with 2 white bands on the underside. These are borne in distant whorls of 10–30 in the axils of scale-leaves. The female cones ripen in the second year and are 6–12 cm long, ovoid-oblong, their scale-ends with a transverse furrow separating a convex upper half from a concave lower half. Each fertile scale bears 7–9 seeds with an unequal pair of lateral wings. Umbrella-pine is one of the famous "five trees of Kiso" that were for many centuries protected by the emperors of Japan: the other four are all members of the cypress family (Cupressaceae). Its unique "double-needles" distinguish it from all other conifers. This pine is not very often seen in cultivation in the British Isles and few specimens exceed 20 m in height.

Other genera of the Taxodiaceae are *Cunninghamia*, including the occasionally planted **Chinese Fir** (*C. lanceolata*), recognizable by its narrowly triangular or lanceolate leaves, 3–7 cm long and up to 4 mm wide at the base, and interestingly one of the trees associated with *Metasequoia* where first seen in South-western China; *Glyptostrobus*, with the single species *G. lineatus*, deciduous and much resembling swamp cypress, also from China; and *Athrotaxis*. This last includes the Tasmanian cedars, with small alternate scale-like leaves, close-pressed to the stem throughout or with spreading tips, and the **King William Pine** (*A. selaginoides*), with small rigid sharp-pointed and spreading leaves about 1 cm long, lanceolate and with 2 broad white bands beneath. None of these is grown at all commonly.

scale for trees 2, 3, & 4

1 AMERICAN THUYA (*Thuja occidentalis*) 2 CHINESE THUYA (*T. orientalis*) 3 HIBA (*Thujopsis dolabrata*)
6 HINOKI CYPRESS (*C. obtusa* 'Nana Gracilis') 7 SAWARA CYPRESS (*C. pisifera* 'Filifera')
10 MONTEREY CYPRESS (*C. macrocarpa*) 11 SMOOTH ARIZONA CYPRESS (*C. glabra* 'Pyramidalis')—detail only.

30 m

25

20

15

10

5

0

scale for trees 1, 5, 6, 7, 8, 9, & 10

4 INCENSE CEDAR (*Calocedrus decurrens*)   5 NOOTKA CYPRESS (*Chamaecyparis nootkatensis*)
8 LEYLAND CYPRESS (× *Cupressocyparis leylandii*)   9 ITALIAN CYPRESS (*Cupressus sempervirens*)
Details × ⅔ (for details of trees 3, 4, 10 see pp. 104–5). Text pp. 130–1

INTRODUCED CONIFERS: Parks and Gardens

The conifers illustrated on pp. 128–9 all belong to the cypress family (Cupressaceae, p. 103). The thuyas (*Thuja*), hiba (*Thujopsis*), and incense cedar (*Calocedrus*) all have in common the restriction of the higher orders of branching to a single plane—giving flat sprays of foliage, the scale-like appearance of their leaves, and the overlapping margins of the scales of their female cones (in cypresses the cone-scales touch only along their edges). The table on p. 207 shows the main differences between the three genera.

THUYAS (*Thuja*). There is a brief account of the genus on p. 115 with a description of western red cedar (*T. plicata*). This and the other two species commonly seen in gardens may be distinguished by the table on p. 207.

1 **American Thuya** or **White Cedar** (*T. occidentalis*), native in eastern North America, is a tree up to 20 m in height, narrowly conical at first, with short spreading branches, but becoming irregular in shape later. The stout trunk has thick fibrous brown bark with a network of shallow ridges. The leaves are abruptly pointed, dark green above and uniformly pale yellowish-green beneath with no white markings, and each has a more or less conspicuous translucent gland, readily visible if the shoot is held up to the light. The ripe female cone is 8 mm long. American thuya is seen in gardens mainly in one or other of its dwarf varieties.

2 **Chinese Thuya** or **Chinese Arbor-vitae** (*T. orientalis*), native in China and Korea, is a large shrub or small tree, sometimes 15 m in height, with almost erect branches and branchlets so that its crown is very dense and quite narrowly conical or columnar. The bark is red-brown, peeling in vertical strips. The flat sprays of foliage are held vertically or nearly so and are dark green on both sides, with no white markings; and the leaves are blunt-tipped and with an oval translucent gland. The ripe female cones are broadly ovoid, 2 cm long, each scale with a stout down-curved hook from just below the tip. The cone is bluish in colour and remains fleshy until shortly before opening, and the seeds are wingless. The cones distinguish it from forms of cypresses with vertically flattened foliage-sprays. Chinese thuya is not much grown in gardens but is sometimes seen in parks and churchyards.

HIBA

3 **Hiba** (*Thujopsis dolabrata*), native only in Japan, has a conical crown and reaches a height of 20 m or more in the British Isles. The bark is reddish-brown, peeling in long vertical strips. The leafy shoots are much broader than those of any other scale-leaved conifer, 4–6 mm across, and are also more conspicuously and completely white beneath, with only a narrow surrounding green border. The ripe female cones are 1–2 cm long, each scale with a protuberance, often hooked, near its tip. Hiba is frequently grown in gardens in the west, less commonly elsewhere.

INCENSE CEDAR

4 **Incense Cedar** (*Calocedrus decurrens*, formerly *Libocedrus*), native in Oregon and California in western North America, is a tall narrowly columnar tree reaching heights of 45 m (up to 35 m in the British Isles). The bark is reddish-brown or cinnamon-coloured and has scaly ridges. The flat foliage-sprays are held horizontally. The leaves on the sides of shoots are much longer than those on upper and lower faces so that, especially on main shoots, the leaf-tips are in whorls of 4. The leaves have short raised tips, and those on branchlets have each a rather indistinct translucent gland. The underside of the branchlets is uniformly yellowish-green, somewhat paler than the upper side. The ripe female cones are 2–2·5 cm long, narrow and almost cylindrical, each scale with a down-turned point near its tip. The seeds have large asymmetrical terminal wings, in contrast with the symmetrical lateral wings of thuya seeds (apart from the wingless seeds of *T. orientalis*). Incense cedar is commonly planted in parks and large gardens on account of its narrowly columnar habit.

FALSE CYPRESSES (*Chamaecyparis*). Lawson's cypress (*C. lawsoniana*) was described on p. 115. The table on p. 205 summarizes the main differences between it and the three following species but does not attempt to include all the numerous horticultural varieties.

Nootka Cypress (*C. nootkatensis*), native in western North America from Oregon to Alaska, is a narrowly conical tree with the lower branches upturned at their ends and the branchlets drooping; it reaches 40 m in height. The bark is brownish, irregularly fissured, and scaling. The branchlets are much less flattened than in other false cypresses and are either cylindrical or almost equally 4-sided. The leaves, 2–3 mm long, are rather longer and more pointed than in other species. The scale-ends of the ripe cones have an erect pointed protuberance. Nootka cypress is a shapely tree with attractively pendulous branchlets and is frequently grown in parks, large gardens, and churchyards, sometimes in yellow-leaved and long-weeping forms.

Hinoki Cypress (*C. obtusa*) is native in Japan where it is a broadly conical tree reaching 40 m in height, with reddish peeling bark. It differs from other false cypresses in its very blunt leaves and the white X-shaped markings on the underside of the shoot as well as in its orange-brown ripe cones which are rather less than 1 cm across. Wild-type Hinoki is not infrequent in western gardens and can reach a height of 20 m, but elsewhere only culti-

vated forms, many of them small or miniature bushes, are commonly seen. The illustration is of 'Nana Gracilis', a conical bush or small tree up to 5 or 6 m high and said to be the most commonly planted dwarf conifer. The pale yellow-leaved variety 'Crippsii' is also much grown, even in small gardens. Other forms have markedly bunched foliage or long pendulous sprays, but most have normal scale-leaves in contrast with many forms of Sawara cypress.

Sawara Cypress (*C. pisifera*), also native in Japan, is in its wild form a narrowly conical tree up to 35 m high, differing from *C. obtusa* in the incurved pointed tips of its leaves and its smaller cones, brown when ripe and only 6 mm across. It is much grown in the British Isles but almost entirely in one of its innumerable horticultural varieties, several of them with permanently juvenile foliage, the leaves being needle-like and more or less spreading. The illustration is of 'Filifera', a broadly conical large shrub or small tree which can be 20 m high and has long whip-like hanging branchlets. Also very commonly grown are 'Plumosa' and the golden-leaved 'Plumosa Aurea', both with feathery sprays of juvenile foliage.

HYBRID CYPRESS (x *Cupressocyparis*)

Leyland Cypress (x *C. leylandii* = *Chamaecyparis nootkatensis* x *Cupressus macrocarpa*) is the name given to several different hybrids between the same parents. The one most commonly grown had Nootka cypress as the female parent and was first raised in 1888: there are now well-grown trees, 30 m high, narrowly columnar but

tapering to a pointed tip. The foliage is in slightly drooping sprays like those of Nootka cypress but less flattened because some branching is at right angles to the usual plane. Leyland cypress grows very fast and has become popular for hedges and shelter-belts.

TRUE CYPRESSES (*Cupressus*). See also table p. 205.

Italian Cypress (*C. sempervirens*) is native in Southeastern Europe and Western Asia and is a forest tree in Crete and Cyprus. The wild tree is flat-topped with spreading horizontal branches, but the familiar tree of the Mediterranean landscape is narrowly columnar, like a closed umbrella—contrasting with the open umbrella of the stone pine (*Pinus pinea*, p. 123), and it is this form that is occasionally seen in gardens in the British Isles, chiefly in the south-west. It reaches 15 m or more in height and has steeply ascending branches and dark green foliage. The branchlets taper at their ends: in Monterey cypress they are slightly expanded and the leaf-tips are also slightly swollen, but the differences are not very great. The cones are 2–3·5 cm long and are dullish grey-brown when ripe.

Monterey Cypress (*C. macrocarpa*), native only near Monterey in California, is a tree up to 25 m in height, at first conical but later flat-topped. Old trees, such as can be seen in South-western England and in Ireland,

develop a broadly ovoid crown with steeply ascending lower branches or may come to resemble an old cedar of Lebanon. The slender branchlets are almost cylindrical and the blunt-tipped leaves are dark green with paler margins. The ripe cones are 2·5–4 cm long and glossy reddish-brown. Monterey cypress was formerly much planted for hedges but is being superseded by Leyland cypress.

Smooth Arizona Cypress (*C. glabra*, often misnamed *C. arizonica*), native in Arizona, is a tree up to 20 m high with a dense conical crown and purplish bark flaking into red-brown patches. The ascending branches bear horizontally-spreading branchlets of greyish foliage, and the glossy ripe cones are up to 3 cm long. The illustration is of 'Pyramidalis', with steeply ascending branches and branchlets and silvery blue-grey foliage. This cypress is quite commonly planted in gardens and often used as a hedge plant, and is best identified by its white-spotted greyish leaves.

m 25

20

15

10

5

0

scale for trees 1, 2, 3, 4, 6, 7, 8, & 9

1 CHINESE JUNIPER (*Juniperus chinensis*)   2 BLUE CHINESE JUNIPER (*J. chinensis* 'Columnaris glauca')
6 GOLDEN YEW (*T. baccata* 'Aurea')—detail only   7 CALIFORNIAN NUTMEG (*Torreya californica*)
Details × ⅔. See also pp. 104–5; text pp. 134–5.

PENCIL CEDAR (*J. virginiana*)   4 PLUM-FRUITED YEW (*Podocarpus andinus*)   5 IRISH YEW (*Taxus baccata* 'Fastigiata')
MONKEY-PUZZLE TREE (*Araucaria araucana*)   9 MAIDEN-HAIR TREE (*Ginkgo biloba*). a = young shoot; b = autumn leaves.

INTRODUCED CONIFERS: Parks and Gardens

JUNIPERS (*Juniperus*); ill. p. 132. Junipers belong to the family Cupressaceae (p. 103). They differ from other members of the cypress family in having female cones that remain fleshy and berry-like up to the time of ripening, which may be in the first, second, or third year after their appearance. Birds eat the "berries" and disperse the wingless seeds. In some junipers, like our native *J. communis* (p. 39), all the leaves are short spreading needles, usually borne in whorls of 3. In others some or all are scale-like, like those of cypresses, and are usually borne in opposite pairs. Most scale-leaved junipers have leaves of both kinds on the same plant, the needles commonly at the beginning or end of each season's growth (see ill. p. 104), and for this reason such junipers can almost invariably be distinguished from a cypress. Those cypress cultivars in which needle-like juvenile foliage is retained throughout life usually have softer needles, less rigid and prickly than those of junipers, and mostly in opposite pairs rather than in threes (but see **3** below). Junipers, too, usually have male and female cones on different plants. Some species are trees of considerable stature but many are shrubs.

Two scale-leaved junipers with slender cylindrical branchlets are frequently grown in parks and gardens, both trees with male and female cones on different plants. There is a table on p. 205.

1 **Chinese Juniper** (*J. chinensis*), native in China and Japan, is a narrowly conical tree up to 18 m high with dark brown peeling bark. Old trees may become many-stemmed and broader. The "berries" take two years to mature. There are many horticultural varieties.

2 **Blue Chinese Juniper** (*J. chinensis* 'Columnaris Glauca') differs from the wild tree in being more densely columnar, tapering only slightly towards the tip, and in having all its leaves needle-like and bluish-green in colour.

3 **Pencil Cedar** or **Red Cedar** *(J. virginiana)*, native in Eastern U.S.A., is a conical tree reaching up to 30 m in North America and 15 m in the British Isles, with reddish-brown peeling bark and ascending or spreading branches. It differs from Chinese juniper in having pointed scale-leaves and needle-leaves which are mostly at the ends of shoots. The "berries" ripen in one year. The wood is used for making pencil-casings.

The next four illustrations are all of conifers that resemble junipers in having ripe female cones with fleshy parts of one kind or another which are sufficiently conspicuous to attract birds.

YELLOW-WOODS (*Podocarpus*); ill. p. 132. Yellow-woods belong to the family Podocarpaceae (p. 103). They are evergreen trees and shrubs which are native chiefly in mountain forests of warmer parts of the southern hemisphere but with some species extending northwards to India, China, and Japan. The leaves are alternate and vary in shape from linear to oblong-lanceolate, and the female cones have 2–4 scales of which only 1–2 are fertile, each bearing a single inverted ovule with an outer fleshy covering. The ripe seed is fleshy-walled and in some species the top of the cone-stalk also becomes fleshy and coloured.

4 **Plum-fruited Yew** (*P. andinus*, formerly *Prumnopitys elegans*) is a large shrub or small tree to 15 m or more in height, with black bark and leafy shoots (see ill. p. 105) somewhat like those of yew but with the stem not ridged and with the underside of each leaf marked with 2 broad bluish-white bands. The leaves are linear and up to about 2·5 cm long, more or less in 2 rows but crowded and pointing forwards. Male and female cones usually develop a single ovoid-oblong seed about 2 cm long and with an outer yellowish-green covering. Ripe seeds are not often seen in the British Isles.

Willow Podocarp (*P. salignus*, formerly *P. chilinus*), up to 20 m high and with orange-brown bark, is readily distinguished by its long slender leaves, 5–12 cm long. It is occasionally seen in gardens in the south and west.

YEWS (*Taxus*); ill. p. 132. Yews belong to the family Taxaceae (p. 103). Our native yew (*T. baccata*, p. 27) is much grown in parks and gardens, often in one of its horticultural varieties which include the two following.

5 **Irish Yew** (*T. baccata* 'Fastigiata') is grown all over the country, especially in churchyards and formal gardens. It is an upright bush or small tree up to 15 m high with a columnar crown because of its crowded erect branches. The leaves are very dark green and are arranged all round the stem (see ill. p. 105) instead of being twisted into 2 rows as in the wild tree. Most Irish yews are female.

6 **Golden Yew** (*T. baccata* 'Aurea') is the name given to various forms with golden-yellow leaves, often planted in gardens. They are usually large shrubs rather than trees but are otherwise similar to wild yew.

CALIFORNIAN NUTMEGS (*Torreya*); ill. p. 133. These belong to the family Taxaceae (p. 103). They differ from yews most obviously in having the ripe seed completely enclosed in the fleshy cup or aril instead of being exposed at its top, and further in that the aril is green or purplish, not scarlet-red.

Californian Nutmeg (*T. californica*), native in California, is often a large shrub but can be a broadly conical tree up to 20 m high, with brownish bark which is smooth or narrowly ridged. The first-year stem is green and hairless, becoming brown in the second year, and the winter-buds are ovoid, sharp-pointed, and with brown scales. The alternate evergreen leaves are linear, 3–7 cm long, spine-pointed, and with 2 narrow white bands beneath. The ripe seed (see ill. p. 105) is 2–3·5 cm long, ovoid-oblong or broadest above the middle, and green in colour, tinged with purple. This tree is grown chiefly in the south and west but is nowhere common.

MONKEY-PUZZLE TREES (*Araucaria*); ill. p. 133. Monkey-Puzzles belong to the family Araucariaceae (p. 103). There are about 15 species of *Araucaria* in tropical and subtropical parts of the southern hemisphere. All are large trees with whorls of horizontal branches and evergreen leaves which vary greatly in size and shape between species.

Monkey-Puzzle Tree or **Chilean Pine** (*A. araucana*). This, the only hardy member of the Araucariaceae, is native in the Chilean Andes, Tierra del Fuego, and Northern Patagonia, where it can reach 30 m in height. It is recognizable from afar by its more or less broadly rounded crown and its regular whorls of stout branches, horizontal in the upper part of the crown but drooping below and all upturned at their ends. Branchlets usually droop. The stems are densely clothed with very rigid and very spiny-pointed leaves, ovate-lanceolate, 2·5–5 cm long, lying forward over the stem and overlapping but with the spiny tips raised and spreading (see ill. p. 105) so that it would indeed puzzle a monkey to climb the tree. The leaves remain green and functional for the unusually long time of 10–15 years and may not fall for several further years. Male and female cones, both very large, are usually on different trees. The male are 8–12 cm long, erect, and with many long slender pollen-sacs attached to the end of each scale. The female cones (see ill. p. 105), which take two years to mature, are broadly ovoid or almost spherical and 15 cm or more across. They stand erect on the tree and fall to pieces, the scales becoming detached from above downwards, each carrying a single wingless seed up to 4 cm long which remains attached to it. The seeds are edible. This striking tree thrives best in the moist cool climate of the lower slopes of the Chilean Andes. The tallest specimens in the British Isles are about 25 m high and are mainly in the west; in drier parts the tree grows slowly and loses its lower branches.

Norfolk Island Pine (*A. heterophylla*, formerly *A. excelsa*), with regularly whorled branches bearing small and curved awl-shaped leaves, is much grown as a decorative pot- or tub-plant but can be planted in the open in the extreme south-west.

MAIDEN-HAIR TREE (*Ginkgo*). The following species is the only member of the family Ginkgoaceae and that family is the only one in the order Ginkgoales.

Maiden-hair Tree (*G. biloba*); ill. p. 133. This is not a conifer but resembles them in lacking true flowers with ovules enclosed within an ovary. Its special features are given on p. 102. Maiden-hair tree has reached nearly 30 m in height in the British Isles and has a slender trunk with greyish fissured bark. The deciduous leaves, many of them borne on woody short-shoots, are 5–12 cm long, somewhat broader than long and of very distinctive shape (see ill. p. 105). Trees do not often flower in the British Isles and those that do are usually male, bearing yellowish male catkins, 6–8 cm long, with the leaves. The maiden-hair tree has never been found certainly wild and it seems likely that its survival is due to its having been a sacred tree, planted round shrines and temples in China for untold centuries.

m 20

10

5

0

scale for tree 1

1a

1a

1a

1

1

m 10

5

0

scale for trees 2, 3, 4, 6, & 8

3

3

2

1

4

2

(M)

(F)

4

1 HOLM OAK (*Quercus ilex*)   2 SWEET BAY (*Laurus nobilis*)   3 HODGIN'S HOLLY (*Ilex* x *altaclarensis* 'Hodginsii')
7 *Eucryphia* x *intermedia*—flower detail only   8 EVERGREEN MAGNOLIA (*M. grandiflora*).

4 *Cotoneaster frigidus*   5 TASMANIAN SNOW GUM (*Eucalyptus coccifera*)—details only   6 CIDER GUM (*E. gunnii*)
(M)=male flowers; (F)=female flowers; a=various leaf shapes; b=juvenile leaves. Details × ⅔. Text pp. 138–9

INTRODUCED FLOWERING TREES: Evergreen

EVERGREEN OAKS (*Quercus*); ill. p. 136. (For deciduous oaks see pp. 14, 159.)

1 **Holm Oak** or **Evergreen Oak** (*Q. ilex*). This handsome tree, reaching 25 m or more in height, has a broad dense crown and smooth grey bark eventually becoming finely scaly. The twigs are densely tomentose during the first year but later are almost hairless. The leaves, 3–7 cm long, vary in shape from lanceolate to ovate-oblong and have smooth or, especially in young plants, distantly spine-toothed margins. They are glossy dark green and almost hairless above but paler and densely tomentose beneath. The greenish male flowers are in catkins 3–5 cm long, the female, also green, in short spikes of 1–4, both opening mid-June. The acorns, 2–4 cm long, taper to a point and are dark chestnut-brown; their grey-tomentose cups are covered with small flat scales. This is the tree called "ilex" by the Romans. It is native in the Mediterranean region and up the Atlantic coast of Europe northwards to Brittany. It is commonly planted all over the British Isles except in Northern Scotland, is abundant in many coastal areas, and has become naturalized in Southern England.

Cork Oak (*Q. suber*) is a smaller tree, not exceeding 20 m in the British Isles, with the thick soft pale-coloured bark that is the cork of commerce. The leaves are more usually toothed than those of holm oak but are otherwise similar, and the upper scales of the acorn-cup are longer and erect or spreading. Cork oak is native in the west Mediterranean region, much cork being exported from Spain, Portugal, and North Africa. It thrives less well than holm oak in the British Isles and is rarely seen except in Southern England. The semi-evergreen Lucombe oak is a hybrid between cork oak and Turkey oak (p. 159).

LAUREL

2 **Sweet Bay, Bay Laurel,** or **Poets' Laurel** (*Laurus nobilis*); ill. p. 136. This member of the laurel family (Lauraceae) is a vigorously suckering shrub or small tree up to 3 m high, densely branching and pyramidal in form, its blackish bark patterned with pale lenticels. The simple hairless evergreen leaves are 5–10 cm long, elliptic and about three times as long as broad, short-pointed. They are dull dark green above, paler and markedly net-veined beneath, with untoothed narrowly white-translucent and usually wavy margins. The leaf-stalk is 6 mm long and dark red. The leaves, strongly aromatic when crushed, have long been used for flavouring. The small greenish flowers, opening in late April, male and female on separate plants, have 2 sepals and 2 petals similar in size and colour. The male flower has about 12 stamens from which pollen is released by the raising of small valve-like flaps. In the female flower there are usually 2–4 sterile stamens and a single ovary ripening to a black single-seeded berry about 12 mm long. Sweet bay is native in the Mediterranean region and forms woods locally. It was used in classical times for making ceremonial crowns and garlands. In the British Isles it is frequent in gardens in the south and near the sea but is liable to frost-damage in colder parts.

HYBRID HOLLIES; ill. p. 136.

3 **Hybrid Hollies.** By far the commonest cultivated holly is our native *Ilex aquifolium* (p. 38) with its numerous horticultural varieties. Other evergreen hollies frequently to be seen in gardens are hybrids of this with one or other of two related species—Azorean Holly (*I. perado*) and Canary Island Holly (*I. platyphylla*), neither grown except in the mildest parts of the country. They differ from *I. aquifolium* in having larger and less spiny leaves with winged leaf-stalks. As a matter of convenience all the hybrids are treated as cultivated varieties of the Highclere holly (*I. x altaclarensis*), a name originally given to a presumed cross between our native holly and Azorean holly. The hybrids are usually more vigorous than native holly, and their leaves are larger, often almost spineless, and commonly variegated. Some have yellow fruits. Certain forms are female and fruit freely, like 'Golden King', which has almost spineless yellow-margined leaves. Others are exclusively male so that they never fruit, like the purple-stemmed but spiny-leaved 'Hodginsii' illustrated. This holly grows to about 14 m and has white purple-tinged flowers, 1·2 cm across. Most of the hollies of this group can be used for hedges and are the more valuable because they thrive in both coastal and industrial areas.

COTONEASTERS; ill. p. 136. Cotoneasters have small white flowers, much visited by bees, and usually red berry-like fruits. They are related to hawthorns (p. 30) and firethorns but differ in having the leaf-margins neither lobed nor toothed and in not being thorny. Some are deciduous, some evergreen, and others are semi-evergreen—retaining a few leaves throughout a normal winter. Most are shrubs and several are low-growing or even prostrate, but a few are small trees.

4 *C. frigidus*, native in the Himalayas, is usually a small tree up to about 6 m high with pale grey bark. Its deciduous leaves are 6–12 cm long, broadly elliptic, and tomentose beneath when young but becoming hairless later. The many-flowered corymbs appear in late June and are succeeded by heavy clusters of crimson fruits which may persist through much of the winter. The tree is often planted along woodland rides to provide winter feed for pheasants.

C. x watereri is the collective name for commonly grown hybrids between *C. frigidus* and either *C. henryanus* or the closely related *C. salicifolius*, both from China. These hybrids have long narrow semi-evergreen leaves up to 12 cm long and more or less tomentose beneath. The branches are usually arching and carry numerous large clusters of fruits in autumn and winter. In some cultivated forms the fruits are red or orange-red but in others yellow or apricot-coloured, becoming pink-tinged when ripe.

GUM-TREES (*Eucalyptus*); ill. p. 137. The many hundred species of *Eucalyptus* are mainly natives of Australia with a few in Papua-New Guinea, Indonesia, and the Philippines. They range in size from small shrubs to magnificent trees over 100 m in height and surpassed only by the Californian redwood (p. 126). All are evergreen, and there is usually a marked difference between the juvenile leaves of young plants and stump-shoots—which are pale blue-green, unstalked, and borne in opposite pairs— and the adult leaves, darker and greener, stalked, alternate, and hanging vertically down. The leaves have aromatic oils in glands which appear as shining dots when viewed against the light. The usually white flowers appear in summer and have many conspicuous, often brightly coloured stamens. Only a few gum-trees are hardy in the British Isles, chiefly those from upland areas and especially from the mountains of Tasmania.

Tasmanian Snow Gum (*E. coccifera*) is fairly hardy. It has smooth white but grey-streaked bark and broadly elliptical adult leaves 2·5–4·5 cm long and ending in a narrowly hooked and down-curved tip.

Cider Gum (*E. gunnii*), also Tasmanian, is perhaps the most commonly planted gum in the British Isles. It can be grown northwards to the Moray Firth and reaches 20 m in height, with smooth bark scaling into green, grey, and orange patches. The juvenile leaves are broadly rounded, the adult elliptic, 4–8 cm long by 2·5–4·5 cm wide. The name comes from the smell of the crushed leaves.

Southern Blue Gum (*E. globulus*) is native in Australia. It thrives in Ireland, where it has reached 40 m in height, and some have been planted in Cornwall. Its trunk peels to expose a smooth grey-white underbark and its glossy adult leaves are 10–30 cm long, narrow, and usually curved into a sickle-shape—all characteristic features of the blue gums. It and some of its hybrids have been planted in more or less frost-free temperate areas all over the world for their fast-growing and valuable timber. The dried leaves yield medicinal oil of eucalyptus.

EUCRYPHIA; ill. p. 137. This genus consists of five or six large shrubs or small trees confined as natives to Chile and South-eastern Australia, including Tasmania. Their leaves are in opposite pairs and are either simple or pinnate and either evergreen or deciduous. The flowers have early-falling sepals, large white petals, numerous conspicuous stamens, and a 5–12-chambered ovary ripening to a hard dry fruit that splits open to release many small winged seeds.

E. x *intermedia* is a frequently grown hybrid between the Chilean *E. glutinosa* and the Tasmanian *E. lucida*. *E. glutinosa* has deciduous pinnate leaves with glossy toothed leaflets and flowers 6 cm across. *E. lucida* has evergreen simple untoothed leaves, oblong-lanceolate with broadly rounded tips, dark green above but bluish-white beneath, and fragrant flowers 3–4 cm across. The hybrid has some of its leaves simple and some with 3 leaflets, all evergreen and pale bluish beneath. Its flowers are not more than 5 cm across and have 4 petals.

E. x *nymansensis,* a hybrid of *E. glutinosa* with *E. cordifolia*, also has some of its evergreen leaves simple and some with 2–3 leaflets, all glossy and toothed. Its flowers open in late August to mid-September: they are 6–8 cm across, with either 4 or 5 petals. This striking tree is to be seen in many gardens in the south and west and may grow to 15 m.

MAGNOLIA. For an introduction to the genus see p. 146.

Evergreen Magnolia or **Southern Magnolia** (*M. grandiflora*); ill. p. 137. Most magnolias are deciduous but this tree of South-eastern U.S.A. is an exception. Its large alternate laurel-like leaves are broadly elliptic, 12–20 cm long and 5–7·5 cm across, dark glossy green above, rusty beneath. The large white flowers, 15–20 cm across with 6–12 perianth segments, are borne singly in late summer and early autumn and are pleasantly fragrant. Evergreen magnolia is commonly seen as a wall plant but can be grown in the open in sunny and sheltered places as a small tree up to 10 m high. It is much grown in Southern Europe in parks and gardens and also as a street tree.

m 8

scale for trees 1, 2, 3, 4, 5, & 7

1 *Rhododendron ponticum*   2 *R.* × *nobleanum*   3 CHERRY LAUREL (*Prunus laurocerasus*)
7 CHILEAN FIRE-BUSH (*Embothrium coccineum*).   Details × ⅔. Text pp. 142–3

4 PORTUGAL LAUREL (*P. lusitanica*)   5 LAURUSTINUS (*Viburnum tinus*)   6 JAPANESE PRIVET (*Ligustrum ovalifolium*)

INTRODUCED FLOWERING TREES: Evergreen

RHODODENDRONS. The vast genus *Rhododendron* (ill. pp. 140–1), with over 600 species and innumerable cultivated hybrids, includes the azaleas of horticulturists. They are members of the heather family (Ericaceae) and share with many others of the family an intolerance of calcareous soils, which cause them to develop yellowish leaves owing to a failure to obtain sufficient iron. Their flowers, commonly in compact, almost globular racemes, are usually showy. The petals are united at the base into a short tube or cup and the stamens converge at the lower side of the flower and then turn upwards, their pollen being released through apical pores. The leaves are alternate, simple, and untoothed, and may be either evergreen or deciduous. Broadly speaking, the "rhododendrons" of horticulturists are evergreen and have 10 or more stamens, while the "azaleas" are deciduous or, if evergreen, quite small-leaved, and have only 5 stamens; but there are some exceptions which make it impossible to recognize two distinct genera. Most are shrubs, though of very varying size, but there are some arboreal species and several may grow either as shrubs or trees.

Many of the more definitely arboreal rhododendrons have very large leaves and on this account require some shelter from strong winds. Most, too, are damaged by hard frosts and for these two reasons are chiefly grown in woodland and only in our milder counties.

1 **R. ponticum**, the most widely grown large rhododendron, is usually a shrub up to 3 m. Its laurel-like evergreen leaves, 6–12 cm long, and the brown-spotted purple flowers which open in May–June are now very familiar because the plant has become extensively naturalized in woods and in the open on suitably acid soils. *R. ponticum* is native in Asia Minor and a few localities in Portugal, Spain, and Greece. It is of interest, in view of its ready naturalization, that it was native in Ireland during at least one of the long interludes between successive advances of the ice in the recent Ice Age.

R. arboreum, the first Himalayan species to be introduced, can be a tree up to 12 m high. Its leaves are up to 20 cm long, with white or rusty hairs beneath, and its cup-shaped white to blood-red flowers are borne in dense spherical clusters from January to April and are often spoilt by frost.

2 **R. x nobleanum** is a hardy hybrid of *R. arboreum* with *R. caucasicum*, with leaves buff beneath and rich rose-pink flowers opening from January to March. It grows up to 10 m.

R. sinogrande, the most impressive of the tree rhododendrons in cultivation, comes from China. It can reach 10 m and has leaves typically 60 by 25 cm and occasionally up to 90 cm long. It flowers in April. The closely related **R. grande**, which flowers from February to April, comes from the Himalayas. It has smaller leaves, not exceeding 30 cm in length, and is hardier than *R. sinogrande*. The flowers of both are creamy-white with a dark crimson basal blotch on each petal.

R. falconeri and related species are taller and hardier than the *grande* series and their leaves are smaller. *R. falconeri* itself may reach 16 m and has attractive reddish bark, but its leaves, dark green with sunken veins above, rust-coloured beneath, do not exceed 30 cm and are often shorter. The flowers, which are whitish with a basal crimson blotch on each petal, open in April. *R. falconeri* is native in the central Himalayas. Related and somewhat hardier are *R. fictolacteum* and *R. rex*, both from China.

"LAURELS"

3 **Cherry Laurel** (*Prunus laurocerasus*); ill. p. 140. The subgenus *Laurocerasus* of the large genus *Prunus* (see also pp. 22, 30, 178–9, 182) comprises evergreen shrubs or trees with white flowers in elongated racemes in April–June. The two species commonly grown in this country are called cherry laurel and Portugal laurel respectively from the resemblance of their leaves to those of the true laurel or sweet bay (*Laurus nobilis*, p. 138). Cherry laurel is usually a large shrub but may grow as a tree to 6 m high. Its firm leathery leaves, 5–15 cm long, are oblong-obovate, narrowed abruptly to a long point, and usually have a few distant marginal teeth. They have one or more circular glands near the base of the pale underside of the leaf, which contrasts with the darker green and glossy upper side; they are quite hairless. The young twigs and leaf-stalks are green and hairless. The erect racemes are 5–12 cm long and the cherry-like purple-black fruits are 10–12 mm across—they are quite pleasant to eat. Cherry laurels are native in the Eastern Balkans and Asia Minor; in the British Isles they are commonly planted and have become more or less naturalized.

The crushed leaves emit prussic acid in sufficient amounts for their use in entomologists' killing-bottles.

Portugal Laurel (*P. lusitanica*); ill. p. 140. This is a shrub or tree to 8 m or more with leaves 6–12 cm long, darker green above, less leathery and more regularly toothed than those of cherry laurel and lacking glands on the underside. It has smooth, almost black bark. Leaf-stalks and young twigs are dark red. The suberect racemes of white flowers appear in April–June and are 10–25 cm long; the purple-black fruits are about 9 mm across. Portugal laurel is native in South-western Europe and the Azores; it is often planted in the British Isles though less commonly than cherry laurel.

Laurustinus (*Viburnum tinus*); ill. p. 141. This is a species of the large genus *Viburnum* and therefore a relative of the guelder rose (p. 35), but it differs from our native species in being evergreen and in flowering throughout the winter. It is a shrub reaching about 3 m high and its opposite leaves, 5–7·5 cm long, are ovate-oblong, pointed, dark glossy green and hairless above, downy on the veins beneath. The margin is untoothed and usually turned downwards. The flowers are in somewhat rounded clusters 5–7·5 cm across and are pink outside, white within. The berry-like fruits turn blue and then black. Laurustinus is native in the Mediterranean region. It is much grown both as a free-standing shrub and also as a hedge plant in the British Isles.

Spotted Laurel (*Aucuba japonica*) belongs to the same family as the dogwoods and is related neither to the true laurel nor to cherry and Portugal laurel. Growing up to 3 m, it is always shrubby in form and its leaves are in opposite pairs, unlike those of the other "laurels". They are 8–20 cm long, broadly elliptical-ovate and with distant marginal teeth. The wild plant has leaves that are glossy green on both sides, but much more commonly planted are the forms with yellow-spotted leaves. The flowers are small and purplish, male and female being borne on separate plants in March–April. Female plants bear dense panicles of bright red berries, each with a single seed, in late autumn. Spotted laurel, which is native to Japan, is very widely grown in the British Isles because it thrives on all types of soil, endures shade, and tolerates a good deal of atmospheric pollution.

PRIVETS (see also p. 39)

Japanese Privet (*Ligustrum ovalifolium*); ill. p. 141. This is perhaps the most widely used of all our hedge plants, except only the hawthorn of our field hedges. The semi-evergreen elliptic ovate leaves, 2·5–6 cm long, are both longer and relatively broader than those of wild privet and the white flowers, which open in July, are in larger panicles with the petals joined into a tube 2 or 3 times as long as the free lobes (the tube equals the lobes in wild privet). The Golden Privet (*L. ovalifolium* 'Aureum') is popular as a hedge plant because of its yellow leaves, either green-centred or uniformly yellow. Japanese privet, if left unpruned, can reach heights of 5 m or so but remains shrubby in habit.

Shining Privet (*L. lucidum*) can grow as a tree to 12 m high with smooth grey bark. Its dark glossy evergreen leaves are narrowly ovate, 3–6 cm long, and its white flowers are in upright panicles up to 25 cm long. The petal-tube of the individual flower is about as long as the free lobes. This handsome tree, flowering in August and September, is grown occasionally in gardens, and a few other tree privets are also in cultivation. It is native in Eastern Asia.

CHILEAN FIRE-BUSH

Chilean Fire-Bush (*Embothrium coccineum*); ill. p. 141. This very striking plant can unfortunately be grown successfully only in the mildest parts of the country. It is a small and short-lived evergreen tree which can reach 10–12 m in height when growing well. Its leaves are rather variable in shape but usually elliptic or lanceolate, 6–12 by 2–4 cm but sometimes up to 20 cm long, narrowing both to the base and to the tip which is blunt or even rounded. They are glossy green above, paler and bluish beneath, hairless and somewhat leathery, and have untoothed margins. The scarlet-crimson flowers, borne in May and June, are in numerous short terminal and axillary racemes and make a brilliant display. Each flower has a long slender tube, 2·5–4 cm long and dividing above into 4 strap-shaped lobes with a stamen united to each. The lobes curl back to reveal the long erect style. The fruit is a pinkish capsule. This plant is native in Chile and a member of the family Proteaceae, almost confined to the Southern Hemisphere.

scale for trees 1, 3, 4, & 6

1 CUCUMBER TREE (*Magnolia acuminata*)   2 LILY TREE (*M. denudata*)—flower and buds, spring; leaves, late summer
spring   5 *M.* × *loebneri* 'Leonard Messel'   6 TULIP TREE (*Liriodendron tulipifera*).   Details × ⅔. Text pp. 146–7

3 *M.* × *soulangeana*—tree in flower, early spring; winter-buds   4 STARRY MAGNOLIA (*M. stellata*)—tree and flower,

INTRODUCED FLOWERING TREES: Deciduous

The family Magnoliaceae includes the magnolias (*Magnolia*) and tulip trees (*Liriodendron*) together with eight other genera. Its members are of great interest to botanists because their flowers are thought by many to resemble those of very early flowering plants and their wood also shows a number of features regarded as primitive in the evolutionary sense. In addition three of the genera, including both *Magnolia* and *Liriodendron*, have curiously interrupted ranges of distribution, with representatives in Eastern Asia but nowhere else except the eastern side of North America with or without extensions into the Caribbean area. This posed a difficult problem of explanation for early plant geographers, but it is now realized from finds of plant fossil remains that magnolias and tulip trees were living over much of the north temperate region of both Old and New Worlds before the last Ice Age. They remain as native plants in quite small parts of their known former range, showing what are termed "relict" distributions. This seems due to the fact that these trees cannot tolerate climates as cold as those readily withstood by birches, aspens, and many oaks, elms, maples, and beeches, and only down the broad coastal plains of the eastern sides of Asia and North America were they able to migrate southwards in front of the advancing ice without having their retreat fatally cut off by mountainous country such as prevented their survival in Europe, Western Asia, and the western part of North America. Several genera in other families show similarly discontinuous distributions, notably the witch hazels (*Hamamelis*, p. 150), Indian beans (*Catalpa*, p. 199), and *Wisteria*, all absent from Europe though found in Eastern Asia and the eastern part of North America. The horse-chestnuts (*Aesculus*, pp. 190–1) and planes (*Platanus*, pp. 194–5) differ in having survived also in the Balkan Peninsula and South-western Asia: there seem to have been other possible migration routes into the Balkans and also into the country round the Caspian Sea.

MAGNOLIAS. The genus *Magnolia* (ill. pp. 144–5) includes both trees and shrubs, mostly deciduous but a few evergreen. The leaves are alternate, simple, and untoothed but sometimes lobed; their large stipules, which enclose the next youngest leaf in bud, usually fall early and leave scars completely encircling the stem. The large flowers are borne singly at the ends of stems. They have 3 sepals and 6 or more petals, but the distinction between sepals and petals may be very slight. There are very many stamens and numerous ovaries borne in close spiral sequence on a long floral axis, the ovaries above the stamens. The fruits split open to reveal usually 2 seeds which are at first suspended on long slender threads but then fall or are taken by birds. Magnolias are native in tropical and Eastern Asia and in the eastern part of North America and the Caribbean area, but are widely grown for their large and attractive flowers which in most deciduous species appear before the leaves and in this country need protection from strong winds and severe frosts. Most are intolerant of calcareous soils but *M.* x *loebneri* and *M. kobus* grow well on chalk.

1 **Cucumber Tree** (*M. acuminata*) is a large deciduous tree, 20–30 m high, with narrowly fissured bark and shining red-brown twigs. The leaves, 15–25 cm long, are broadly elliptic to ovate, hairless or nearly so. The not very conspicuous flowers, opening with the leaves in May or June, are 4–5 cm across, greenish-yellow, with 3 narrow reflexed sepals and 6 broader petals. They are succeeded by the "cucumbers" of developing fruits, 5–8 cm long, at first green but turning red. Cucumber trees are native in North-eastern America and are quite hardy in the British Isles.

2 **Lily Tree** or **Yulan** (*M. denudata*) is a deciduous shrub or small tree up to 9 m high with downy young twigs and furry buds. The obovate-oblong leaves are 10–15 cm long with a broadly rounded but short-pointed tip. The large white flowers are 12–15 cm across and appear in March–May, before the leaves. Their sepals and petals are indistinguishable. Lily tree is native in China.

M. liliiflora is a deciduous lime-hating shrub, 3 m or more high, with broadly elliptic leaves 10–18 cm long. Its tulip-like flowers, purplish outside and creamy-white within, appear in April–June. The sepals are small, greenish, and early-falling. *M. liliiflora* is native in China. It is an attractive shrub but much less commonly grown than the following.

M. x soulangeana, a hybrid of *M. denudata* with *M. liliiflora* and the most popular of all magnolias, is a large deciduous shrub or tree up to 10 m. The leaves are much like those of *M. denudata* but are often broadest at or below the middle. The flowers, which appear in April or May before the leaves, are large and tulip-shaped; the sepals which are about half as long as the petals are sometimes greenish but more usually white, like the petals, with rose or purplish staining towards the base of the outer side. Some horticultural varieties are uniformly white and some are purple-tinged inside as well as outside, and there are also variations in size of flowers. This magnolia is not successful on shallow chalky soils.

Pink Tulip Tree (*M. campbellii*), from the Himalayas, is a tree up to 20 m high with large fragrant flowers that open widely and are of various colours from white or palest pink to a deep rose-purple. Its hybrid with *M. denudata*, **M. x veitchii**, is also a tree. It is covered with large pink-flushed flowers in April and is one of the finest magnolias in cultivation, though not as hardy as some and definitely a lime-hater.

Starry Magnolia (*M. stellata*). This is usually a rounded shrub, growing to 3 m high, with very furry winter-buds and obovate-oblong to elliptic deciduous leaves 4–10 cm long. The fragrant white (rarely pink) flowers are about 8 cm across and the sepals and petals, 12–18 in all, are all alike, narrow and spreading. The flowers open in March or April and may be damaged by frost. It is native in Japan.

M. kobus, a related Japanese species, is a large shrub or small tree up to about 8 m high with broadly obovate deciduous leaves up to 15 cm long. Its flowers have only 6–9 perianth segments, broader than those of *M. stellata*. They are white but commonly with a purple line down the outer side of each, and they appear in April–May.

5 *M. x loebneri* 'Leonard Messel' is a hybrid between *M. kobus* and a pink-flowered form of *M. stellata* and is intermediate between its parents in stature and in the size and shape of its leaves. The flowers are star-like, with numerous narrow spreading perianth segments, lilac-pink in colour. They are deep pink in bud and open in March–April before the leaves.

A few other deciduous magnolias are occasionally to be seen in gardens in the milder counties of the south and west and in Ireland. These include the two large-leaved species, **M. macrophylla** of the South-eastern U.S.A. and **M. obovata** of Japan. Both have obovate leaves up to 30 cm or more long, those of *M. macrophylla* sometimes reaching 60 cm and having large ear-like basal lobes. Both have cream-coloured fragrant flowers. They may grow as trees and *M. obovata* can reach a height of 15 m. An evergreen magnolia is described on p. 139.

LIRIODENDRON

Tulip Tree (*Liriodendron tulipifera*); ill. p. 145. This is a lofty deciduous tree of North-eastern America where it can reach a height of 60 m. The brown twigs show encircling stipule-scars like those of the magnolias. The alternate long-stalked hairless leaves, 7–12 cm long and almost equally wide, usually have 2 broad long-pointed basal lobes and a central part ending in a pair of upper lobes with a wide and shallow straight-sided notch between them, so that the end of the leaf may give the appearance of having been cut across with scissors. The fragrant tulip-shaped flowers open in June or July and are 4–5 cm high, each with 3 spreading greenish-white sepals, soon falling, and 6 erect petals, pale greenish with a broad orange band near the base. The fruits are in a dense cone-like aggregate, the individual fruit having 1–2 seeds, dry and winged rather like an ash-key and similarly wind-carried when the aggregate breaks up. It is a very handsome tree, both when in flower and when the leaves turn a rich yellow in autumn, and often planted in parks and large gardens. In North America it is called "yellow poplar" because of its long-stalked fluttering leaves. The useful timber is called whitewood. A very closely related species, *L. chinense*, grows in China.

m 7

6

5

scale for trees 1, 2, 3, 5, 6, 7, & 8

4

3

2

1

0

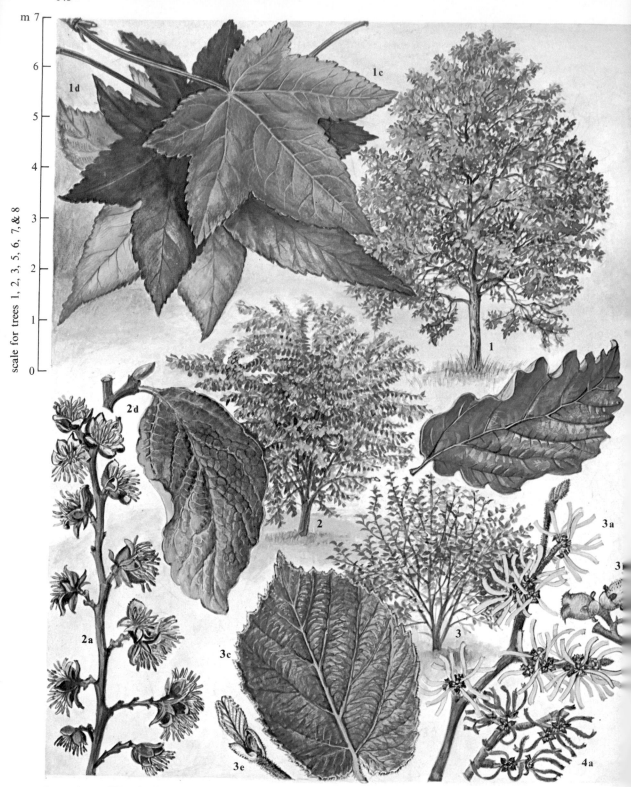

1 SWEET GUM (*Liquidambar styraciflua*)—young tree   2 PERSIAN IRONWOOD (*Parrotia persica*)
5 POCKET-HANDKERCHIEF TREE (*Davidia involucrata*)—young tree   6 FLOWERING DOGWOOD (*Cornus florida*)
e=shoot. Details × ⅔. Text pp. 150–1

3 CHINESE WITCH HAZEL (*Hamamelis mollis*)   4 *H*. x *intermedia* 'Red Glow'—flower details only
7 CORNELIAN CHERRY (*C. mas*)   8 *C. officinalis*—February. a=flowers; b=fruits; c=summer leaves; d=autumn leaves;

INTRODUCED FLOWERING TREES: Deciduous

SWEET GUM

1 **Sweet Gum** (*Liquidambar styraciflua*); ill. p. 148. This and the two following trees belong to the witch hazel family (Hamamelidaceae), comprising woody plants with simple alternate stipulate leaves and small flowers made conspicuous chiefly by aggregation. Their fruits are dry and woody, 2-celled, and splitting open to release the seeds. Sweet gum is a North-east American tree with close relatives in Asia. In the British Isles it is found mainly in the south. It reaches 30 m or more in height and has a deeply fissured grey-brown bark. Older twigs commonly have conspicuous corky ridges. The deciduous leaves have 5–7 narrowly triangular, long-pointed, and finely toothed palmate lobes so that they resemble those of maples—but they are arranged alternately, not in opposite pairs as in maples. They turn bright crimson in autumn. Male and female flowers are borne in separate globular heads on the same tree, the male short-stalked and in conical clusters, the female long-stalked, solitary. The individual flowers lack petals and are very inconspicuous. The male flower has numerous stamens, the female 4 non-functional stamens and a 2-celled ovary. The globular fruiting clusters, 2·5–4 cm across, hang on long stalks and resemble those of planes but are woody and made spiny by the pairs of persistent styles of the component flowers.

IRONWOOD

2 **Persian Ironwood** (*Parrotia persica*); ill. p. 148. This small tree reaches 10–12 m in height but it is often shrubby in form. It is native round the southern end of the Caspian Sea, in Northern Iran, and the Caucasus. It has scaling pinkish-grey or grey-brown bark and is deciduous, with short-stalked, ovate, downy leaves, 7–12 cm long and half as wide, coarsely toothed above the middle, and turning brilliant gold and crimson in autumn. The flowers, in dense clusters, open before the leaves. They have no petals but are bisexual and are made conspicuous by their bright red stamens. The fruit consists of 3–5 deep brown nuts surrounded by pale green bracts. The leaves resemble those of witch hazels.

WITCH HAZELS (*Hamamelis*); ill. p. 148.

3 **Chinese Witch Hazel** (*H. mollis*), native in China, is a deciduous shrub or small tree to 10 m high with rounded leaves broadest above the middle, downy above, densely felted beneath, and with distantly toothed margins. In general form, and in their abruptly short-pointed tip, the leaves resemble those of our native hazel. They turn red and yellow in autumn but not as brilliantly as those of *Parrotia*. The bisexual flowers each have 4 long and very narrow parallel-sided yellow petals and 4 stamens. They open in mid-winter on the leafless twigs and are pleasantly fragrant. The dry fruit opens along 2 lines to release 2 shining black seeds. The autumn colouring of the leaves adds to the attractions of this very popular plant. **Japanese Witch Hazel** (*H. japonica*) differs in having more or less hairless leaves, not or barely heart-shaped at the base.

4 *H.* x *intermedia*, the hybrid between *H. mollis* and *H. japonica*, is commonly grown. It has larger flowers and in several varieties the petals are orange rather than yellow and often tinged with red as in the variety 'Red Glow' illustrated. *H.* x *intermedia* flowers in winter.

H. virginiana, native in the eastern part of North America and there called simply witch hazel, is a deciduous shrub or small tree reaching to about 5 m in height. It has ovate to obovate leaves 10–15 cm long, usually with a markedly asymmetric rounded or slightly heart-shaped base and rather deep and widely spaced wavy marginal teeth. The underside is hairless or nearly so. They turn golden-yellow in autumn, and the abundant yellow flowers also appear in September–November. This is the commercial source of the "witch hazel" used medicinally to stop bleeding and also of an oil used in perfumery. It is not very commonly grown except as a stock on which other species are grafted.

Ozark Witch Hazel (*H. vernalis*), native in central U.S.A., with yellow to red flowers appearing from January to March, grows only as a shrub up to 3 m high.

DOVE TREE

5 Pocket-handkerchief Tree or **Dove Tree** (*Davidia involucrata*); ill. p. 149. This tree, native in China, is now usually placed in the Nyssaceae with the sour-gums (*Nyssa*). This is a deciduous tree to 20 m high, with purplish flaky bark. It has simple alternate broadly ovate leaves, 8–14 cm long, heart-shaped at the base and long-pointed at the tip, and resembling those of common lime. They have pointed teeth along their margins and are silky-hairy beneath. The small flowers lack petals and are in dense heads, each with numerous male flowers and 1 bisexual flower: they are made to some extent conspicuous by the stamens but particularly by the pair of large white bracts hanging down from the base, the larger up to 16 cm or so long and 10 cm across, the other about half that size. The whole crown is draped with these white handkerchiefs in May and early June. The ripe fruits are green with a purple bloom and are about 3·5 cm long, pear-shaped.

DOGWOODS (*Cornus*); ill. p. 149.

The genus *Cornus* is a very large one which some botanists choose to split into a number of smaller genera but others prefer to retain intact. The simple leaves are usually in opposite pairs but are alternate in some species. The flowers are small but aggregated into panicles, umbels, or heads. In some of the most popular species in cultivation the flower-clusters have 4–5 large white or coloured bracts close beneath them so that the whole cluster looks like a single large flower. The parts of the individual flowers are in fours, with only 4 stamens. The fruit is berry-like but with a 2-celled stone, each cell having a single seed. There are two native species, the shrubby dogwood (*C. sanguinea*, p. 35) and the dwarf cornel (*C. suecica*), a moorland herb with the umbels of tiny dark purple flowers surrounded by 4 white bracts.

C. controversa is a deciduous tree to 20 m with alternate broadly elliptic leaves, 7–12 cm long, bluish and somewhat downy beneath. The cream-coloured flowers appear in corymbs in May–June and the blue-black fruits in August. *C. macrophylla* has larger opposite leaves, 10–16 cm long. Both are native in Eastern Asia.

6 Flowering Dogwood (*C. florida*) is a large deciduous shrub or small tree up to about 6 m in height. The short-stalked ovate leaves are in opposite pairs. They are 8–15 cm long, abruptly narrowed into a long pointed tip and rounded or tapering at the base, and they are hairless above, bluish beneath. The small greenish flowers are in heads surrounded by 4 broad white bracts 4–5 cm long (rosy-pink in var. *rubra* and other cultivated forms). This dogwood is much cultivated in the U.S.A. both for its white "flowers" and for the rich red autumn colours of the leaves. It is native in the Eastern U.S.A. southwards from Massachusetts. It is a lime-hater, suffers damage from late frosts, and requires a hot summer to ripen its wood: in the British Isles it thrives best on acid soils in southern and western counties.

C. kousa, native in Japan (var. *chinensis* in China), makes a bigger tree than *C. florida*, sometimes reaching 9 m, and is hardier. Its wavy-margined elliptic leaves are only 6–9 cm long and its bracts creamy rather than pure white. It flowers in June. The fruits are united in strawberry-like heads, but they are not often seen in the British Isles.

Cornelian Cherry (*C. mas*) is a deciduous shrub or small tree to 8 m, with dark brown scaling bark and greenish finely-hairy young twigs. The opposite leaves are ovate-elliptic and much like those of our native British dogwood but with tufts of whitish hairs in vein-axils on the underside. The small yellow flowers are in globular clusters surrounded by 4 yellowish-green bracts which are shorter than the flowers. They open in February and March, well before the leaves, and a plant in full flower is a very attractive sight at that time of year. The fruits ripen in August: they are up to 1·5 cm long, tapering at both ends, bright red, and edible. It is native in central and Southern Europe and abundant in some limestone areas.

8 *C. officinalis*, the related Japanese species, is taller (up to 10 m) and less spreading and has somewhat larger leaves with large tufts of reddish-brown hairs in vein-axils on the underside. The bright yellow heads of flowers are produced even earlier than those of cornelian cherry, and the scarlet fruits ripen in August.

Two shrubby dogwoods with corymbs of white flowers, and lacking the conspicuous bracts of *C. florida* and its relatives, are often seen in gardens. One is the **Red-Osier Dogwood** (*C. sericea*) of North America, with blood-red branches, some prostrate and some arching down to the ground, and all readily rooting so that a single plant soon forms an extensive thicket. The flowers open in May–June, in corymbs 3–5 cm across, and the white to bluish fruits ripen in September–October. This dogwood grows to 2 m or more in the British Isles. The **Tartar Dogwood** (*C. alba*), which is 2–3 m in height, resembles *C. sericea* but its red shoots are erect, the leaves are longer-pointed, the fruit ripens earlier, and the stone of the fruit is longer than broad (the reverse in *C. sericea*). It is native in Siberia and Northeastern Asia.

m 15

10

5

0

scale for trees 1, 3, 4, 5, 6, 7, 8, & 10

1 FILBERT (*Corylus maxima*)   2 PURPLE-LEAVED FILBERT (*C. maxima* 'Purpurea')—leaf details only
5 JAPANESE LARGE-LEAVED BIRCH (*Betula maximowicziana*)   6 CANOE BIRCH (*B. papyrifera*)
9 GREY ALDER (*A. incana*)—twig and leaf detail only   10 CUT-LEAVED ALDER (*A. glutinosa* 'Imperialis').

3 TURKISH HAZEL (*C. colurna*)—tree only   4 EUROPEAN HOP-HORNBEAM (*Ostrya carpinifolia*)
7 YOUNG'S WEEPING BIRCH (*B. pendula* 'Youngii')   8 ITALIAN ALDER (*Alnus cordata*)
Details × ⅔. Text pp. 154–5

INTRODUCED FLOWERING TREES: Deciduous

HAZELS (*Corylus*); ill. p. 152. A general description of the genus is given on p. 34.

1–2 **Filbert** or **Kentish Cob** (*C. maxima*) (**1**), native in South-eastern Europe and Western Asia and grown throughout the British Isles, is a large shrub or small tree up to 10 m in height with short-stalked leaves resembling those of our native hazel (*C. avellana*) but somewhat larger, 7–14 cm long against 5–10 cm in hazel. The male catkins are also longer than in hazel but are otherwise similar. The chief difference from hazel is that the green cup round the nut is longer and more tubular than in hazel and ends in several irregular toothed lobes which extend well beyond the enclosed nut. The nut itself is longer and less rounded than the hazel nut. A purple-leaved variety (***C. maxima* 'Purpurea'**) (**2**), is frequently grown for its foliage. Hybrids between *C. avellana* and *C. maxima*, with nuts intermediate in size and shape and the cup shorter than in filbert and often split almost to its base, are sometimes seen in gardens.

3 **Turkish Hazel** (*C. colurna*), native in South-eastern Europe and across Asia to China, is a large tree up to 25 m high. It has pale scaling bark, later fissured and corky, and leaves like those of *C. avellana* but rather larger and with a stalk 2 cm long against only 1 cm in *C. avellana*. The nuts are in dense clusters and their cups end in long narrow lobes that curl downwards.

Corkscrew Hazel (*C. avellana* 'Contorta'), occasionally seen in gardens, is a curious horticultural variety in which the twigs and branches are grotesquely bent and twisted. It is similar to *C. avellana* in other respects.

HORNBEAMS (*Carpinus*). A general description of the genus is given on p. 18. Our native hornbeam (*C. betulus*) is frequently planted in all parts of the country and is much used for hedges. Also frequent in gardens and as a street tree is the horticultural variety 'Fastigiata', with a compact broadly conical crown. American hornbeam (*C. caroliniana*) is very like *C. betulus* but the 3-lobed wing of the nutlet is only about half as long and the winter-buds are hairy. Eastern hornbeam (*C. orientalis*) and Japanese hornbeam (*C. japonica*) have toothed but unlobed ovate fruit-wings. None of the three is common in gardens.

HOP-HORNBEAMS (*Ostrya*), like the related hazels and hornbeams, have simple alternate deciduous leaves with early-falling stipules, and their small greenish male and female flowers, opening in early spring, are in separate catkins on the same plant. The male catkins are slender and drooping, with flowers consisting only of stamens. The female catkins are initially erect, with 2 flowers in the axil of each scale and each female flower has a basal tube which later enlarges into a loose bladder-like envelope round the nutlet. By this time the fruiting catkins are directed downwards and come to resemble ripe hops.

4 **European Hop Hornbeam** (*O. carpinifolia*) ill. p. 152. This is a shrub or small tree up to 20 m high with greyish bark at first smooth but later developing vertical and horizontal fissures. The young twigs are downy and the leaves are very like those of hornbeam but rather more finely toothed and with some hairs on the upper surface. It is native in Southern Europe and Asia Minor and is characteristically a plant of shady north-facing slopes. **American Hop-Hornbeam** (*O. virginiana*) has shorter leaf-stalks, which are usually sticky with glandular hairs, and narrower nutlets; and **Japanese Hop-Hornbeam** (*O. japonica*) has the leaves more softly hairy, both above and beneath. Both are occasionally seen in gardens.

BIRCHES (*Betula*); ill. pp. 152–3. A general description of the genus is given on pp. 18–19. Birches commonly grown in gardens include forms of the native silver birch (*B. pendula*) and a few other species which are usually recognizable as birches without difficulty even though some have much larger leaves than our silver birch and others do not have white bark.

5 **Japanese Large-leaved Birch** (*B. maximowicziana*) is a large tree up to 30 m high, native in Japan. The trunk is at first orange-brown but peels in papery flakes to turn first green and then greyish. The leaves are strikingly large for a birch and resemble those of a lime, being 8–14 cm long, broadly ovate, and deeply heart-shaped at the base, with sharp-pointed tip. They turn a beautiful clear yellow in autumn.

6 **Canoe Birch** or **Paper-Bark Birch** (*B. papyrifera*) is a tree reaching heights of 30 m or more, with the initially warm brown bark peeling to expose a white underbark which is continually renewed by further peeling. The leaves are ovate and long-pointed, 4–10 cm long, rounded or wedge-shaped at the base. They differ from leaves of our silver birch in being downy on the veins beneath, but like them they turn yellow in autumn. Canoe birch is native in a broad belt across North America from Labrador to Alaska in the north and from Connecticut to Washington state in the south. The bark was used by North American Indians to make birch-bark canoes and wigwam covers as well as baskets, dishes, and trays.

7 **Young's Weeping Birch** (*B. pendula* 'Youngii') is a cultivated variety of our native silver birch in which the main branches spread outwards and then curve down to form a rather irregular dome-shaped crown from which the very slender branchlets hang vertically. This attractive weeping tree is very popular. Cut-leaved Birch (*B. pendula* 'Dalecarlica'), with deeply cut and lobed leaves, is also planted occasionally.

More rarely seen in gardens are **Transcaucasian Birch** (*B. medwediewii*), with upturned branches and broad dark green leaves, 6–12 cm long, resembling those of alder (Northern Persia); **Erman's Birch** (*B. ermanii*), with orange-brown branches, cream-white pink-tinged bark, and handsome glossy leaves, 6–10 cm long (North-eastern Asia and Japan); **River Birch** (*B. nigra*), with dark reddish and very shaggy bark and diamond-shaped leaves with strikingly double-toothed margins (Eastern U.S.A.); **Cherry Birch** (*B. lenta*), with dark reddish-brown or purple bark (eastern North America); and **Yellow Birch** (*B. lutea*), with shining golden-brown or amber-coloured bark (eastern North America).

ALDERS (*Alnus*); ill. p. 153. For a general description of the genus see p. 19.

8 **Italian Alder** (*A. cordata*), native in Corsica, Southern Italy, and Western Asia, is a tree up to about 15 m high with a usually smooth brown bark and hairless pointed winter-buds. The leaves are broadly rounded, heart-shaped at the base and blunt or abruptly short-pointed at the tip, and with finely toothed margins. They are 5–10 cm long with stalks about a third as long. The woody female "cones" are up to 2·5 cm long—much larger than in our native alder (*A. glutinosa*). This attractive tree is less commonly grown than it deserves.

Grey Alder (*A. incana*), a very hardy species of mountain valleys and subarctic forests of Northern and central Europe and across Northern Asia, is a freely suckering shrub or tree up to 20 m high, with smooth pale grey bark. It has broadly elliptic leaves, 4–10 cm long, rounded at the base and with pointed tip, and the margins are doubly toothed and often slightly lobed. The upper surface is dull green with sunken veins, and the lower bluish-green and hairy when young but later becoming hairless. The woody fruiting "cones" are 1·5 cm long. Grey alder is frequently planted for shelter and for improving poor soils through its capacity for nitrogen-fixation. It is locally naturalized, especially in Scotland. **Oregon Alder** (*A. rubra*), of North-western America, differs in having more definitely lobed leaves with narrowly down-turned margins.

10 **Cut-leaved Alder** (*A. glutinosa* 'Imperialis') is a form of our native alder in which the leaves are deeply and finely cut. It is commonly planted for its decorative value. There are also fastigiate and variegated forms in cultivation.

1 AMERICAN BEECH (*Fagus grandifolia*)—leaf detail only   2 COPPER BEECH (*F. sylvatica* 'Purpurea')
5 ROBLE BEECH (*N. obliqua*)   6 RAOUL BEECH (*N. procera*)—leaf detail only
9 CHESTNUT-LEAVED OAK (*Q. castaneifolia*)—leaf details only   10 TURKEY OAK (*Q. cerris*)—July
13 AMERICAN RED OAK (*Q. rubra*)—October   14 SCARLET OAK (*Q. coccinea*)—October

3 CUT-LEAVED BEECH (*F. sylvatica* 'Heterophylla')   4 MOUNTAIN BEECH (*Nothofagus solandri* var. *cliffortioides*)
7 ANTARCTIC BEECH (*N. antarctica*)—leaf details only   8 ALGERIAN OAK (*Quercus canariensis*)—leaf and shoot details only
11 LUCOMBE OAK (*Q.* x *hispanica* 'Lucombeana')—details only, May   12 HUNGARIAN OAK (*Q. frainetto*)
All details × $\frac{2}{3}$, except 12 which is shown at both $\frac{2}{3}$ and $\frac{1}{4}$. Text pp. 158–9

INTRODUCED FLOWERING TREES: Deciduous

BEECHES (*Fagus*); ill. p. 156. A general description of the genus is given on p. 14.

1 **American Beech** (*F. grandifolia*) is occasionally grown in the British Isles but does not thrive here. It resembles native beech in its smooth grey bark and in the general form of its leaves but these are larger, more strongly toothed, and have 9–14 pairs of veins (against only 5–9 pairs in *F. sylvatica*). It is native in eastern North America from New Brunswick to Florida and Texas and there reaches a height of 30 m or more.

Oriental Beech (*F. orientalis*), of South-eastern Europe and Western Asia, differs from our native beech in its slightly larger elliptic-obovate leaves which tend to be broadest beyond the middle, and in the longer stalks of its fruit-cups which are 2 cm or more (against 1·5 cm or less in *F. sylvatica*), but there are intermediates. Some East Asiatic beeches are also grown occasionally.

2 **Copper Beech** (*F. sylvatica*, several cultivated varieties collectively named 'Purpurea'). Amongst varieties of native beech commonly planted in the British Isles, by far the most conspicuous are the various purple- and copper-leaved forms called copper beech or purple beech, with leaves ranging in colour from dark purple to reddish-green.

3 **Cut-leaved** or **Fern-leaved Beech** (*F. sylvatica*, several cultivated varieties collectively named 'Heterophylla'). Also commonly grown in gardens and parks are these forms of native beech with narrow leaves variously cut and lobed, often strikingly unlike those of the wild tree.

Weeping Beech (*F. sylvatica* 'Pendula') is frequently planted. It varies greatly in general shape, some forms being quite narrow in outline, others spreading, but all with markedly pendulous branchlets.

SOUTHERN BEECHES (*Nothofagus*); ill. p. 156. The close relatives of beech in the southern hemisphere include both evergreen and deciduous species. They flower in May and resemble beech in having 3-sided nuts enclosed in a scaly cup but differ in having the male flowers solitary or in groups of no more than 3 and in having usually 3 nuts in each cup instead of only 2. Their leaves are often less than 2·5 cm long. Evergreen species both from New Zealand and from Chile are sometimes seen in gardens, but the only deciduous species likely to be encountered in the British Isles come from Chile (**5** and **6** below).

4 **Mountain Beech** (*N. solandri* var. *cliffortioides*) is a small tree up to 20 m high, native in mountain areas of both the North and South Islands of New Zealand. It is readily recognized by the small triangular untoothed evergreen leaves, only about 1 cm long, which are often upturned at the tips but with downcurved margins. **Black Beech** (*N. solandri*) has slightly larger flat leaves, and a third New Zealand species, **Silver Beech** (*N. menziesii*), has toothed leaves. Two evergreen species from Chile, *N. dombeyi* and *N. betuloides*, have leaves more than 2·5 cm long but are rarely seen in the British Isles.

5 **Roble Beech** (*N. obliqua*) is a tall tree up to 30 m high with ovate to ovate-oblong deciduous leaves 3–8 cm long, rounded to broadly wedge-shaped at the base and more or less blunt-tipped, with toothed margins. The male flowers are solitary, each with 30–40 stamens.

6 **Raoul Beech** or **Rauli Beech** (*N. procera*) also reaches almost 30 m in height but its oblong leaves, 4–10 cm long, are rounded at both ends and finely double-toothed. Both Roble and Raoul show promise of being useful timber trees in the British Isles.

7 **Antarctic Beech** (*N. antarctica*), also deciduous and also from Chile, has leaves only 1·5–3 cm long, more or less heart-shaped at the base and with irregular teeth and short lateral lobes. It is less hardy than the two preceding species.

OAKS (*Quercus*); ill. pp. 156–7. For a general description see p. 14. Apart from the evergreen oaks described on p. 138, many non-native deciduous oaks are much grown in the British Isles, some for their handsome leaves as well as their beautiful autumn colouring.

8   Algerian Oak (*Q. canariensis*, formerly *Q. mirbeckii*) grows to 30 m or more, and has deeply fissured bark and a rounded crown. The leaves are 5–18 cm long, elliptic-ovate, broadly toothed, glossy dark green above and pale or bluish beneath. The stalked acorns have the cup reaching to about halfway. Native in North Africa, Spain, and Portugal, it is a handsome tree whose leaves commonly persist until the end of the year so that it may be termed semi-evergreen. The hybrid with pedunculate oak, with smaller obovate and shallowly lobed leaves, is also grown and is perfectly hardy in the British Isles.

9   Chestnut-leaved Oak (*Q. castaneifolia*) grows to 25 m high in the British Isles. It has dark grey fissured bark and oblong-elliptic leaves 7–16 cm long, with pointed tip and narrowly rounded or wedge-shaped base, dark green above and downy beneath; the stipules are persistent. The acorn is 2–3 cm long with the cup extending half-way up, its scales curled downwards. It is a native in Iran and the Caucasus. A semi-fastigiate form is also in cultivation. Chestnut-leaved oak can be grown as far north as Yorkshire.

**   Turkey Oak** (*Q. cerris*) is a large and fast-growing tree with dark brown fissured bark and hairy buds surrounded by narrow stipules up to 2·5 cm long. Leaves are 5–10 cm or more long, very variable in shape and lobing but oblong or obovate-oblong in outline, usually pointed at the tip and with 6–9 pairs of more or less pointed lobes; they are dull green and rough above, paler and downy beneath. The acorn ripens only in the second year after flowering and is 2–4 cm long, its cup covered with narrow spreading scales up to 2·5 cm long. It is native in central and Southern Europe and South-western Asia, but commonly planted and perfectly hardy in Britain and naturalized in many places, especially in Southern England.

11   Lucombe Oak (*Q.* x *hispanica* 'Lucombeana'). The semi-evergreen hybrid between Turkey oak and cork oak (p. 138), first raised in Exeter in the eighteenth century, is a variable tree, the most frequently planted form having a short trunk and widely spreading crown. The bark is dark, deeply fissured, and corky, and the leaves are more like those of cork oak than Turkey oak but they vary in the degree of lobing. The leaves, except in very hard winters, are retained until late spring. The acorn-cup has down-curved scales.

12   Hungarian Oak or **Macedonian Oak** (*Q. frainetto*, formerly *Q. conferta*) grows to 30 m in the British Isles and has pale grey fissured bark and large buds surrounded by persistent stipules. The leaves are short-stalked, obovate, 10–18 cm long, tapering to the narrowly heart-shaped base and with about 8 pairs of lobes extending halfway to the midrib—these often further lobed. They are dark green above, grey-green and hairy beneath. The acorn is about 2·5 cm long and the cup has rather loosely overlapping oblong scales. This very fine tree, native from Southern Italy to the Black Sea and locally in Hungary and Czechoslovakia, thrives throughout the British Isles.

13   American Red Oak (*Q. rubra*, including *Q. borealis*). This fine large tree grows well in most parts of the British Isles and some are 30 m or more high. Its bark is grey, becoming fissured only in old trees. The twigs soon become hairless and dark red; buds are reddish-brown. The leaves, 12–25 cm long, are ovate or obovate in out-line with 3–5 pairs of lobes reaching half-way to the mid-rib, each tapering to a long fine point and with a few fine-pointed lateral teeth. The leaves are dull green above, pale beneath and smooth except for tufts of brown hairs in the vein-axils. They turn to various shades of red in the autumn. The short-stalked acorns, ripening in the second year and not often seen in the British Isles, are up to 2·5 cm long and have only the base enclosed in the shallow flat-scaled cup. This oak is native in North-eastern America but frequently grown in Britain for its brilliant autumn colouring.

14   Scarlet Oak (*Q. coccinea*), also grown for its fine autumn colours, is native in North-eastern America but does not extend as far north as red oak, from which it differs in having leaf-lobes that reach more than half-way to the midrib. The leaves are glossy green above and a richer scarlet in autumn, and the cup encloses the lower half of the acorn. Scarlet oak has been planted chiefly in South-eastern England and has reached heights of 25 m.

1 DUTCH ELM (*Ulmus* x *hollandica* 'Hollandica')   2 HUNTINGDON ELM (*U.* x *hollandica* 'Vegeta')
5 JERSEY ELM (*U. minor* var. *stricta* 'Sarniensis')—leaf detail both summer and autumn
8 BLACK MULBERRY (*Morus nigra*). Details × $\frac{2}{3}$. Text pp. 162–3

40 m

35

30

25

20

15

10

5

0

scale for trees 1, 2, 3, 4, 5, 6, 7, & 8

3 SMOOTH-LEAVED ELM (*U. minor*)—autumn 4 CORNISH ELM (*U. minor* var. *stricta* 'Cornubiensis')
6 WEEPING ELM (*U. glabra* 'Pendula')—tree only 7 CAUCASIAN ELM (*Zelkova carpinifolia*)

INTRODUCED FLOWERING TREES: Deciduous

ELMS (*Ulmus*); ill. pp. 160–1. A brief general description of the genus is given on p. 15. Elms are particularly difficult to name with confidence because there are many local types with no very clear-cut differences between them and also because they readily intercross so that naturally-occurring hybrids may bridge the gaps between species that might otherwise be easily distinguished. A possible reason for these peculiarities is that some of our elms, which do not seem to occur as components of our natural woodland, may have been introduced into England in late prehistoric or early historic times so that cattle and sheep could be fed on their palatable and nutritious leafy branches, valuable as fodder even in winter. They may therefore not have had time in which to come into stable balance either with their new environments or with each other. Several of these forms have been planted along roads and in parks and gardens, together with some others that have arisen more recently through hybridization or otherwise.

1 **Dutch Elm** (*U.* x *hollandica* 'Hollandica'). This and the following elm are presumed hybrids between wych elm (*U. glabra*) and the very variable smooth-leaved elm (*U. minor*, including what was formerly named *U. carpinifolia*), and seem to have arisen in the late seventeenth or early eighteenth century. It is a rounded tree up to 35 m high, with the upper branches ascending but the lower spreading widely. The brown bark is shallowly fissured and eventually develops a pattern of squarish plates. There are very numerous sucker shoots and also many epicormic shoots—that is, shoots springing from buds on the trunk and main branches: all these shoots have narrow corky ridges up to 2 cm high. The twigs are stout, downy at first but becoming chestnut-brown. The leaves are 6–12 cm long, broadly rounded, broadest at or just above the middle, asymmetric at the base but not concealing the leaf-stalk which is up to 1 cm long. The leaf-tip is pointed but not as long as in wych elm and the margin is coarsely toothed. The upper surface is rough but soon becomes hairless and shining; the lower is rough and has prominent tufts of hairs in the vein-axils. The seed usually reaches the apical notch of the fruit-wing. Dutch elm is frequent along roads in Southern England but uncommon elsewhere.

2 **Huntingdon Elm** (*U.* x *hollandica* 'Vegeta'), which reaches 30 m in height, differs in having a rather short trunk and branches ascending at a narrow angle to form a crown broadening upwards to a rounded top. The bark is brown with a network of low ridges with intervening deep fissures. There are usually few suckers and few epicormic shoots. The twigs, sparsely downy at first, become smooth and dark brown in the second year. The leaves are 8–14 cm long, narrowly obovate, narrower than in Dutch elm and broadest just beyond the middle, very asymmetric at the base but far from concealing the stalk, which is 1–2 cm long. The leaf-tip is long-pointed and the margin sharply toothed. The upper surface is smooth and shining and the lower has tufts of hairs in the vein-axils. The seed is about half-way between the centre and the apical notch of the fruit-wing. Huntingdon elm is widely planted in parks and gardens and especially along roads.

3 **Smooth-leaved Elm** (*U. minor*) is described briefly on p. 15. The name is now given to a whole large complex of wayside elms which cannot be divided into clearly distinct species. Some of the populations in East Anglia have small leaves with almost symmetrical bases and short stalks, and it was to these that the name *U. minor* was first applied, but they grade into the rather larger-leaved forms formerly called *U. carpinifolia* or *U. nitens* which tend to have shining upper leaf-surfaces, very asymmetric bases, and quite long stalks. The more or less fastigiate Cornish and Jersey elms may be regarded as variants of *U. minor* (**4** and **5** below).

4 **Cornish Elm** (*U. minor* var. *stricta* 'Cornubiensis') grows wild in Devon and Cornwall, and perhaps also in South-western Ireland, but as a wayside tree and not a component of natural woodland. Cornish elm is a tall semi-fastigiate tree up to 35 m high with grey-brown fissured bark and steeply ascending branches, the lower branches shorter and less stout than in Huntingdon elm and the crown narrower and thinner. The twigs are brownish and the ovate leaves, 5 cm long, are dark green, smooth and shining above, not very unequal at the base and normally folded along the midrib so as to be concave above and boat-shaped. The fruit is narrow with the seed close to the apical notch. Cornish elm is occasionally planted along roads.

5 **Jersey, Guernsey,** or **Wheatley Elm** (*U. minor* var. *stricta* 'Sarniensis') are names for local elms in the Channel Islands and Southern England, like Cornish elm but with rather less steeply ascending and more regular branches, giving a neatly conical crown. The leaves are up to 7 cm long, rounder and flatter than those of Cornish elm, not folded upwards. Jersey elm is commonly planted along roads and in parks throughout England and Southern Scotland but rarely further north. It can reach 35 m or more in Southern England.

6 **Weeping Elm** (*U. glabra* 'Pendula') is one of two weeping forms of wych elm seen in gardens. It is a tree up to 20 m high with spreading branches whose branchlets hang down from their ends. The **Camperdown Elm** (*U. glabra* 'Camperdown'), which is normally grafted on ordinary wych elm, has twisted boughs forming a rounded dome from the edges of which long branches are directed downwards to the ground. The leaves, up to 20 cm long, are larger than those of 'Pendula' or of wild wych elm. This is the common weeping elm of parks and gardens.

ZELKOVA. This genus is closely related to the elms, but differs in having some of the flowers unisexual and the fruit green and somewhat fleshy, not winged.

Caucasian Elm (*Z. carpinifolia*, formerly *Z. crenata*) ill. pp. 160–1. This is a tree up to 25 m high, native in the Caucasus and the southern coastal strip of the Caspian Sea. In the British Isles it usually has a short stout trunk only 1–3 m high and a large broom-like crown of ascending branches. The trunk is often fluted and has smooth scaling bark, and the winter-buds are dark brown with numerous scales. The elliptic leaves, 3–5 or more cm long, are rounded at the base, pointed at the tip, and have a few large broadly rounded teeth along the margins. They are dark green and smooth or nearly so above, downy on the veins beneath. The leaf-stalks are only 1–2 mm long. The flowers, opening with the leaves, have 4–5 stamens and no petals; and the small fruits are green, ridged, and about 5 mm across. This is a tree of very unusual appearance and is seen only occasionally in parks and large gardens.

MULBERRIES (*Morus*) are placed with the figs (*Ficus*, p. 201) in the family Moraceae, differing from the elm family (Ulmaceae) in having milky juice and aggregates of flowers that give rise to composite fruits. The leaves are alternate and stipulate. The flowers have no petals and each of the 5 stamens is opposite to a sepal. The ovary has a single ovule and the individual fruits are therefore single-seeded.

Black Mulberry (*M. nigra*); ill. pp. 160–1. Probably native of Western Asia, this is a tree up to 12 m high with a short trunk and widely spreading zig-zag branches forming a wide low crown. The bark is reddish-brown, irregularly fissured and burred, and the young shoots are downy, green at first and later dark brown. The broadly ovate leaves are 6–12 cm or more long, deeply heart-shaped at the base and more or less abruptly pointed at the tip, with coarsely toothed margins and sometimes with a lobe on one or both sides. They are dark green and rough above, paler and downy beneath. Male and female flowers, open in April–May, are usually on different trees, both in short dense spikes. In fruit the female flowers aggregate into a dark red-purple blackberry-like composite fruit, 2–2·5 cm long, the fleshy parts consisting of the enlarged sepals of the crowded flowers. Black mulberry is frequent in parks and gardens in Southern England and there are many historic old trees.

White Mulberry (*M. alba*), native in China, is usually a narrow-crowned tree up to 15 m high with shallowly ridged grey or brownish bark and rather larger and more often lobed leaves than those of black mulberry, downy only on the veins beneath. The spikes of female flowers, open in April–May, have stalks of about their own length —in contrast with the short-stalked flowers of *M. nigra*. The aggregate fruits are 1–2·5 cm long, white or pinkish and very sweet when ripe. The leaves are the chief food of silk-worms. White mulberry is less often grown in the British Isles than black mulberry.

164

1 BASFORD WILLOW (*Salix* x *rubens* 'Basfordiana') 2 GOLDEN WILLOW (*S. alba* 'Vitellina')
5 PURPLE-TWIG WILLOW (*S. acutifolia*) 6 WEEPING WILLOW (*S. babylonica*)

15 m

10

5

0

scale for trees 5, 6, 7, & 8

3 SCARLET WILLOW (*S. alba* 'Chermesina')   4 VIOLET WILLOW (*S. daphnoides*)
7 GOLDEN WEEPING WILLOW (*S.* x *chrysocoma*)   8 CRICKET-BAT WILLOW (*S.* 'Coerulea'). Details × ⅔. Text pp. 166–7

INTRODUCED FLOWERING TREES: Deciduous

WILLOWS (*Salix*); ill. pp. 164–5. A brief general description of willows is given on p. 34 with the account of native sallows, and other native tree-willows are described on p. 90. Many willows are grown as ornamental plants, especially, but by no means exclusively, by streams and lakes or in other wet places. Many of these are cultivated forms of native species, but willows hybridize so freely that it is often very difficult to be sure how some of the forms originated.

1 **Basford Willow** (*S.* x *rubens* 'Basfordiana') is probably a hybrid between crack willow (*S. fragilis*) and a form of white willow (*S. alba*) with yellow twigs, and in many ways it is intermediate between the supposed parent species. The twigs are glossy and orange-coloured and the tapering leaves are 10–15 cm long but only up to 2 cm across, so that they are narrower than those of crack willow and are also more finely toothed, but they differ from those of white willow in being silky-hairy only when young. The trees in cultivation are mostly male, with slender drooping catkins, 5–10 cm long. Basford willow is an attractive and popular tree.

2 **Golden Willow** (*S. alba* 'Vitellina'), a tree reaching 20 m or more in height, is a commonly planted form of white willow in which the first-year twigs are almost the colour of egg-yolk. The leaves are somewhat narrower than those of typical white willow and are bluish and only slightly silky beneath, but in other respects the tree is similar to white willow. Only male trees are known, presumably because the original mutant was a male plant and propagation has always been by vegetative means, not by seed. The colour of the twigs of golden willow suggests that it might have been one of the parents of Basford willow (**1** above).

3 **Scarlet Willow** or **Orange-twig Willow** (*S. alba* 'Chermesina') is yet another form of white willow in which the young twigs are orange-scarlet. It can be a tree up to 25 m high but is usually cut back at frequent intervals to encourage the growth of long new shoots.

4 **Violet Willow** (*S. daphnoides*), native in Norway and Sweden, is a tall shrub or small tree up to 10 m in height, with purple bark and slender twigs covered with a bluish waxy bloom for about three years, after which the underlying purple colour is revealed. The leaves are 5–10 cm long, lanceolate, up to 4 times as long as wide, with finely toothed or almost untoothed margins. They soon become hairless and are then dark glossy green above and pale bluish-green beneath. The cylindrical catkins appear in March before the leaves and are 3–4 cm long, with black-tipped scales. Violet willow is much grown for the attractive bloom on its twigs in winter.

5 **Purple-twig Willow** (*S. acutifolia*), native in Western U.S.S.R., is closely related to violet willow and is sometimes regarded as merely a subspecies of it. It differs chiefly in the narrower and somewhat longer linear-lanceolate leaves, 6–12 cm long, and its fatter catkins, ovoid rather than cylindrical as in violet willow. The twigs are covered with a blue-white bloom but eventually darker in colour than those of violet willow.

6 **Weeping Willow** (*S. babylonica*), native in China but thought by Linnaeus to come from Mesopotamia, is a tree up to 10 m high with long slender pendulous branches, brownish in colour. The leaves are narrowly lanceolate, 8–16 cm long, dark green above but paler beneath, hairless, with finely toothed margins. Most of the trees in cultivation in the British Isles are female, with slender curved catkins up to 2 cm long, appearing with the leaves in early May. The tree was introduced into the British Isles in the early eighteenth century and was soon widely planted, but it has been superseded in recent years by the golden weeping willow.

7 **Golden Weeping Willow** is of doubtful origin but often regarded as a hybrid, *S.* x *chrysocoma*, between *S. babylonica* and *S. alba* 'Vitellina'. Others believe it to be merely a weeping form of *S. alba* 'Vitellina'. A much planted and very beautiful tree, it has a widely domed crown, sometimes reaching 20 m in height, and arching branches ending in very long slender pendulous branchlets which touch the ground and are golden-yellow in colour. The narrowly lanceolate leaves are 6–10 cm long and are slightly silky-hairy on both sides, glossy pale green above and somewhat bluish beneath. The catkins appear with the leaves in April and are unusual in that most have both male and female flowers in the same catkin.

S. '**Sepulcralis**', probably a hybrid between *S. alba* and *S. babylonica*, is a tree of much the same size and shape as *S. babylonica* and with similarly brown branches and branchlets but it is less strongly pendulous and the linear-lanceolate leaves are usually silky-hairy and whitish beneath. Its slender catkins appear with the leaves in April–May.

Weeping Peking Willow (*S. matsudana* 'Pendula') is a graceful tree up to about 10 m high and with long slender olive-green branches which arch downwards and end in pendulous branchlets. The leaves are narrowly lanceolate, 5–8 cm long, bluish beneath, with long-pointed tips and sharply toothed margins. The catkins, 2 cm long, appear with the leaves in April–May. This willow is more resistant to various fungal diseases than are the weeping forms described above. The wild form of Peking willow is rare in gardens but *S. matsudana* 'Tortuosa', with twigs and branches twisted into spirals, is sometimes grown.

Two other weeping willows often seen in gardens are **Kilmarnock Willow** (*S. caprea* 'Pendula'), a weeping form of the great sallow (p. 34) and an attractively umbrella-shaped tree no more than 3 m high which is exclusively female; and **Weeping Purple Osier** (*S. purpurea* 'Pendula'), like the wild type in having some of its oblanceolate finely toothed leaves in opposite pairs and in its red-purple twigs. Weeping purple osier can be grown as a standard and is then suitable for the small garden.

Cricket-bat Willow (*S.* 'Coerulea'), a tree up to 25 m or more in height, is regarded by some authorities as a form of white willow (*S. alba*) but by others as derived from a cross between white willow and crack willow (*S. fragilis*). It differs from typical white willow in its higher angle of branching, giving it a conical crown. Further differences are the purplish colour of the young twigs and the broader, less hairy leaves, dark greyish blue-green above and pale bluish beneath. It is exclusively female. The tree is cultivated for its timber, regarded as the best for making cricket-bats. Care is taken to ensure rapid growth and it is then cut at a much earlier age (as little as twelve years old) than any other timber tree to secure wood of the requisite quality. Plantations of cricket-bat willow are chiefly to be seen in the wet lowlands of Eastern England: the tree is said to have arisen in Norfolk round 1700 A.D.

scale for trees 1, 2, 3, 4, 5, & 7

m 25

20

15

10

5
4
3
2
1
0

1
2
3
4
2 & 3
4
2 (M)
1
1 (M)

1 EASTERN COTTONWOOD (*Populus deltoides*)   2 LOMBARDY POPLAR (*P. nigra* 'Italica')
5 WESTERN BALSAM POPLAR (*P. trichocarpa*)   6 BALSAM POPLAR (*P. balsamifera*)—details only

3 FEMALE LOMBARDY POPLAR (*P. nigra* 'Italica Foemina')   4 BERLIN POPLAR (*P.* x *berolinensis*)
7 WHITE POPLAR (*P. alba*). (M) = male catkin; (F) = female catkin; a = shoot. Details × $\frac{2}{3}$. Text pp. 170–1

INTRODUCED FLOWERING TREES: Deciduous

POPLARS (*Populus*); ill. pp. 168–9. Apart from our native poplars and the hybrid black poplars grown for commercial purposes (pp. 94–5), representatives of three sections of the genus are often planted in the British Isles: black poplars, balsam poplars, and smooth-barked poplars.

BLACK POPLARS have fissured bark, sticky but not markedly fragrant buds, leaves with a narrow translucent border, and flattened leaf-stalks. The male catkins are reddish-purple and appear in March–April. The catkin-scales, which fall early, have their margin deeply cut into narrow segments, but these are hairless, not fringed with long hairs as in smooth-barked poplars. The fruits are ovoid.

1 **Eastern Cottonwood** (*P. deltoides*), native in Eastern U.S.A. from the Rocky Mountains to the Atlantic coast, is a tree up to 30 m with a wide-spreading, rather open crown and a grey fissured bark. The young twigs are hairless and vary from very slightly to quite strongly angled, and the shining brown buds are sticky with resin. The leaves are 7·5–15 cm long, broadly ovate to deltoid, truncate or slightly heart-shaped at the base and with a long-pointed tip. The surfaces are hairless but the coarsely rounded-toothed margin is densely ciliate. The leaf-stalk is 3–7 cm long and has 2-4 glands close to the blade. The catkins are 7–10 cm long in flower and the fruiting catkins lengthen to 15–20 cm. The fruits open along 3–4 lines. Cottonwood differs from our native black poplar (*P. nigra*, p. 94) in having ciliate leaf-margins and glands at the top of the leaf-stalk, and from the hybrid black poplars (p. 95) in the usually more strongly angled twigs and the denser and longer hairs along the leaf-margin. The closely related **P. angulata**, never found wild and often regarded merely as a mutant form of *P. deltoides*, is a vigorous large-leaved tree with drooping lower branches and markedly angled twigs and with toothed rather than deeply cut catkin-scales. Neither *P. deltoides* nor *P. angulata* is often grown in the British Isles but most hybrid black poplars have one or other as a parent.

2 **Lombardy Poplar** (*P. nigra* 'Italica'), a narrowly fastigiate tree reaching 30 m or more in height, is very widely grown. It appears to be a mutant form of the continental black poplar (*P. nigra* var. *nigra*) with similar or slightly smaller leaves and with hairless twigs and leaf-stalks. It is known only as a male tree, propagated by cuttings. The dark grey trunk is often fluted and becomes shallowly fissured: epicormic shoots may be numerous. The red catkins open in early April. Some individuals have a whitish trunk and then resemble the east-Mediterranean 'Thevestina', with downy young twigs and white trunk. **Western Lombardy Poplar** (*P. nigra* 'Plantierensis'), now more commonly planted than 'Italica', differs only in its somewhat broader head and in having its young twigs and leaf-stalks hairy at first though becoming almost hairless by early summer. It may be a fastigiate mutant of our native *P. nigra* var. *betulifolia* or a hybrid between it and 'Italica'.

3 **Female Lombardy Poplar** (*P. nigra* 'Italica Foemina') may be a hybrid between 'Italica' and *P. nigra* var. *nigra*. It is less narrowly fastigiate and somewhat looser in the crown than 'Italica' and may have several narrow crowns. It has only female catkins. This poplar is not very commonly grown in the British Isles.

4 **Berlin Poplar** (*P.* x *berolinensis*), said to be a hybrid between Lombardy poplar and the Siberian balsam poplar *P. laurifolia*, is a columnar tree up to 25 m in height with less steeply ascending branches than in Lombardy poplar so that the crown is distinctly broader. The bark is grey and there are commonly many erect epicormic shoots. The young twigs are at first sparsely downy but become hairless. The leaves are 9–10 cm long, ovate to rhombic-ovate, tapering downwards into a long wedge-shaped base and upwards into a pointed tip. The margins are non-ciliate and have a narrow translucent border and rounded teeth. They are hairless, bright green above but grey-green or somewhat whitish beneath. The leaf-stalk is not flattened and glands may or may not be present at the join of stalk and blade. Both male and female trees are known, the catkins appearing in late April, with the crimson male catkins much the more conspicuous. Berlin poplar is not very commonly planted.

BALSAM POPLARS have rough fissured bark and large sticky buds which are strongly and pleasantly aromatic especially when opening in spring. The leaves are pale or whitish beneath, often with a metallic lustre, and with the dark veins very conspicuous. The margin may or may not be ciliate but there is no translucent border and the leaf-stalks are not flattened. The catkin-scales are cut into narrow segments which are not fringed with hairs, and they fall early as in black poplars. The fruits are ovoid.

5 **Western Balsam Poplar** or **Black Cottonwood** (*P. trichocarpa*), native in western North America from Alaska to California, is a tree up to 35 m high in the British Isles, with ascending branches and a conical crown. The bark is finally dark grey and deeply fissured. Young twigs are yellowish and slightly angled, and the long slender terminal buds, 2 cm or more long, are shining red-brown, resinous, and very fragrant. The leaves, up to 15 cm long, or longer on very vigorous shoots, are more or less narrowly ovate, usually rounded at the base and pointed or long-pointed at the tip, with finely rounded-toothed margins. They are dark green above, silvery or rusty-white beneath, and the leaf-stalks are 3–7 cm long. The catkins appear in early April before the leaves, the male dull reddish in colour. This is an attractive tree, very strongly and delightfully fragrant in spring and early summer, and it is the most commonly grown of the balsam poplars. The fruits are downy (not so in **6**).

6 **Balsam Poplar** (*P. balsamifera*, sometimes named *P. tacamahaca*), native in a broad belt across North America from Alaska to Labrador and New England, is a tree 35 m or more in height in the British Isles, with ascending branches and a narrow open conical crown. The bark is finally dark grey with flat scaly ridges separated by narrow fissures. The young twigs are shining brown and not angled, and the terminal buds are dark brown, long-tapering, and fragrantly resinous. The leaves, 8–15 cm long, are broadly ovate to ovate-lanceolate, usually rounded at the base, less commonly broadly wedge-shaped or somewhat heart-shaped, and long-pointed at the tip, with finely toothed margins. The upper surface is shining dark green and hairless, the lower whitish and often downy on the conspicuous veins. The leaf-stalk is 5–8 cm long. Catkins appear in April, the male reddish in colour. Balsam poplar is occasionally grown for the fragrance of its opening buds.

Balm of Gilead (*P. gileadensis*, often misnamed *P. candicans*) is more commonly grown and is a freely suckering tree. Its origin is unknown but it may be a hybrid between balsam poplar and cottonwood. It resembles balsam poplar in its sticky fragrant buds and the whitish netted underside of its leaves but differs in having hairy and angular young twigs, broadly ovate leaves which are usually heart-shaped at the base and downy all over the underside, a more spreading and open crown, and in being female only and therefore propagated by cuttings. 'Aurora' is a variegated form in which the young leaves are creamy-white and pink but turn green later.

SMOOTH-BARKED POPLARS have bark that is initially smooth and grey or silvery-white but becomes rough near the base of old trees. Winter-buds are either tomentose or hairless and are not or only slightly sticky. The leaves have neither a translucent border nor glands at the junction of stalk with blade. The catkin-scales are toothed or cut into long narrow segments, the teeth and segments fringed or bearded with long hairs. The scales remain attached until after the catkins fall. The fruits are long and narrowly conical. Within this section the white poplars (including our native *P. canescens*) have the leaf-stalks not or indistinctly flattened, whereas in the aspens (including our *P. tremula*) they are very markedly flattened.

White Poplar (*P. alba*), native in central and Eastern Europe and eastwards to central Asia, is a freely suckering tree up to 25 m high with smooth whitish bark patterned with rows of dark rhombic lenticels: in old trees the base of the trunk is dark and rough. Young twigs and winter-buds are white-tomentose. Leaves on short-shoots are 3–5 cm long and vary in shape from very broadly ovate to elliptic-oblong. They are rounded or slightly heart-shaped at the base, rounded at the tip and with a few shallow lobes or large blunt triangular teeth on each side, and are dark green above and white-tomentose beneath when young but become greyish later. Leaves on long-shoots and suckers are 6–12 cm long with 3–5 coarsely toothed palmate lobes so that they resemble leaves of many maples: they remain white-tomentose beneath throughout the season. Catkins appear in April, the male 4–8 cm long, crimson and grey, the female 2–6 cm, pale green. White poplar has long been a popular tree for roadside planting as well as for parks and gardens and is locally common all over the British Isles. A fastigiate form, 'Pyramidalis', is sometimes planted.

scale for trees 1, 6, 9, 10, 11, & 12

m 15

10

5

0

$1 \times \frac{2}{3}$

$2 \times \frac{2}{3}$

$3 \times \frac{2}{3}$

$8 \times \frac{2}{3}$

$1 \times \frac{2}{3}$

$3 \times \frac{2}{3}$

$8 \times \frac{2}{3}$

$4 \times \frac{2}{3}$

1

6

$7 \times$

$5 \times \frac{2}{3}$

$6 \times \frac{2}{3}$

1 RED HAWTHORN (*Crataegus laevigata*) 2 ORIENTAL THORN (*C. laciniata*)—details only
5 COMMON QUINCE (*Cydonia oblonga*)—details only 6 MEDLAR (*Mespilus germanica*)
9 WILD SERVICE TREE (*S. torminalis*) 10 FONTAINEBLEAU SERVICE TREE (*S. x latifolia*)

$11 \times \frac{2}{3}$

$10 \times \frac{2}{3}$

$12 \times \frac{2}{3}$

11

$\times \frac{1}{5}$

9

10

11

12

9

$9 \times \frac{2}{3}$

$\times \frac{1}{5}$

$12 \times \frac{1}{5}$

3 COCKSPUR THORN (*C. crus-galli*)—details only   4 GLASTONBURY THORN (*C. monogyna* 'Praecox')—details only
7 BRONVAUX MEDLAR (+ *Crataegomespilus dardari*)—details only   8 SERVICE TREE (*Sorbus domestica*)—details only
11 FINNISH WHITEBEAM (*S.* x *hybrida*)   12 HYBRID ROWAN (*S.* x *thuringiaca*). Details × $\frac{2}{3}$. Text pp. 174–5

INTRODUCED FLOWERING TREES: Deciduous

HAWTHORNS (*Crataegus*); ill. p. 172. There is a brief general description of the genus on p. 30. The illustrations of cultivated hawthorns (p. 172) include forms of our two native species, also described on p. 30. All the following flower in May or early June.

1 **Red Hawthorn** (*C. laevigata*, various cultivars) is the popular name given to a number of forms of Midland hawthorn (p. 30) which have pink or red flowers and which are very common in gardens. Wild plants of common hawthorn often have pale pink flowers, especially just before fading.

2 **Oriental Thorn** (*C. laciniata*, formerly *C. orientalis*), native in Southern Europe and South-western Asia, is a shrub or small tree up to 10 m high with woolly-hairy young twigs which later become hairless and blackish. The leaves, 3–5 cm long, are shaped much like those of common hawthorn but the 3–7 lobes are narrow and very deep, sharply toothed near their ends and tomentose on both sides but more densely beneath. The flowers, 1·5–2 cm across, are in dense tomentose corymbs, and the orange to brick-coloured fruits are 1·5–2 cm across, woolly when young and crowned by the persistent and down-turned sepals. *C. tanacetifolia* has the leaf-lobes toothed throughout and larger fruits, 2–2·5 cm across.

3 **Cockspur Thorn** (*C. crus-galli* and hybrids). The cockspur thorn is native in North-eastern America and is a small tree to about 10 m high with a flat-topped spreading crown and smooth grey bark. The hairless purple-brown twigs carry numerous spines, 7–10 cm long. The unlobed obovate leaves are 3–8 cm long, hairless and shining above, rounded at the end, and sharply toothed except for the wedge-shaped base: they turn orange in autumn. The flowers are 1·5 cm across, in hairless corymbs, and the red fruits are 1 cm across. Two hybrids with other North American species are also grown: *C.* x *lavallei*, with downy shoots and corymbs and narrower leaves, and *C.* x *prunifolia*, with hairless dark purple-brown twigs, shorter spines (1·5–2 cm), and downy corymbs, and with broadly ovate-elliptic leaves. The leaves of both are glossy dark green above, turning red in autumn.

4 **Glastonbury Thorn** (*C. monogyna* 'Praecox') is a form of common hawthorn in which leaves and flowers commonly appear in mid-winter and again in spring. It is popularly believed to have arisen from the staff of Joseph of Arimathea which he thrust into the ground on Christmas Day and which at once burst into flower. Weeping and fastigiate forms of common hawthorn are also grown.

QUINCES

5 **Common Quince** (*Cydonia oblonga*); ill. p. 172. Quinces resemble pears in having unjoined styles and pear-shaped fruits but they have untoothed leaves and solitary flowers. The common quince, probably of Asiatic origin, is a shrub or small tree up to 6 m high with ovate leaves 5–10 cm long, very woolly beneath. The pale pink or white flowers open in May and are 4 cm across and the

broadly pear-shaped fruit may reach 12 cm in diameter in cultivated plants. It is yellow and fragrant and is used in cookery and for making preserves: the word "marmalade" comes from Spanish *marmelo*, a quince.

Japanese Quince or **Japonica** (*Chaenomeles speciosa*), a shrub much grown on walls for its scarlet-red flowers, belongs to a related genus in which the leaves are toothed and the styles joined below.

MEDLARS; ill.p.172.

6 **Medlar** (*Mespilus germanica*), native in South-eastern Europe and Western Asia, is a tree up to 6 m high with grey-brown fissured bark and downy twigs: the wild tree is thorny but cultivated forms are non-thorny. The oblong-lanceolate leaves are almost unstalked, dull green and sparsely hairy above but more densely hairy beneath, short-pointed and with margins untoothed or with a few small teeth near the tip. The solitary flowers, opening in late May or June, are 3–4 cm across, with long narrow sepals extending between and equalling the broad white petals. The brown, almost globose fruit, 2–3 cm across, is crowned by the long persistent sepals. It is eaten when over-ripe and makes a good jelly.

7 **Bronvaux Medlar** (+ *Crataegomespilus dardari*) is a graft-hybrid which arose in a garden at Bronvaux near Metz from near the point where a medlar had been grafted on a hawthorn stock and has since been propagated by grafting on hawthorn. There are several such graft-hybrids, some, like this, resembling medlar and others more like hawthorn, and they seem to have a skin of medlar over a hawthorn core. The plant illustrated has leaves like medlar but is spiny, and the flowers and fruits are only about 1·5 cm across. There are also sexual hybrids between hawthorns and medlar, resembling medlar but with smaller flowers which may be in clusters of 2–3.

SERVICE TREES (*Sorbus*); ill. pp. 172–3. There is a general account of the genus on p. 22.

8 **Service Tree** (*S. domestica*), native in Southern Europe, is a tree up to 20 m high with a rough bark coming away in strips. The leaves are pinnate, with 5–10 pairs of narrowly oblong sharply toothed leaflets and a similar terminal one, all 3–8 cm long. The cream-coloured flowers, 1·5 cm across in pyramidal panicles, are succeeded by yellowish or dull red fruits 1·5–3 cm across, shaped either like apples or pears and best eaten when over-ripe. They have been used in continental Europe for making a kind of cider. The larger leaflets and fruits and the elongated panicles rather than corymbs of flowers distinguish this fine tree from mountain ash. Service tree was once thought a native because of a solitary tree in Wyre Forest, but it was almost certainly planted there.

Other pinnate-leaved species seen in gardens include **Kashmir Rowan** (*S. cashmiriana*) and **Hupeh Rowan** (*S. hupehensis*), both white-fruited, the latter more frequently planted and having berries only 6 mm across (12 mm in Kashmir rowan). **S. 'Joseph Rock'** from China but of unknown origin, has small silvery grey-green leaves only 15 cm long and yellow fruits.

9 **Wild Service Tree** (*S. torminalis*) is described on p. 22.

10 **Fontainebleau Service Tree** (*S. x latifolia*) is one of a number of local whitebeams which appear to have arisen as hybrids between common whitebeam (*S. aria*) and wild service tree (*S. torminalis*) and of which there are three or four in South-western England. It is a tree up to 15 m high, with broadly ovate leaves 6–15 cm long, rounded at the base and having short broadly triangular sharply toothed lateral lobes, greyish-tomentose beneath. The tomentose corymbs are 7–10 cm across and the flowers 1·5 cm across. The ripe fruit is orange or brown-red, dotted with lenticels, and is 1–1·5 cm across. This tree is occasionally planted in parks or streets.

11 **Finnish Whitebeam** (*S. x hybrida*, formerly *S. fennica*, hybrid of Swedish whitebeam and mountain ash) is a tree up to 12 m high with tomentose young twigs and leaf-stalks. The ovate to oblong leaves are 7–12 cm long and have 1–3 pairs of separate oblong pointed leaflets below but are lobed above, the lobes becoming shallower towards the tip: leaflets and lobes are all sharply toothed, and green above but grey-tomentose beneath. The flowers are 1 cm across and the globose crimson fruits are 12 mm in diameter.

12 **Hybrid Rowan** (*S. x thuringiaca*, hybrid of common whitebeam and mountain ash) is very like Finnish whitebeam but the leaves are more narrowly oblong in outline (about twice as long as wide—about one and a half times in Finnish whitebeam), and the 1–3 pairs of free leaflets are blunt-ended, with shorter and broader teeth. The scarlet fruits are only 8–10 mm across. Some leaves have no free leaflets. This hybrid is sometimes planted as a street tree.

Swedish Whitebeam (*S. intermedia*, formerly *S. suecica*) is a shrub or tree to 10 m high, with tomentose young twigs. The broadly elliptic leaves are 7–12 cm long, with broad lateral lobes which curve towards the leaf-tip and extend up to one-third of the way to the midrib. The leaves and their lobes are toothed and are hairless above, grey-tomentose beneath. The corymbs are about 10 cm across and the individual flowers up to 2 cm across, white with pale pink stamens. The fruits are ovoid, 1·5 cm long, bright orange-red. Swedish whitebeam is often planted as a street tree.

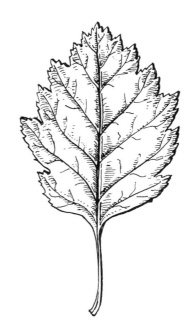

scale for trees 1, 2, 3, 4, 5, 6, 7, & 9

1 *Prunus conradinae*   2 AUTUMN CHERRY (*P. subhirtella* 'Autumnalis')   3 SARGENT'S CHERRY (*P. sargentii*)
6 *P.* 'Kanzan'   7 *P.* 'Kiku-zakura'   8 GREAT WHITE CHERRY (*P.* 'Tai Haku')—detail only   9 *P.* 'Amanogawa'.

4 DOUBLE GEAN (*P. avium* 'Plena')   5 WEEPING YOSHINO CHERRY (*P.* x *yedoensis* 'Shidare Yoshino')
Details × ⅔. Text pp. 178–9

INTRODUCED FLOWERING TREES: Deciduous

FLOWERING CHERRIES (*Prunus*). The flowering cherries of our gardens are characterized by deciduous leaves, axillary clusters of not more than 6 flowers, and small fruits having neither the downy skin of the apricots and peaches of sub-genus *Amygdalus* nor the bloom of true plums and cherry plums of subgenus *Prunus*.

The flowering cherries illustrated on pp. 176–7 belong to subgenus *Cerasus* and fall into two groups: forms of our wild cherry (*P. avium*), with down-turned sepals and white petals; and the so-called Japanese cherries which have erect or spreading sepals and petals ranging in colour from white to deep pink. These latter are derived from a small group of East Asiatic species which have been in cultivation for a very long time in Japan and China and have given rise there to innumerable horticultural varieties and hybrids. The most important of the parent species are the hill cherry (*P. serrulata*), the closely related Oshima cherry (*P. speciosa*), Sargent's cherry (*P. sargentii*), and finally the spring cherry or rosebud cherry (*P. subhirtella*). All have smooth shining bark and horizontally-extended lenticels, the bark chestnut-brown except in *P. speciosa* where it is pale grey, and all have stalked ovate-elliptic to obovate-elliptic leaves with rounded base, abruptly long-pointed tip, and sharply toothed margin. The leaves are commonly reddish when young and assume bright autumn colours. The flowers are white or pink and the small fruits are ovoid or globular, about 8 mm long and usually black or nearly so but reddish-yellow in *P. speciosa*. These four species are described below with their most commonly grown cultivars, many of them of unknown hybrid origin, and with one or two other species sometimes seen in gardens. Most of the Japanese cherries grown in the British Isles are grafted on wild cherry (*P. avium*) but some are on Japanese stocks and some can be raised from seed. They flourish on all types of well-drained soil and can be grown on chalk. For descriptions of other introduced species see pp. 142–3, 182. Native species are described on pp. 22, 30.

1   **P. conradinae**, native in China, is a small tree with a rounded crown and grows up to about 8 m high. The young twigs and leaf-stalks are hairless. The abundant fragrant flowers, white or pinkish in colour, are in unstalked clusters of 1–4 and open in February before the leaves. The flowers are only about 2 cm across, but the cultivar 'Malifolia' has deeper pink flowers up to 3 cm across.

2   **Autumn Cherry** (*P. subhirtella* 'Autumnalis'), introduced from Japan but not known there as a wild plant, is a small tree up to about 8 m high with slender ascending branches that curve outwards to form an open spreading crown. Young twigs are reddish and downy. The narrowly ovate-elliptic to oblong-lanceolate leaves, 4–6 cm long, are abruptly and narrowly pointed at the tip and have sharp irregular teeth some of which are further toothed. The downy red leaf-stalk is only 1–1·5 cm long. There are two main flowering periods, October–November and March–April, but there are usually some open flowers throughout the winter. They are semi-double, with downy calyx-tube and fringed petals, white or very pale pink at first but later turning deeper pink. The illustration is of 'Autumnalis Rosea', with flowers deep pink from the first.

Weeping Rose-bud Cherry or **Weeping Spring Cherry** (*P. subhirtella* 'Pendula'), with long weeping branches from above the graft-union, is often grown for its graceful habit, its white, pink, or deep rose flowers in March–April, and its bright autumn colouring.

P. 'Accolade' is an attractive but not very commonly grown hybrid between *P. subhirtella* and *P. sargentii*.

It is a small tree to about 8 m in height with spreading branches, hairless twigs, and narrowly ovate-elliptic glossy green leaves which have closely and finely toothed margins and downy red leaf-stalks 2 cm long. The pink semi-double flowers have fringed petals and are borne profusely in clusters that hang down beneath the shoots and open in March–April.

3   **Sargent's Cherry** (*P. sargentii*), native in Sakhalin and Korea, is naturally a tree to 12 or more in height with a spreading crown and purplish-brown bark, but it is usually grafted on our wild cherry and grown as a standard. The young twigs are dark red and hairless. The leaves are obovate-elliptic, 7–15 cm long, abruptly long-pointed and with sharp marginal teeth drawn out into narrow points but not distinctly awned as in *P. serrulata* or *P. speciosa* below. The leaf-stalk is about 4 cm long, deep red and hairless. The leaves open reddish-purple but then turn green. The flowers, opening shortly before the leaves in mid-April, are single and pink, 3–4 cm across, and borne in unstalked clusters. The calyx-tube is hairless. The leaves turn bright orange and red in autumn, earlier than most trees—making this one of the finest of Japanese flowering cherries. It is much planted in streets.

4   **Double Gean** or **Double White Cherry** (*P. avium* 'Plena') is a double-flowered form of our native wild cherry (p. 22) It is a beautiful tree, 20 m or more high, much grown for its drooping clusters of white flowers and attractive autumn colour.

Oshima Cherry (*P. speciosa*), native in Japan, is a tree
10–15 m high with pale grey bark and ovate-elliptic leaves
up to 15 cm long with hairless leaf-stalks. The leaves end
in a long narrow-pointed tip and the margins have fine
teeth drawn out into long awn-like points, longer even
than in *P. serrulata* (see below). They are only slightly
reddish when opening and soon become bright green,
turning pale gold and red in autumn. The fragrant white
or pinkish long-stalked flowers open in April. Oshima
cherry is believed to be the ancestor of many of the
Japanese cherries including 'Shirotae', often called the
Mount Fuji cherry, a small tree up to 9 m high with
wide-spreading branches that may reach the ground
and hanging clusters of fragrant single or semi-double
white flowers up to 6 cm across. It is also believed to be a
parent of several hybrids.

5 Yoshino Cherry (*P. x yedoensis*, believed to be *P. sub-hirtella* x *P. speciosa*), introduced from Japan but not
known as a wild plant, is a tree up to about 12 m high
with smooth pale grey bark and low-arching branches.
The young twigs are somewhat downy. The obovate-elliptic leaves, 8–15 cm long, are abruptly long-pointed
and have finely-pointed marginal teeth and somewhat
downy veins on the underside. The leaf-stalk is 4 cm
long, pink and a little downy. The leaves open green.
The flower-buds are pink but the scented single flowers,
3–3·5 cm across, are white or slightly pink-tinged and
open in late March or early April, usually before the
leaves. The sepals are toothed and the calyx-tube downy,
and the petals are deeply notched. The illustration is of
weeping Yoshino cherry, 'Shidare Yoshino', with pale
pink flowers.

A more common weeping Japanese cherry is **'Kiku-shidare Sakura'**, a form of hill cherry (*P. serrulata*)—
often wrongly called 'Cheal's weeping cherry'. It makes
an attractive standard when its branches are covered
with deep pink double flowers. They open with the
leaves, which are reddish when young and have awned
marginal teeth.

P. serrulata itself is a small flat-topped tree up to about
9 m high, with obovate-elliptic leaves up to 15 cm long,
long-pointed at the tip and with marginal teeth drawn
out into awns but these are not as long and fine as in
P. speciosa, from which *P. serrulata* differs further in its
chestnut-brown bark and hairless young twigs. The
flowers are white and double, showing that this tree is a
garden variety of an apparently lost wild type. Among
many cultivars other than 'Kiku-shidare Sakura' are
6, 7, 8, and **9** below.

6 *P.* **'Kanzan'**, perhaps the most popular of all Japanese
cherries in the British Isles, is a vigorous tree up to about
15 m high. Its stiffly ascending branches form an inverted
cone-shaped crown tending in older trees to spread out-wards at the top. The large leaves are obovate-elliptic,
up to 18 cm long with a stalk 3 cm long. They open red,
become dark green in summer, and then turn pale gold
to deep pink in autumn. The flower-buds are bright red
and open with the leaves in late April and early May in
crowded clusters of large semi-double purplish-pink
flowers which turn pink later.

7 *P.* **'Kiku-zakura'** is a small tree with reddish-green young
leaves. The soft pink flowers open only in late April to
mid-May and are strongly double, their numerous petals
crowded in a rounded mass.

8 Great White Cherry (*P.* 'Tai Haku') is a vigorous tree up
to 12 m high with rich copper-red young leaves and pale
pink flower-buds. The large single white flowers, 6–8 cm
across, with broad petals and red centres, open in late
April and are borne in large rounded clusters.

9 *P.* **'Amanogawa'** is a much-grown narrowly fastigiate
cultivar up to 8 m high with only slightly reddish young
leaves and fragrant semi-double pink flowers opening
in late April or early May.

Fuji Cherry (*P. incisa*) is a shrub or small tree said to
reach 9 m in height in Japan, where it is native. Its
purplish twigs are hairless and the ovate- to obovate-elliptic leaves, 2·5–5 cm long, have sharply double-toothed margins. They are downy, especially beneath,
and are purplish when young, become green in summer,
and are richly coloured again in autumn. The leaf-stalks
are about 1 cm long. The small flowers, 2–2·5 cm across,
open in late March or early April and are single and
white but appear pinkish because of the red sepals. The
cultivar 'Praecox' flowers in January and February.
P. x hillieri is a hybrid between *P. incisa* and *P. sargentii*,
and its cultivar 'Spire' is a conical tree up to 8 m high,
with soft pink flowers in April and rich red autumn
colours.

180

1 ALMOND (*Prunus dulcis*)   2 PURPLE-LEAVED PLUM (*P. cerasifera* 'Pissardii')
5 WILLOW-LEAVED PEAR (*Pyrus salicifolia* 'Pendula')   6 SNOWY MESPIL (*Amelanchier lamarckii*)   7 *Malus* x *micromalus*
Details of flowers and leaves × ⅔. Text pp. 182–3

3 BLACK-LEAVED PLUM (*P. cerasifera* 'Nigra')—details only   4 PEACH (*P. persica* 'Klara Mayer')
8 JAPANESE CRAB (*M. floribunda*)   9 SIBERIAN CRAB (*M. baccata*)   10 CHINESE CRAB (*M. spectabilis*).

INTRODUCED FLOWERING TREES: Deciduous

PRUNUS. For a general description of the genus see p. 22. Almond and peach belong to the subgenus *Amygdalus*, with flowers in unstalked or very short-stalked clusters of 1–3, appearing before the leaves. A terminal bud continues the growth of the shoot and each leaf has 3 axillary buds, the outer ones flower-buds. The fruit is usually downy, though not in the variety of peach called nectarine (*P. persica* var. *nucipersica*), and its stone is usually pitted or furrowed all over. Cherry plum, on the other hand, belongs to subgenus *Prunus*, as do sloe and the other true plums: they have no terminal bud, and have leaves each with a single axillary bud and non-downy fruit with a whitish bloom, the stone smooth or wrinkled but not deeply pitted or furrowed all over.

1 **Almond** (*P. dulcis*); ill. p. 180. Almond, which is probably native in Western Asia and North Africa, is a small tree up to 8 m high with oblong-lanceolate leaves, 7–12 cm long, finely toothed and usually with glands at the junction of leaf-stalk with blade. The large pink flowers, 3–5 cm across, are borne singly or in pairs and open in March or April. The fruit is 3–6 cm long, ovoid-oblong but somewhat flattened, grey-green and downy, the hard leathery "flesh" splitting to release the flattened stone, finely pitted all over and enclosing the single seed which is the edible almond. The tree is much planted for its early and attractive flowers and there are several forms in cultivation, some with white and some with double flowers as well as weeping, semi-fastigiate, and variegated-leaved varieties.

2–3 **Cherry Plum** or **Myrobalan** (*P. cerasifera*); ill. p. 180. Cherry plum is native in the Balkan Peninsula and the Crimea and is a shrub or small tree up to 8 m high, with hairless twigs which may become thorny. Its leaves are 3–7 cm long, elliptic or nearly so, with a pointed tip and blunt-toothed margins. The upper surface is hairless and somewhat glossy, the lower downy on the midrib when young but becoming hairless. The white flowers, 2–2·5 cm across, are mostly solitary and open just before or with the leaves. The fruit is globose, 2–2·5 cm across, yellow or red and with a slight bloom. Cherry plum is often mistaken for sloe, but this latter has downy twigs and smaller leaves which are dull above and broadest beyond the middle, and its fruit is much darker in colour. Cherry plum is often used for hedges but more commonly as an ornamental tree and then usually in one of its horticultural varieties. Ill. **2** is of **Purple-leaved Plum** (*P. cerasifera* 'Pissardii'), which is extremely popular. The dark purple-red leaves unfold in late March or early April, at the same time as the pink buds open into small white flowers. The purplish fruits are rarely seen. Ill. **3** is of **Black-leaved Plum** (*P. cerasifera* 'Nigra') which has still darker leaves and stems, blackish-purple in colour, and flowers opening rather later than those of 'Pissardii'—pink at first but paling before they fade.

4 **Peach** (*P. persica*); ill. p. 180. Native in China, peach is a tree to 6 m high with leaves rather longer (to 15 cm) and broader than those of almond and broadest at or just beyond the middle. There are glands at the junction of leaf-stalk and blade. The flowers are usually solitary, pink, smaller than in almond (2·5–3·5 cm across), and open 2–3 weeks later. The fruit is the familiar peach, fleshy and juicy, 5–7 cm in diameter. There are many variant forms with single, semi-double, or fully double flowers which may be white, pink, or almost crimson in colour. The illustration is of 'Klara Mayer', with deep pink double flowers.

The remaining illustrations are of members of the subfamily Pomoideae of the family Rosaceae, in which the ovary is "inferior"—standing at the top of the flower-stalk but below the sepals, so that the remains of the sepals are at the top of the fruit instead of round its base. Representatives of three genera are illustrated and described: a pear (*Pyrus*), an *Amelanchier*, and crab apples of the genus *Malus*. Pears and apples are closely related but pears have reddish and apples yellow stamens, pears have 2–5 styles separate to the base while apples have them joined below, and the characteristically-shaped fruits of pears have the flesh markedly "gritty" because of stone-cells round the core and under the skin. Amelanchiers are related to hawthorns but differ in being non-thorny, having unlobed but toothed simple leaves, and blue-black berry-like fruits with a single seed in each of 4–10 compartments of the ovary: there are no "stones" enclosing the seeds as in hawthorns.

PEAR

5 **Willow-leaved Pear** (*Pyrus salicifolia*); ill. p. 180. This pear is native in the Caucasus, and in the British Isles it is a small tree up to 8 m high with slender pendulous branches and narrow leaves resembling those of some willows. The leaves are 3–9 cm long and taper gradually to both ends. They are at first white-tomentose all over and remain so beneath but the upper side loses its tomentum and becomes glossy. The dense corymbs are also white-tomentose and the individual white flowers, open in mid-April, are 2 cm across. The small brown fruits are 2–3 cm long. The pendulous form grown in gardens is often named 'Pendula'.

AMELANCHIER

6 **Snowy Mespil** or **June-berry** (*Amelanchier lamarckii*); ill. p. 181. This is a shrub or small tree with a low rounded crown and up to 12 m in height, native in eastern North America. The leaves are 3–7 cm long, ovate-elliptic or ovate-oblong, short-pointed, becoming hairless. The unfolding leaves are purplish-pink and downy. The flower-racemes are slender and nodding and the individual flowers, open in April–May, are 2·5–4·5 cm across, the narrow petals giving a star-like form. The globose fruits, 6 mm in diameter, first turn red and then, in July, purple-black. This amelanchier is much grown and has become locally naturalized on sandy soils in Southern England.

CRAB APPLES (*Malus*); ill. p. 181. Ornamental crab apples have deep red to white flowers borne in April–May in drooping umbels and each with many yellow stamens. The fruits are usually globose but may be elongated: they range in colour from pale yellow to scarlet or purple, and crabs have become popular garden trees as much for their decorative fruits as for their flowers. A number of Asiatic species have been introduced and these, with their numerous varieties and hybrids, raise many problems of naming. The table below shows the main differences between the three species illustrated. (The native British species is described on p. 31.)

	Japanese Crab	Siberian Crab	Chinese Crab
Leaf-stalk	3 cm	2–5 cm	1–3 cm
Flowers:			
diameter	2·5–3 cm	3–3·5 cm	4–5·5 cm
colour	Very pale pink, buds crimson	White, buds pale	Pale pink, buds deep rose
fullness	Single, petals touching	Single, petals separated	Semi-double, 6–8 petals
sepals	Hairy, long-pointed	Hairless, long-pointed	Hairless or nearly so, short-pointed
Fruits:			
diameter	6–8 mm	10–15 mm	About 20 mm
colour	Red or yellow	Red or yellow	Yellowish

M. x micromalus (probably *M. spectabilis* x *M. baccata*) is a hybrid crab, raised and long cultivated in Japan. The ovate-elliptic leaves have stalks 2–3 cm long and the pink flowers are about 4 cm across with pointed sepals that are finally hairless. The almost round fruits are 10–15 mm in diameter.

Japanese Crab (*M. floribunda*) is a widely grown shrub or small tree up to 10 m high with ovate-elliptic leaves 4–8 cm long, long-pointed and toothed. It comes from Japan and is attractive because of the changing colour of its very abundant flowers.

Siberian Crab (*M. baccata*), native in North-eastern Asia, is a round-crowned tree up to 14 m high with ovate-elliptic leaves on long slender stalks.

10 **Chinese Crab** (*M. spectabilis*) is a narrow-crowned tree up to 8 m in height with elliptic short-stalked leaves 5–8 cm long and large flowers. This very beautiful crab comes from China but is said not to be known as a wild tree.

Other much-grown crabs are **'John Downie'**, with elongated orange-scarlet fruits; and **'Eleyi'**, of complex hybrid origin from Asiatic species other than those listed above, which has red-purple fruits 3–4 cm long.

184

m 10

scale for trees 1, 2, & 3

5

0

1 COMMON LABURNUM (*Laburnum anagyroides*)   2 SCOTTISH LABURNUM (*L. alpinum*)
5 FALSE ACACIA (*Robinia pseudacacia*)   6 TREE OF HEAVEN (*Ailanthus altissima*)
Details × $\frac{2}{3}$. Text pp. 186–7

scale for trees 5, 6, & 7

3 JUDAS TREE (*Cercis siliquastrum*)   4 SILVER WATTLE (*Acacia dealbata*)—leaf detail only
7 PAGODA TREE (*Sophora japonica*)—young tree in early June. (M) =male flowers; a=mature leaflet; b=fruits.

INTRODUCED FLOWERING TREES: Deciduous

The large pea family (Leguminosae), comprising several thousand species of trees, shrubs, and herbs and with representatives all over the world, has flowers with a single-celled ovary which develops in most genera into the kind of fruit called a pod or legume, drying as it ripens and opening along both edges to release the seeds. It is readily divisible into three sub-families. Our native British members, including gorse and broom (pp. 38–9), all belong to the single sub-family Lotoideae which is the most readily recognizable from the distinctive shape and arrangement of the petals, well seen in the large flowers of sweet pea. One petal, standing at the top or back of the flower, is usually larger than all the others and encloses them in bud. This is called the "standard". Next to it are the 2 "wings" forming the sides of the flower, and finally at the bottom or front, are the innermost 2 petals which adhere along both top and bottom edges to form the "keel", shaped like the keel of a boat. The second sub-family is the Caesalpinoideae, differing from the Lotoideae in that the top petal is the innermost in bud and often the smallest, while the 2 front petals enclose all the others in bud. The general form of the flower is variable but quite often it is very different from that of a sweet pea. Finally there is the sub-family Mimosoideae, in which the tiny flowers, massed in dense heads or spikes, have petals all similar in size and shape. Silver wattle belongs to this sub-family.

LABURNUMS (*Laburnum*); ill. p. 184. Laburnums belong to the sub-family Lotoideae. They are extremely poisonous, especially in their pods and seeds.

1 **Common Laburnum** or **Golden Rain** (*L. anagyroides*) is a small tree of central and Southern Europe which may reach 7 m in height. Its bark is smooth, dark green at first but becoming brownish-green, and the twigs are grey with appressed hairs. The compound leaves have 3 elliptic to obovate leaflets, 3–8 cm long, rounded at the end but usually with a very short point and silky with appressed hairs beneath. The leaf-stalk is 5–8 cm long. The pea-like yellow flowers, up to 2 cm long, open in late May or early June and are in pendulous silky-hairy racemes 10–30 cm long. The pods are 4–6 cm long, appressed-hairy when young, with the upper edge somewhat thickened but not winged. The seeds are black. Common laburnum is very widely grown and has become locally naturalized.

2 **Scottish Laburnum** (*L. alpinum*), native in mountain woods in central Europe and southwards to Italy and Albania, is a tree up to 10 m high and differs from common laburnum in having almost hairless twigs and leaflets hairy on the margins but not or sparsely so beneath. The almost hairless racemes are longer (up to 40 cm) and denser than in common laburnum, and the pods are also hairless and with the upper edge winged. The seeds are brown. Scottish laburnum flowers two or three weeks later than common laburnum and the flowers are somewhat smaller, up to 1·5 cm long. The most commonly planted laburnum is now the hybrid between common and Scottish laburnums, **L. x watereri** (formerly called *L. vossii*), which has the long slender late-opening racemes of Scottish laburnum but with individual flowers as large as those of common laburnum. It is intermediate between its parents in hairiness and the pod has a narrow wing along its top edge.

Adam's Laburnum (+ *Laburnocytisus adami*). This interesting though not very decorative plant appeared in 1825 in the garden near Paris of a nurseryman named Adam who had budded a common laburnum stock with purple broom (*Cytisus purpureus*). The bud died but a shoot grew out from nearby and this proved to be different from either stock or bud-parent. All plants in cultivation have derived from this original shoot by vegetative propagation. They are small laburnum-like trees often with shoots of one or both parent types as well as of the intermediate type with small hairless leaves and pinkish-brown flowers in May–June. Adam's laburnum seems to be a graft-hybrid or "plant-chimaera", with a thin skin of purple broom over a core of common laburnum.

JUDAS TREE

3 **Judas Tree** (*Cercis siliquastrum*); ill. p. 184. Judas tree belongs to the sub-family Caesalpinoideae and is native in the Mediterranean region. It is a small deciduous tree up to 10 m high with purplish-grey finely fissured bark and dark red-brown twigs and winter-buds. The leaves are alternate and neatly arranged in 2 rows. They are 8–12 cm long, almost circular but deeply cordate at the base, and are hairless with untoothed margins. The pinkish-purple flowers are in short-stalked hanging clusters on twigs and branches of all sizes and even on the main trunk. They open in May, before or with the leaves, and are pea-like but with the standard quite small and enclosed by the wings, and the 2 front petals are the largest and outermost. The flat pods, up to 10 cm long and conspicuously purplish throughout the summer, remain on the tree until well into winter.

HONEY LOCUST

Honey Locust (*Gleditsia triacanthos*) also belongs to the sub-family Caesalpinoideae. A large North American tree, reaching 20 m high in the British Isles, it has yellowish-green male and female flowers in separate racemes on the same tree and is remarkable for the stout and usually branched spines, up to 15 cm long, borne on the trunk and branches. Its enormous pods, sickle-shaped and twisted and up to 45 cm long, rarely mature here, though the tree is occasionally seen in parks and large gardens.

KENTUCKY COFFEE-TREE

Kentucky Coffee-tree (*Gymnocladus dioicus*), another member of the sub-family Caesalpinoideae, has very large doubly-pinnate leaves from 30 to 90 cm or more long on very stout twigs. It is grown in a few gardens in Southern England.

WATTLES or MIMOSAS (*Acacia*). Most of the acacias grown in the British Isles are in cool greenhouses. The true acacias belong to the sub-family Mimosoideae.

Silver Wattle or **Mimosa** (*A. dealbata*); ill. p. 184. An Australian tree, silver wattle may occasionally be seen growing out-of-doors in the British Isles and it reaches a height of 15 m in Ireland. But it may be killed back to the ground in hard winters even in the mildest counties, although it fares better against a wall. The silvery fern-like leaves are doubly pinnate and the bright yellow flowers, which open from January onwards, are small but massed in globular heads of about 30 which are themselves in panicles.

Sydney Golden Wattle (*A. longifolia*) is a shrub or small tree to 5 m high, with simple narrow leaves, 5–10 or even up to 15 cm long, and flowers in axillary spikes in March. It is somewhat more hardy than silver wattle.

FALSE ACACIA

False Acacia or **Locust Tree** (*Robinia pseudacacia*); ill. p. 185. False acacia belongs to the sub-family Lotoideae and is native in eastern North America. It has been extensively planted in the British Isles and is locally naturalized. It is a freely suckering tree up to 27 m high and with deeply and coarsely fissured bark by which it can readily be recognized in winter. The alternate pinnate leaves have stipules which commonly persist and become spiny. The leaves are 15–20 cm long and with 7–19 elliptic or ovate leaflets each 3–5 cm long. The fragrant white pea-like flowers are in pendulous racemes, 10–20 cm long, and open in June. The pods turn dark brown and remain on the tree well into the winter. It has no relationship with the true acacias.

TREE OF HEAVEN

Tree of Heaven (*Ailanthus altissima*); ill. p. 185. Tree of heaven belongs to the family Simaroubaceae and is native in China. It is a large suckering tree, 20 m or more in height, with stout ascending zig-zag main branches. The bark is smooth, grey-brown, patterned with vertically-running but sinuous lenticels. The leaves, which have an unpleasant smell when crushed, are alternate, pinnate, up to 60 cm long, with 13–25 narrowly ovate red-stalked leaflets having 1–4 large teeth near the base, each tooth with a raised gland beneath it. The small greenish flowers, open in late July, are borne in large terminal panicles, and in late summer the fruiting ovary splits into oblong winged "keys", like those of ash. Tree of heaven is much grown in Southern and Eastern England, including the London area, for its magnificent form and the red colour both of its young leaves and its ripe fruits.

PAGODA TREE

Pagoda Tree (*Sophora japonica*); ill. p. 185. This is a member of the sub-family Lotoideae, native in China and Korea. It is a large wide-crowned tree, reaching over 20 m high in the British Isles, with heavy spreading branches and green twigs. The leaves are pinnate, 15–25 cm long, usually with 11–15 leaflets up to 5 cm long. The white pea-like flowers are in loose erect panicles 15–25 cm high, and the pods are constricted between the seeds. This fine tree is occasionally seen in parks and gardens.

m 20

15

10

5

0

scale for trees 1, 2, 6, & 7

1

2

6

7

$7 \times \frac{1}{4}$

$3 \times \frac{2}{3}$

$4 \times \frac{2}{3}$

$5 \times \frac{2}{3}$

$7 \times \frac{2}{3}$

$1 \times \frac{2}{3}$

$2 \times \frac{2}{3}$

$6 \times \frac{2}{3}$

$1 \times \frac{2}{3}$

$5 \times \frac{2}{3}$

1 NORWAY MAPLE (*Acer platanoides*)   2–4 JAPANESE MAPLES   2 *A. palmatum* 'Atropurpurea'
5 BOX ELDER (*A. negundo*)—details only   6 PAPER-BARK MAPLE (*A. griseum*)   7 HERS'S SNAKE-BARK MAPLE (*A. hersii*)
10 YELLOW BUCK-EYE (*A. flava*)   11 INDIAN HORSE-CHESTNUT (*A. indica*)—flower detail only

30 m

25

20

15

10

5

0

scale for trees 8, 9, & 10

$12 \times \frac{1}{4}$

$8 \times \frac{1}{4}$

$9 \times \frac{1}{4}$

$10 \times \frac{1}{4}$

12×1

8×1

9×1

10×1

11×1

3 *A. palmatum* 'Dissectum'—details only   4 *A. palmatum* 'Heptalobum'—details only
8 RED HORSE-CHESTNUT (*Aesculus* x *carnea*)   9 COMMON HORSE-CHESTNUT (*A. hippocastanum*)
12 PRIDE OF INDIA (*Koelreuteria paniculata*)—leaf and flower details only. Text pp. 190–1

INTRODUCED FLOWERING TREES: Deciduous

MAPLES (*Acer*); ill. p. 188. A general description of the genus is given on p. 26 and a key to commonly planted species on p. 206.

1 **Norway Maple** (*A. platanoides*) is native throughout much of continental Europe from Southern Norway and Finland southwards to Southern France, Northern Greece, and the Crimea. It is a tree up to 30 m in height with a broad spreading crown and smooth dark grey bark later becoming shallowly fissured. The young twigs are hairless and brownish and the winter-buds, up to 1 cm long, are green below and reddish-brown above. The leaves are 10–15 cm long and equally wide with usually 5 palmate lobes, the two basal short and triangular, the others parallel-sided below and ending in long narrow points, each with a few large and similarly long-pointed teeth. They are bright green and hairless above, paler beneath, and turn a beautiful yellow in autumn. The leaf-stalk is 5–20 cm long and exudes a milky juice when broken. The greenish-yellow flowers, about 8 mm across, are in erect corymbose panicles and open in late March before the leaves. The fruit-wings diverge at a very wide angle. Norway maple is quite often planted and is locally naturalized. Forms with red-purple or variegated leaves or of columnar shape are also grown in gardens. It can readily be distinguished from sycamore by its bark, its longer-pointed leaf-lobes, and the wider angle between its fruit-wings. From the North American sugar maple (*A. saccharophorum*), with rather similar leaves, it differs in the milky-juice of its leaf-stalk.

2–4 **Japanese Maple** (*A. palmatum*), native in Japan and Korea, is a shrub or small tree up to 8 m high with smooth brown bark and deeply 5–7-lobed leaves, the lobes ovate-lanceolate or narrower and extending more than half-way to the top of the slender leaf-stalk, 2–5 cm long. Each lobe, about 8 cm long, tapers into a long point and has the margins finely-toothed: both surfaces are bright green and hairless. The flowers are purple-red, 6–8 mm across, opening in April in small erect corymbs which droop in fruit, and the fruit-wings diverge at an obtuse angle. The illustrations on p. 188 show three of the very many garden forms of this widely planted maple: 'Atropurpurea' (**2**), the most popular of all, with deep red-purple leaves; 'Dissectum' (**3**), with leaves divided almost to the base into narrow coarsely-toothed lobes; and 'Heptalobum' (**4**), with larger usually 7-lobed doubly-toothed leaves. Japanese maples are quite hardy in the south and west but elsewhere may suffer from late frosts.

5 **Box Elder** or **Ash-leaved Maple** (*A. negundo*), a tree to 20 m high with smooth grey bark, native in Eastern U.S.A., is unusual amongst maples in having pinnate leaves with 3–5 or more leaflets and in having wind-pollinated flowers with male and female on different trees. The leaves are 5–20 cm long, varying with the number of leaflets, each of which is 5–10 cm long, ovate-lanceolate, long-pointed, and coarsely toothed or lobed. The leaflets are bright green and hairless above, paler and often slightly downy beneath. The flowers are yellow-green and open before the leaves in early March, the male in pendulous clusters and the female in loose pendulous racemes. The fruit-wings diverge at an acute angle with the broad tips incurved. Box elder is usually grown in gardens in a variegated-leaved form, 'Variegatum'.

6 **Paper-bark Maple** (*A. griseum*), native in China, has reached 13 m in height in the British Isles but, so far, is usually a smaller tree grown chiefly for its chestnut-coloured bark which separates and peels in papery flakes to expose a cinnamon-coloured underbark. The twigs are dark brown and the leaves have 3 ovate-oblong leaflets, the middle one distinctly stalked and all coarsely toothed and somewhat lobed, dark green and hairy above, paler and downy beneath. The pale yellow-green flowers, opening with the leaves in late May, are in pendulous clusters, each flower 1·5 cm across, and the large fruit-wings diverge at an acute angle. The leaves turn red and scarlet in autumn.

7 **Hers's Snake-bark Maple** (*A. hersii*), a small tree up to 15 m high, native in China, is one of a group of maples with smooth olive-green bark strikingly patterned with vertical white stripes of varying width. The leaves are broadly ovate, heart-shaped at the base and usually with 2 short triangular lateral lobes above the middle, but these are sometimes lacking (in the related Père David's maple, *A. davidii*, the leaves are more usually unlobed). The green flowers are in drooping racemes and give rise to long hanging strings of fruits in which the wings diverge so widely as to be almost in a straight line.

HORSE-CHESTNUTS (*Aesculus*) ill. p. 189. These are deciduous trees and shrubs with large winter-buds and opposite pairs of palmately-compound leaves which lack stipules. The flowers are in erect many-flowered panicles and have each 4–5 sepals, the same number of unequal-sized petals and usually 5–8 stamens. The ovary is 3-celled and the ripe fruit splits along 3 lines to release the one or more large seeds, the chestnuts. The seed-leaves emerge during germination.

8 Red Horse-Chestnut (*A.* x *carnea*, a hybrid between common horse-chestnut, *A. hippocastanum*, and the red-flowered *A. pavia*) is a tree up to about 20 m in height with slightly roughened brown bark and twigs with pale orange-brown lenticels. The winter-buds are not sticky. The leaves are like those of common horse-chestnut but darker and somewhat smaller, the leaflets very coarsely toothed. The flowers open in May–June, are in panicles 12–20 cm long, and are of varying shades from flesh-pink to deep red. The fruits are almost globose and only slightly prickly, 3–4 cm across and with 1–3 small chestnuts.

Common Horse-chestnut (*A. hippocastanum*), native in the Balkan Peninsula, is a fine tree with a tall domed crown up to 30 m or more in height and brown flaking or scaling bark. The twigs are reddish-brown with pale lenticels, and the strikingly large winter-buds, up to 2·5 cm long, are resinous and very sticky. The leaves have 5–7 leaflets each 10–25 cm long, obovate but with a prolonged wedge-shaped base, doubly-toothed. The panicles, opening in May, are 20–30 cm long and the flowers have white petals tinged and blotched with pink and yellow. The spiny fruit is globose, 6 cm across, and has either a single rounded seed or 2 3 that are smaller and flattened. This horse-chestnut is very commonly planted, especially in the southern half of the country, and is occasionally self-sown.

10 Yellow Buck-eye (*A.flava*, formerly *A. octandra*), native in Southern and Eastern U.S.A., is a tree up to 25 m high with smooth or scaling pinkish-brown bark. The winter-buds are smooth and non-sticky. The leaves have 5 oblong-obovate to elliptic long-pointed and finely toothed leaflets, each 10–15 cm long and distinctly stalked. The panicles are 10–15 cm long and the crowded flowers, open in May–June, have very unequal yellow petals and usually 7 stamens. The smooth fruit is almost globose, 5–6 cm in diameter and usually with 2 seeds.

11 Indian Horse-chestnut (*A. indica*), native in the Himalayas, is a tree to 20 m high with smooth greyish bark. The shiny-brown winter-buds are 1·5 cm long and sticky. The leaves are of 5–9 obovate-lanceolate leaflets, long-pointed and finely toothed, 15–30 cm long and on a reddish common stalk 10–18 cm long. The leaflets are dark green above, hairless and bluish beneath. The panicles, opening in late June, are 15–30 cm or more long and the flowers have white petals flushed with pink. The fruits are smooth and the seeds large and glossy dark brown. Indian horse-chestnut flowers later than common horse-chestnut and is useful for prolonging the flowering-time in parks and large gardens.

PRIDE OF INDIA (*Koelreuteria*) belongs to the large family Sapindaceae which consists chiefly of woody plants, many of them climbers, which are widely distributed through the tropics and subtropics but with a few extending into temperate regions. They strongly resemble horse-chestnuts and maples but their usually pinnately or palmately compound leaves are almost always alternate. Apart from Pride of India one other member of the family, the attractive pinnate-leaved and white-flowered *Xanthoceras sorbifolia*, is occasionally seen in gardens.

12 Pride of India or **Golden Rain Tree** (*K. paniculata*); ill. p. 189. Native in Eastern Asia, this is a small tree that may reach 10 m in height and has brown bark with short fissures down to the orange-coloured underbark. The alternate leaves are 15–40 cm long, pinnate or bipinnate at the base, with 9–16 ovate-oblong leaflets each 3–8 cm long, coarsely and irregularly toothed or pinnately lobed, dark green and hairless above, paler beneath. The flowers are in loose panicles up to 40 cm long and are 1 cm across, yellow, with only 4 petals and 8 or fewer stamens. The ovary is 3-celled and ripens to a dry thin-walled fruit opening to release the black seeds.

m 30

20

10

5

0

scale for trees 1, 2, 4, 6, & 7

$1 \times \frac{2}{3}$

$3 \times \frac{2}{3}$

$\times \frac{1}{6}$

$\times \frac{2}{3}$

$\times \frac{1}{3}$

1 COMMON LIME (*Tilia* x *vulgaris*) 2 CAUCASIAN LIME (*T.* x *euchlora*) 3 WEEPING SILVER LIME (*T. petiolaris*)
6 COMMON WALNUT (*Juglans regia*) 7 HYBRID WING-NUT (*Pterocarya* x *rehderana*) 8 PIGNUT (*Carya glabra*).

10 m

5

4

3

2

1

0

scale for trees 3 & 8

6

7

7

$7 \times \frac{2}{3}$

$\times \frac{1}{6}$

$\times \frac{2}{3}$

8

7

$\times \frac{1}{6}$

5

6

$8 \times \frac{1}{6}$

$6 \times \frac{1}{6}$

$6 \times \frac{2}{3}$

$8 \times \frac{2}{3}$

4 LONDON PLANE (*Platanus hybrida*)   5 ORIENTAL PLANE (*P. orientalis*)—details only

Text pp. 194–5

INTRODUCED FLOWERING TREES: Deciduous

LIMES (*Tilia*); ill. p. 192. A general description of the genus is given on p. 18, preceding a table showing differences between the native British limes.

1 **Common Lime** (*T. x vulgaris*) is a natural hybrid between our two native species, small-leaved lime (*T. cordata*) and large-leaved lime (*T. platyphyllos*), and the table on p. 18 shows how it may be distinguished from its parent species. It is a tree commonly reaching 30 m and individuals up to 46 m are the tallest non-coniferous trees in the country. The ascending branches form a high rounded crown, but the lower branches arch downwards and then turn up again near their ends. The grey bark is smooth at first but later develops shallow vertical fissures and irregular bosses. The branchlets are slender and the young twigs green or red-tinged, hairless or nearly so, and the winter-buds are reddish with 2 or 3 scales visible. The leaves are 6–10 cm long, broadly ovate and abruptly short-pointed with an obliquely heart-shaped base and sharp-toothed margins. They are dark green and hairless above, paler and hairless or nearly so beneath except for tufts of whitish hairs in vein-axils; and the leaf-stalk is 3–5 cm long. The flowers are in pendulous 4–10-flowered clusters and are yellowish-white, opening in early July. The fruits are 8 mm across, broadly ovoid, downy, and slightly ribbed; the supporting wing is yellowish-green. Common lime is very widely planted in parks and gardens and along roads and city streets. It tolerates extreme mutilation and its chief drawbacks are the unsightly bosses on the trunk and the frequent infestation with aphids, causing the drip of honey-dew.

2 **Caucasian Lime** (*T. x euchlora*) is believed to be a hybrid of small-leaved lime (*T. cordata*) and the Caucasian *T. dasystyla* and originated in the Caucasus. It is a tree up to 20 m in height, with smooth grey bark and a tall crown of branches which ascend and then arch downwards. The young twigs are green and the winter-buds red and yellow. The broadly ovate leaves, 5–10 cm long, are much like those of common lime but are shining green above and have tufts of reddish hairs in the vein-axils beneath. The flowers open in late July and the pendulous clusters have only 3–7 bright yellow flowers. The downy, slightly 5-ribbed fruits are tapered at both ends. The glossy leaves, the absence of bosses on the trunk, and the less frequent infestation with aphids make this an attractive substitute for common lime, but it is not yet commonly planted.

3 **Weeping Silver Lime** (*T. petiolaris*) is of unknown origin but may be a garden form of the silver lime (*T. tomentosa*) of South-eastern Europe and Western Asia. It is a tree up to 30 m high with a tall narrow crown and smooth grey bark. The branches ascend initially but then arch downwards and the branchlets are pendulous. The young twigs are downy and the winter-buds are green. The leaves are up to 12 cm long, broadly ovate, heart-shaped at the base and long-pointed at the tip, and with sharply toothed margins—all as in many other limes, but they are dark green above and white-tomentose beneath and the slender downy leaf-stalks are more than half as long as the blade (less than half as long in *T. tomentosa*). The large, very fragrant, and very pale yellowish flowers open in late July and are in pendulous clusters of 5–10 with the supporting wing 9 cm long. The warty fruits are 8–10 mm long, flattened-globose, 5-angled, and nearly always sterile. This is a very beautiful tree but as yet seen only in parks and large gardens or occasionally as a street tree.

PLANES (*Platanus*); ill. p. 192. This is the only genus of the family Platanaceae. They are deciduous trees with scaling bark and have unisexual flowers of both sexes on the same tree. The flowers are crowded into globose clusters on long pendulous stalks and have both sepals and petals with the same number of stamens in the male flowers and 3–6 separate ovaries in the female flowers. Pollination is by wind and the small single-seeded nuts are 4-angled by mutual pressure in the globose aggregate-fruit. The planes have alternate long-stalked palmately-lobed leaves with the enlarged and hollow end of the leaf-stalk enclosing the axillary bud: the large stipules surround the stem above the leaf. Planes are readily distinguished from maples, which also have palmately-lobed leaves, by the alternate leaves and the enlarged base of the leaf-stalk, as well as by the fruits.

4 **London Plane** (*P. hybrida*, sometimes named *P. x acerifolia* or *P. x hispanica*) is of unknown origin but probably arose in the seventeenth century in continental Europe. It has long been regarded as a hybrid between the Balkan and West Asian *P. orientalis* (**5** below) and *P. occidentalis* from the eastern part of North America, but it may equally possibly have arisen as a new garden variety of *P. orientalis*. In London plane the 3–5 leaf-lobes usually extend no more than half-way to the midrib and the terminal lobe is hardly longer than wide; the base of the leaf is truncate or shallowly heart-shaped. It flowers in May: there are normally 2 flower-clusters on each hanging stalk, occasionally 1 or 3. This fine tree, reaching 35 m or more in height, has a tall trunk with brownish bark that flakes off in large patches to expose the pale yellow underbark. The crown is tall and rounded with the lower branches drooping at their ends. There is a good deal of variation from tree to tree in the details of leaf shape. London plane is much planted in parks and along roads in Southern and Midland England.

5 **Oriental Plane** (*P. orientalis*), native in South-eastern Europe and Asia Minor, is a tree to 30 m with a more broadly rounded crown than London plane and with its 5–7 leaf-lobes reaching up to or beyond half-way to the midrib, the terminal lobe much longer than its basal width and the leaf-base commonly wedge-shaped though sometimes truncate or heart-shaped. Like London plane

it flowers in May: there are usually 2–6 flower-clusters on each stalk. While most trees are readily distinguishable from London plane there are individuals that cannot be confidently assigned to one or other. Oriental plane has been planted only infrequently in the British Isles.

WALNUTS (*Juglans*), **WING-NUTS** (*Pterocarya*), **and HICKORIES** (*Carya*); ill. p. 193. These genera are placed in the family Juglandaceae, characterized by having alternate pinnately compound leaves, which lack stipules, and having separate male and female flowers on the same tree, neither with petals and the male usually in long drooping catkins. The female flowers have an ovary with a single ovule, ripening to a single-seeded fruit.

6 **Common Walnut** (*Juglans regia*). Walnuts are deciduous trees, rarely shrubs, in which the pith of small twigs, as seen when they are slit lengthwise, is discontinuous, with air-spaces between plates of tissue—a "chambered" or "septate" pith. The leaves are gland-dotted and aromatic. The flowers have 3–5 inconspicuous sepals; the male flower has numerous stamens and the female an ovary beneath the sepals. The large green fleshy fruit does not split open but rots to release the pitted stone (the walnut) which encloses a single seed with a strangely convoluted surface. Common walnut is native in the Balkans and across central Asia to China and is a tree to 30 m high with a spreading crown and zig-zag lower branches. The bark is grey and at first smooth but later fissuring. The young twigs are dark greenish and hairless but turn dark brown, and the winter-buds are broad and almost black. The leaves have a terminal and usually 3–4 pairs of lateral leaflets, elliptic and 6–15 cm long, becoming hairless except for tufts of hairs in the vein-axils beneath, and with almost untoothed margins. The flowers open in June, the male in catkins 5–15 cm long, the female in single-flowered erect spikes with few flowers. The fruit is 4–5 cm long, oblong-globose, green, and gland-dotted, with the stone splitting readily into 2 halves. Walnut is widely grown, especially in the southern half of the country where there is usually a tree on every old farm. **Black Walnut** (*J. nigra*), from the eastern part of North America, with 11–23 toothed leaflets, is occasionally planted.

7 **Hybrid Wing-nut** (*Pterocarya* x *rehderana*), a hybrid between the Caucasian *P. fraxinifolia* and the Chinese *P. stenoptera*, belongs to a genus of freely suckering deciduous trees with septate pith, naked buds, leaves lacking aromatic glands, and with female as well as male flowers in drooping catkins. The fruit is a ribbed nutlet surrounded by the semi-circular halves of a whitish wing-like collar. The wing-nuts are uncommon in cultivation.

8 **Pignut** (*Carya glabra*) is one of the hickories. A deciduous tree, it differs from walnut in its non-septate pith, non-aromatic leaves, and a fruit-husk that splits along 4 lines to release a smooth-walled and often angled nut. Its bark is dark grey and fissured. Pignut is native in the eastern part of North America where it grows to 40 m high. Its leaves have only 5 leaflets and the obovoid fruit is 2·5 cm long. Pignut is planted as a timber tree in Germany. **Bitternut** (*C. cordiformis*), with slender pointed bright yellow winter-buds (green or brown in other species), is the most frequently planted hickory in the British Isles. Its leaves have 5–9 leaflets and its rounded fruits are 4-winged in the upper half.

196

m 20

15

10

5

0

scale for trees 1, 2, 3, 5, & 7

1

2

$3 \times \frac{1}{3}$

3×1

$2 \times \frac{1}{3}$

4

4×1

$4 \times \frac{1}{3}$

m 5

4

3

2

1

0

scale for tree 4

$2 \times \frac{1}{3}$

2×1

1 WEEPING ASH (*Fraxinus excelsior* 'Pendula')   2 MANNA ASH (*F. ornus*)   3 NARROW-LEAVED ASH (*F. angustifolia*)
6 FARGES'S CATALPA (*C. fargesii*)—leaf and fruit details only   7 PAULOWNIA (*Paulownia tomentosa*). Text pp. 198–9

3

5

7

6 × 1

5 × 1

5 × ⅓

7 × ⅓

7 × ⅓

7 × ⅓

5 × ⅓

4 COMMON LILAC (*Syringa vulgaris*)   5 INDIAN BEAN-TREE (*Catalpa bignonioides*)

INTRODUCED FLOWERING TREES: Deciduous

ASHES (*Fraxinus*); ill. pp. 196 7. There is a general description of the genus on p. 23, preceding that of the European or common ash (*F. excelsior*). Among the ashes commonly grown in gardens are cultivated forms of this native ash. Flowering ashes have flowers with both sepals and petals, but those of European ash have neither sepals nor petals.

1 **Weeping Ash** (*F. excelsior* 'Pendula') is always grafted on common ash and its shoots grow stiffly downwards making a quite small angle with the vertical, so that the hollow crown has the shape of a truncated or round-topped cone. It is often to be seen in gardens.

2 **Manna Ash** or **Flowering Ash** (*F. ornus*), native in the Mediterranean region and northwards to Austria, Czechoslovakia, and Rumania, is a tree up to more than 20 m high, with a smooth grey bark. The young twigs are olive-green and the winter-buds like those of common ash but with only the 2 outer scales dark-coloured, the inner being pale and downy. The leaves have 5–9 ovate-oblong leaflets, 3–9 cm long, the terminal leaflet being broadest, all abruptly long-pointed and with small irregular marginal teeth. The fragrant flowers open in late May and are in dense erect terminal panicles up to 15 cm long. They have 4 sepals and 4 very narrow white petals up to 6 mm long. The winged fruits or "keys" are narrowly lanceolate, 2–2·5 cm long. The manna ash is an attractive tree and is one of several "flowering ashes" of the subgenus *Ornus*.

Chinese Flowering Ash (*F. mariesii*), another member of the subgenus *Ornus*, is less commonly seen in gardens. It is often only a large shrub but is sometimes a small tree up to 10 m or more high, with leaves having only 3–5 leaflets, each with a very short purple-coloured stalk. The ripe fruits are also reddish-purple.

Spaeth's Flowering Ash (*F. spaethiana*) is a similarly small tree, native in Japan, which is remarkable for the swollen and often reddish bases of the stalks of its very large leaves.

White Ash (*F. americana*) has flowers with the general appearance of those of common ash, without petals but with small sepals. White ash reaches a height of 27 m in its native eastern North America and is a fine tree with deeply fissured grey bark, the fissures deep but short, and large leaves up to 35 cm long, each with 7 obovate long-pointed leaflets. The keys are much like those of common ash. In the British Isles white ash is grown in only a few gardens but is perfectly hardy.

3 **Narrow-leaved Ash** (*F. angustifolia*), native in the Mediterranean region and northwards to central Europe, is a tree up to 25 m high with very shallowly ridged dark grey bark. The young twigs are olive and hairless and the winter-buds dark brown, downy. The leaves have 5–13 oblong to linear-lanceolate hairless leaflets, each 3–9 cm long, long-pointed and jagged-toothed. The flowers, opening early spring before the leaves, have neither sepals nor petals and the narrowly oblong "keys" are 3–4 cm long.

Single-leaved Ash (*F. angustifolia* 'Veltheimii') resembles a less commonly grown form of the common ash (*F. excelsior* 'Diversifolia') in having simple non-pinnate leaves. In 'Veltheimii' they are 5–12 cm long, elliptic-lanceolate, hairless both above and beneath and with wedge-shaped base and jagged-toothed margins. In *F. excelsior* 'Diversifolia' the leaves are longer, 15–20 cm, ovate-oblong, rounded at the base, and hairless above but downy alongside the veins beneath: a few leaves have 3 leaflets.

LILACS (*Syringa*); ill. p. 196.

Lilacs, like ashes, belong to the olive family Oleaceae, characterized by having leaves borne in opposite pairs and flowers with 4 sepals and petals but only 2 stamens and a 2-celled ovary. Their petals are joined below into a slender tube and their dry fruits open at maturity to release 2 winged seeds from each cell.

4 **Common Lilac** (*S. vulgaris*). Native in the Northern Balkans, this is a suckering shrub or small tree up to 5 m or so high, with brown fibrous bark. The opposite hairless leaves are 4–8 cm long, ovate and long-pointed with a truncate or shallowly heart-shaped base. The fragrant flowers open in May in erect panicles 10 25 cm long and in the wild plant are lilac-coloured or rarely white, but in cultivated varieties they range from wine-red to white and can be primrose-yellow or cobalt-blue;

and they range also from single to fully double. The fruit is about 1 cm long.

Several other species of *Syringa* are grown in gardens but most are shrubs, like the long-cultivated **Persian Lilac** (*S. x persica*), a hybrid with common lilac as one parent, differing in its lanceolate leaves with wedge-shaped base and small panicles only 5–8 cm long.

INDIAN BEAN-TREES (*Catalpa*); ill. p. 197. This genus belongs to the trumpet-vine family, Bignoniaceae, which consists of woody plants, many of them climbers, usually with opposite compound leaves which in the climbers may have the terminal leaflet modified into a tendril. The flowers are often showy and have 5 sepals joined into a tube below and 5 petals also joined below and more or less unequal in size and shape so that the flower is often not radially symmetrical. There are only 4 stamens and the ovary has a style with a 2-lobed stigma. The fruit is a capsule splitting along 2 lines.

5 **Indian Bean-tree** or **Catalpa** (*C. bignonioides*), native in the South-eastern U.S.A., is a tree to 15 m or more high with a broadly rounded crown and brown scaling bark. The ovate leaves, 10–25 cm long, are borne in opposite pairs or whorls of 3. They are rounded at the base and abruptly short-pointed at the tip, and their margins are untoothed but somewhat wavy and may occasionally be lobed. They are light green and almost hairless above, paler and downy beneath. The flattened leaf-stalk is 8–16 cm long. The flowers open in July and are in erect broadly pyramidal panicles 15–20 cm high, each flower 3–5 cm across with white frilled petal-lobes: the front 3 lobes and the inside of the wide tube are marked with dark purple and yellow spots and stripes. The fruits, "beans", are 20–40 cm long and only about 1 cm wide, and they split along both edges to release numerous seeds with tufts of white hairs at each end. This is a very decorative tree when in flower but is planted frequently only in Southern England.

6 **Farges's Catalpa** (*C. fargesii*), native in China, is a slender upright tree up to about 15 m in height, with fissured bark and differing further from *C. bignonioides* in its smaller and rather more narrowly ovate leaves, 8–14 cm long, with a gradually long-pointed tip. The flowers, open in late June, are in corymbose racemes about 15 cm high, each flower 5 cm across, rose-coloured with purplish spots and yellow blotches. It is less commonly grown than *C. bignonioides*.

PAULOWNIAS (*Paulownia*) belong to the foxglove family, Scrophulariaceae, which consists chiefly of herbaceous plants but includes a few shrubs or trees. They differ from members of the family Bignoniaceae in having leaves much more varied in arrangement, size, and shape and in details of the way in which the ovules are attached within the ovary, but their flowers often closely resemble those of the Bignoniaceae. The petals, usually unequal in size and shape, are joined below into a basal tube, and there are normally fewer than 5 functional stamens. The fruit is either a capsule splitting along 2 lines or a berry.

7 **Paulownia** (*P. tomentosa*); ill. p. 197. Native in China, this is a round-headed tree up to 15 m high with smooth grey bark and stout spreading branches. The opposite leaves are ovate, 12–30 cm long, long-pointed, heart-shaped at the base and untoothed but sometimes with 1–3 large long-pointed teeth or lobes on each side. They are hairy above and more or less densely downy beneath, and the leaf-stalk is 8–20 cm long. Leaves on vigorous sucker-shoots may be up to 1 m across. The fragrant flowers, 3·5–6 cm long, open in late May and are in a pyramidal panicle 20–30 cm high, each flower with 5 rusty-tomentose sepals and a trumpet-shaped corolla, pale violet with dark purple and yellow spots inside, downy and sticky outside. The woody fruit is ovoid and 3–4 cm long, very different from the long narrow "beans" of catalpas. This attractive tree, much grown in South-eastern Europe, is little planted in the British Isles except in a few large gardens.

m 7
6
5
4
3
2
1
0

scale for trees 1, 2, 3, 4, & 5

4

4 a

5

3

1

2

1 CHUSAN PALM (*Trachycarpus fortunei*)   2 CABBAGE TREE (*Cordyline australis*)   3 ADAM'S NEEDLE (*Yucca gloriosa*)
4 STAGHORN SUMACH (*Rhus typhina*)   5 COMMON FIG (*Ficus carica*). a=fruiting panicle and winter shoot × ⅔.
Text p. 201

SOME UNUSUAL FLOWERING TREES

Trees like our native beech may have evolved from unbranched trees with large compound leaves through forms with a few stout branches and leaves of intermediate size. Page 200 shows some trees that may resemble some of those remote ancestors. The first three are monocotyledons.

CHUSAN PALM

1 Chusan Palm (*Trachycarpus fortunei*), a true palm of the family Palmaceae, is native in Eastern Asia and is one of the few palms hardy in the British Isles. It is a slender unbranched tree 5 m or more high, its trunk covered in dark brown fibres from the bases of fallen leaves. It is a fan-palm, with almost circular leaves up to 1 m across and having up to 50 narrow segments radiating from the undivided central portion. The leaf-stalk is up to 1 m long, rounded beneath and with the almost flat

upper side 2·5 cm across and spiny along its edges. The small yellow flowers, open in early summer, are in large drooping panicles about 60 cm long, male and female usually in separate panicles. Each flower has 3 sepals and 3 petals, the male having 6 stamens and the female 3 ovaries separate above but joined at the base. Chusan palm is grown mainly near the south coast of England and in Western Ireland but is occasionally seen in North-west England and Western Scotland.

CABBAGE TREE and YUCCA are often placed in the family Agavaceae, in many respects intermediate between true palms and lilies. They are sometimes tree-like but have long simple leaves.

2 Cabbage Tree or **Cabbage Palm** (*Cordyline australis*), native in New Zealand, is a tree up to about 10 m high, its trunk often covered with dead leaves. Branches arise only after flowering, and each bears a terminal rosette of sword-like leaves 60–90 cm long and up to 7 cm wide, so that old and much-branched plants may have a well-developed crown. The small white fragrant flowers, 6–8 mm across, open in June-July and are borne in large terminal panicles 1 m or more high and half as wide. The fruit is a small bluish berry about 6 mm across. Cabbage palms are common in gardens along the south coast but can be grown near the west coast up to Northern Scotland.

3 Adam's Needle or **Yucca** (*Yucca gloriosa*), native in South-eastern U.S.A. from North Carolina to Florida in a narrow coastal belt, is a tree up to 2·5 m high, not or little branched. Its trunk is rough with horizontally-extended scars of fallen leaves. The stiff spinc-tipped leaves, borne in a dense terminal cluster, are 30–60 cm long and 5–8 cm wide, bluish-green with marginal teeth that are soon shed and often with loose fibres when old. The creamy-white nodding bell-shaped flowers, often reddish outside, open in June–September and are in erect narrowly conical panicles up to 2 m high. Yucca is common in gardens in the warmer parts of Southern England.

SUMACH and FIG are dicotyledons, like most other trees described in this book. They have large leaves on very stout twigs, but are distinctly more branched than the monocotyledonous trees above.

4 Staghorn Sumach (*Rhus typhina*), of the mango family (Anacardiaceae), is a much-grown shrub or small flat-crowned tree that can reach 10 m in height. It suckers very freely. The twigs are velvety with dense brown hairs and the large alternate deciduous leaves, up to 60 cm long, are pinnately compound with 13–21 oblong-lanceolate toothed leaflets each 5–12 cm long. The small greenish flowers, opening in July–September, have 5 sepals and 5 petals and either 5 stamens or an ovary with a single ovule—a few having both. They are borne in dense terminal panicles, 10–20 cm long. On female trees fruiting panicles are made conspicuous by crimson hairs on the fruit-walls. The leaves turn deep crimson in autumn.

5 Common Fig (*Ficus carica*), a member of the family Moraceae, and probably native in Western Asia but long cultivated round the Mediterranean, is a shrub or small tree to 5 m high with rugged grey bark and a spreading open crown. The alternate deciduous leaves, 10–20 cm or more long, have 3–5 obovate blunt-ended lobes. The unisexual flowers are borne on the inside wall of a hollow pear-shaped receptacle, the male above, near the opening, the female below. The edible fruits, 1–2 cm long and green during the first winter, enlarge to 5–8 cm long and turn violet in the second year. In the British Isles figs are usually grown on a south wall and even then seldom ripen.

Key to COMMONLY CULTIVATED SILVER FIRS (*Abies*) (text pp. 110, 118)

1 Leaves standing stiffly at right angles to stem all round stem (i.e. radially arranged) ⇨ 2
   At least some leaves directed sideways, forwards, or backwards ⇨ 3

2 Leaves only 1–2 cm long, short and stout, blunt-ended or with a short point, with lines of white dots on both
     sides = Spanish Fir (*A. pinsapo*) (ill. 5, p. 117)
   Leaves 1·5–3 cm long, stiff and sharp-pointed, and with distinct white bands beneath = Greek Fir (*A. cephalonica*)

3 Leaves distinctly parted above stem, either diverging to form a V-shaped trough or spreading more or less
     horizontally to left and right ⇨ 4
   Leaves not parted or indistinctly parted above stem, those on top of stem usually pointing forwards, at least near
     their base ⇨ 7

4 Leaves spreading horizontally to left and right of stem, more or less in a single plane but in overlapping layers
     with longest below ⇨ 5
   Leaves not in single plane or nearly so but those above stem spreading perpendicular to it while leaving a V-
     shaped trough through short middle leaves = Nikko Fir (*A. homolepis*, formerly *A. brachyphylla*)

5 Longest leaves 2–2·5 cm long; young stem with scattered dark hairs = European Silver Fir (*A. alba*) (ill. 1, p. 116)
   Longest leaves 3–6 cm long; young stem minutely downy with pale hairs ⇨ 6

6 Longest leaves mostly 3–4 cm long; no lines of white dots on upper surface = Grand Fir (*A. grandis*) (ill. 2,
     p. 108)
   Longest leaves mostly 4–5 cm long; lines of white dots on upper surface = Low's White Fir (*A. concolor* var.
     lowiana)

7 Leaves broadest close behind the usually notched tip, mostly 1–2 cm long, with very broad white bands beneath;
     a shrub or small tree = Korean Fir (*A. koreana*) (ill. 3, p. 116)
   Leaves not distinctly broadest close behind tip; large trees ⇨ 8

8 Most leaves simply rounded or pointed at tip, not notched ⇨ 9
   Most leaves clearly notched so as to have double tip ⇨ 11

9 Leaves dark-green, spine-tipped; buds more than 1 cm long = Santa Lucia Fir (*A. bracteata*)
   Leaves blue-green, rounded at tip; buds tiny, much less than 1 cm long ⇨ 10

10 Leaves flat, grooved on top, those on upper side of stem pointing forwards and concealing stem = Noble Fir
     (*A. procera*, formerly *A. nobilis*) (ill. 1, p. 108)
   Leaves almost cylindrical, not grooved on top, those on upper side pointing forwards only at their base, then
     spreading sideways = Californian Red Fir (*A. magnifica*)

11 Buds ovoid, pale brown, not resinous = Caucasian Fir (*A. nordmanniana*) (ill. 4, p. 116)
   Buds globose, reddish or purple, resinous ⇨ 12

12 Buds 2–3 mm long; young shoots pale buff or greyish, later becoming pale brown = Veitch's Silver Fir
     (*A. veitchii*) (ill. 6, p. 116)
   Buds 6 mm long; young shoots rusty-red, later becoming dark purplish-brown = Forrest's Fir (*A. delavayi* var.
     forrestii) (ill. 2, p. 116)

KEY TO COMMONLY CULTIVATED SPRUCE FIRS (*Picea*) (text pp. 110–11, 119)

1 Leaves spreading all round stem, some pointing downwards from underside of stem ⇒ 2
  Leaves parted on underside of stem and spreading to left and right, none pointing downwards ⇒ 5

2 Leaves spreading almost equally in all directions ⇒ 3
  Only a few of the stout and spine-tipped leaves spreading downwards ⇒ 4

3 Leaves rounded in section, uniformly green all round = West Himalayan Spruce (*P. smithiana*) (ill. 9, p. 117)
  Leaves flattened, dark green on top but with white bands beneath = Brewer's Weeping Spruce (*P. brewerana*)

4 Leaves yellowish-green to dark-green, markedly curved and painfully spiny = Tiger-tail Spruce (*P. polita*)
  Leaves blue-green, straight or slightly curved, prickly = Blue spruce (*P. pungens* 'Glauca') (ill. 7, p. 117)

5 Leaves less than 1 cm long = Oriental Spruce (*P. orientalis*) (ill. 8, p. 117)
  Most leaves more than 1 cm long ⇒ 6

6 Leaves green on both sides = Norway Spruce (*P. abies*) (ill. 3, p. 108)
  Leaves with white bands along underside ⇒ 7

7 Leaf tips broad and blunt or abruptly short-pointed; young stem downy = Serbian Spruce (*P. omorika*) (ill. 5, p. 109)
  Leaf-tips pointed; young stem hairless ⇒ 8

8 Leaves 1–2·5 cm long, blue-green on top and so sharp-pointed as to be very prickly to the touch = Sitka Spruce (*P. sitchensis*) (ill. 4, p. 109)
  Leaves 1–2 cm long, dark green on top, not prickly to the touch = Hondo Spruce (*P. jezoensis* var. *hondensis*)

TABLE FOR COMMONLY CULTIVATED LARCHES (*Larix*) (text. p. 114)

	European Larch *L. decidua*	Japanese Larch *L. kaempferi*	Dunkeld Larch *L. x eurolepis*
Twigs	Yellow, with no waxy bloom	Orange-red to dark purple, with whitish waxy bloom	Yellow, with slight waxy bloom
Winter-bud	Golden-brown, not resinous	Red-brown, resinous	Pale reddish-brown, not resinous
Leaves	Bright green, with no whitish bands beneath	Blue-green, with whitish bands beneath	Bluish-green, with pale grey bands beneath
Ripe cone:			
bract-scales	Just visible	All hidden	Some visible
cone-scales	Straight, tips not curved outwards	Tips curled outwards and downwards so that cone is rosette-like seen from above	Tips somewhat bent outwards but not curled downwards

TABLE FOR COMMONLY CULTIVATED 5-NEEDLE PINES (*Pinus*) (text p. 123)

	Arolla Pine *P. cembra*	Bhutan Pine *P. wallichiana*	Weymouth Pine *P. strobus*	Macedonian Pine *P. peuce*
Young stems	Greenish-brown, densely shaggy with orange-brown hairs	Pale green with whitish bloom, hairless	Bright green, hairless but for tufts below leaf spurs	Bright green, hairless
Leaves	5–8 cm, rigid, bunched and ascending	8–20 cm, flexible, drooping	5–14 cm, flexible, bunched, pointing forwards	7–12 cm, rigid, pointing forwards
Cones	5–8 cm long, not opening	15–25 cm long, opening	8–20 cm long, opening	7–12 cm long, opening
Seeds	Wingless or nearly so	Winged	Winged	Winged

KEY TO COMMONLY CULTIVATED TWO-NEEDLE AND THREE-NEEDLE PINES (text p. 123)

1   Most needles in threes ⇨ 2
    Most needles in twos ⇨ 4

2   Young twigs blue-grey with violet bloom; buds non-resinous; ripe cones more than 15 cm long = Jeffrey's Pine
        (P. jeffreyi)
    Young twigs green or brown, without bloom; buds resinous; ripe cones less than 15 cm long ⇨ 3

3   Leaves 10–15 cm long; ripe cones very asymmetric at base and with usually non-persistent prickles on scale-ends =
        Monterey Pine (*P. radiata*)
    Leaves 15–27 cm long; ripe cones symmetric at base and with strong persistent spine on each scale-end = Western
        Yellow Pine (*P. ponderosa*)

4   Most leaves less than 10 cm long ⇨ 5
    Most leaves more than 10 cm long ⇨ 7

5   Bark of upper part of trunk bright reddish or orange; leaves blue-green; cones short-stalked, pendulous, usually
        symmetric, dull brown = Scots Pine *(P. sylvestris)*
    Bark of upper part of trunk not bright reddish or orange; leaves dark or bright green; cone unstalked or nearly so, held
        horizontal or inclining downwards, shining dark brown or reddish brown ⇨ 6

6   Leaves dark green, rigid, twisted; cones very asymmetric, shining brown, prickly, remaining closed on tree for several
        years = Coastal Lodgepole Pine (*P. contorta* var. *contorta*)
    Leaves bright or dark green, rigid, straight, crowded; cones asymmetric, shining red-brown, not prickly, with basal scale
        ends prolonged and down-curved = Mountain Pine (*P. uncinata*). In shrubby form (*P. mugo*) the cones are
        symmetric and basal scales rounded

7   Tree with wide-spreading crown like open umbrella; cone 8–15 cm long, broadly ovoid and blunt-ended or almost
        spherical, mature in 3 years; seeds 16–20 mm long, wingless or nearly so = Stone Pine (*P. pinea*)
    Tree not umbrella-shaped; cone ovoid-conical or oblong-conical, pointed at tip, mature in 2 years; seeds up to 10 mm
        long, winged ⇨ 8

8   Buds not resinous; cones 8–20 cm long, shining brown, pendulous; seeds 8–10 mm long (excluding wing) = Maritime
        Pine (*P. pinaster*)
    Buds resinous; cones 5–8 cm long, dull brown, held almost horizontal; seeds about 6 mm long (excluding wing) ⇨ 9

9   Leaves 10–15 cm long, rigid, straight, clustered, dark or blackish green = Austrian Pine *(P. nigra* ssp. *nigra)*
    Leaves 10–16 cm long, flexible, twisted, spreading untidily, grey-green = Corsican Pine (*P. nigra* ssp. *laricio)*

TABLE FOR COMMONLY CULTIVATED CYPRESSES (text. pp. 130–1)

	False Cypress *Chamaecyparis*	Hybrids x *Cupressocyparis*	True Cypress *Cupressus*
Final branchings of leafy shoot	In single plane, forming flat sprays	Variable	In 2 planes at right angles, giving irregular plumes
Branchlets	Flattened (but not or very slightly in Nootka Cypress)	4-sided	4-sided
Ripe female cone	Up to 1 cm across	Rarely seen	3–4 cm across*
Seeds to each fertile scale	1–5	—	Usually 8–20*

(*Some rarely planted true cypresses have cones only 1 cm across, with few seeds to each fertile scale.)

TABLE FOR COMMONLY CULTIVATED FALSE CYPRESSES (*Chamaecyparis*) (text pp. 115, 131)

	Lawson's Cypress *C. lawsoniana*	Nootka Cypress *C. nootkatensis*	Hinoki Cypress *C. obtusa*	Sawara Cypress *C. pisifera*
Branchlets	Flattened	4-sided, slightly flattened	Flattened	Flattened
Leaf-tip	Pointed, incurved	Sharp-pointed	Blunt	Fine-pointed, incurved
Translucent leaf-gland	Conspicuous	Indistinct or none	None	Indistinct
White markings beneath shoot	White joints between leaves	None	Distinct	Distinct
Diameter of ripe cone	6–8 mm	About 1 cm	8–10 mm	About 6 mm
Smell of bruised foliage*	"Sour parsley"	"Ox-eye daisies"	"Sweet resinous scent, sometimes like Eucalyptus"	"Acrid resinous aroma"

(*from A. L. Mitchell)

TABLE FOR COMMONLY GROWN SCALE-LEAVED JUNIPERS (*Juniperus*) (text p. 134)

	Chinese Juniper *J. chinensis*	Pencil Cedar *J. virginiana*
Branchlets	About 1·5 mm across	Barely 1 mm across
Scale-leaves:		
tip	Blunt	Pointed
colour	Centre dark green, margins distinctly paler	Uniformly green or nearly so
Juvenile leaves	Mainly at bases of shoots	Mainly at tips of shoots
Female cone or "berry":		
diameter	7–8 mm	3–6 mm
colour	Brown, with thick bloom	Blue, with whitish bloom

KEY TO NATIVE AND COMMONLY CULTIVATED MAPLES (*Acer*) (text pp. 26, 190)

1   Leaves compound, with 3 or more separated leaflets ⇨ 3
      Leaves simple, unlobed or more or less deeply palmate-lobed ⇨ 3

2   Leaflets 3–7, often varying on same shoot; bark smooth, grey = Box Elder (*A. negundo*)
      Leaflets always 3; bark red-brown, rolling off in horizontal papery strips = Paper-bark Maple (*A. griseum*)

3   Leaves unlobed or with quite small lateral lobes, often only 1 on each side of leaf ⇨ 4
      Leaves distinctly palmate-lobed ⇨ 6

4   Bark green with conspicuous white stripes (snake-bark maples) ⇨ 5
      Bark brown with buff stripes = Tartar Maple (*A. tataricum*)

5   Young shoots and buds red marked with white; leaves unlobed or with very shallow lobes or large teeth = Père
        David's Maple (*A. davidii*)
      Young shoots and buds green; leaves usually with short pointed lobe or large tooth near middle of each side =
        Hers's Snake-bark Maple (*A. hersii*)

6   Leaves 3-5-lobed, silvery or bluish-white beneath ⇨ 7
      Leaves 3–11-lobed, not whitish beneath ⇨ 8

7   Leaves usually with 5 deep and narrow double-toothed lobes, silvery beneath = Silver Maple (*A. saccharinum*)
      Leaves with 3–5 triangular-ovate toothed lobes, bluish-white beneath = Red Maple (*A. rubrum*)

8   Leaf-stalks exuding white juice when cut or broken; fruit-wings almost in straight line ⇨ 9
      Leaf-stalks not exuding white juice when cut; fruit-wings at various angles ⇨ 10

9   Leaves usually 10–15 cm long and shortly 5-lobed, each lobe with long fine tip and with a few similarly fine-
        pointed marginal teeth = Norway Maple (*A. platanoides*)
      Leaves 4–7 cm long, shortly 3–5-lobed, the lobes blunt-tipped and with a few shallow rounded marginal teeth or
        shallowly 3-lobed = Field Maple (*A. campestre*)

10   Leaf-lobes 5-7, broadly ovate-triangular and with long narrow points, their margins untoothed = Cappodocian
       Maple (*A. cappodocicum*)
      Leaf-lobes with toothed margins ⇨ 11

11   Leaf-lobes ending in very long narrow points and with a few large marginal teeth = Sugar Maple (*A. saccharo-*
       phorum)
      Leaf-lobes with many marginal teeth ⇨ 12

12   Leaves usually with 5 ovate long-pointed and coarsely toothed lobes reaching about half-way down leaf = Sycamore
       (*A. pseudoplatanus*)
      Leaves with finely-toothed lobes ⇨ 13

13   Leaves often red-purple, with 5–7 lobes reaching more than half-way, each long-pointed at tip; leaf-stalks hairless =
       Japanese Maple (*A. palmatum*)
      Leaves almost circular and with 7–11 lobes reaching a quarter to half-way to centre; leaf-stalks hairy at first =
       Downy Japanese Maple (*A. japonicum*)

TABLE FOR THUYA (*Thuja*), HIBA (*Thujopsis*), AND INCENSE CEDAR (*Calocedrus*) GENERA (text p. 130)

	Thuya	Hiba	Incense Cedar
Branchlets	Less than 4 mm across	4–6 mm across	Less than 4 mm across
Leaf-tips on main shoots	In alternating pairs	In alternating pairs	In whorls of 4
Scales of female cone	4–6 pairs, 2–3 fertile	3–4 pairs, 2–3 fertile	2–3 pairs, 1 fertile
Seeds per fertile cone-scale	2–3	3–5	2
Seed-wings	Lateral and symmetrical	Lateral and symmetrical	Terminal and asymmetrical

TABLE FOR THUYAS (*Thuja*) AS COMMONLY SEEN IN GARDENS (text pp. 115, 130)

	Western Red Cedar *T. plicata*	American Thuya *T. occidentalis*	Chinese Thuya *T. orientalis*
Foliage sprays	Horizontal	Horizontal	Vertical
Underside of branchlets	White-streaked	Uniformly pale yellow-green	Uniformly dark green
Ripe female cone	Narrowly oblong-ovoid	Narrowly oblong-ovoid	Broadly ovoid
Cone-scale	Not spiny	Small prickle near tip	Stout down-curled hook near tip
Seeds	Winged	Winged	Wingless

GLOSSARY

Alternate (of leaves): attached singly at any given level on the stem, so that there is 1 leaf at a node, in contrast with **opposite** or **whorled** leaves.

Apomictic: producing good seed without fertilization of the egg in the ovule by a male sexual cell derived from a pollen grain, so that on germination the plant produced is genetically identical with the seed-parent. Many of our native whitebeams, including cliff whitebeam, are apomictic, as are most blackberries and dandelions.

Appressed: lying close-pressed to a surface, like the white silky hairs on both surfaces of the leaves of white willow.

Aril: a fleshy covering, complete or incomplete and often brightly coloured, round the seeds of certain plants, including yew and spindle-tree.

Axil: the angle on the upper or forward side of the join between two parts of a plant. The axil of a leaf is the upper angle between the leaf-stalk and the stem.

Bisexual (of a flower): having both stamens and ovary in the same flower.

Bloom: a film of fine whitish waxy particles on the surface of a leaf, stem, or fruit, removable by rubbing.

Bract: a kind of leaf, usually smaller and of simpler shape than the ordinary foliage leaves, in whose axil either a single flower or a flower-cluster arises. A **bracteole** is like a bract but is borne on a flower-stalk and may have another flower or flower-cluster in its axil, so that the bracteole of one flower may be the bract of another. In the lime the wing of each fruit-cluster is a bracteole.

Bud-scales: the small leaves or stipules, often firm in texture and brownish in colour, that form a protective covering round the growing-tips of stems and the young leaves arising there.

Calyx: a collective term for all the sepals of a flower.

Capsule: a dry fruit opening usually along split-lines from top to bottom but sometimes by the removal of a lid or the development of holes or pores—always with the result that the seeds can be shaken or blown out.

Catkin: an inflorescence usually of small inconspicuous unisexual flowers, unstalked or nearly so and crowded along an unbranched axis. When pollination is by wind the male catkins are commonly long and pendulous and the female much shorter, as in hazel, alder, and oak, but both male and female are long and pendulous in poplars, birches, and hornbeams. The catkins of willows and sweet chestnut are visited by insects and are erect or ascending.

Ciliate: having marginal hairs; literally "provided with eyelashes".

Corolla: a collective term for all the petals of a flower, which may be separate or joined together to varying extents to form a **corolla-tube**.

Corymb: an inflorescence in which the lengths of the stalks of the individual flowers are so adjusted that the flowers all stand at the same level; hence a flat-topped flower-cluster.

Cultivar: a term, shortened from "cultivated variety", used of a variant arising from a wild species, or from a cross between species, which has been selected and grown for its agricultural or horticultural value.

Cyme: a branched inflorescence, usually shaped like an inverted cone, in which the main axis and all its branches end in flowers, so that the youngest flowers tend to be at lower levels than the oldest.

Deciduous (of leaves, etc.): falling, usually through formation of a special separating layer across the stalk or base. In deciduous leaves this takes place in autumn so that the trees or shrubs are leafless throughout the winter.

Decussate (of leaves, etc.): in opposite pairs, the pair at at any given node being at right angles to the pairs at adjacent nodes above and below.

Dicotyledon: see Seed-leaves

Epicormic (of leafy branches): arising from dormant buds on the main trunk or an old branch.

Epiphyte: a plant growing upon another and usually larger plant and therefore not rooted in the ground. The term does not imply any penetration of the host plant nor any parasitic dependence on it.

Evergreen (of a tree or shrub): retaining green leaves throughout the winter or dry season.

Evergreen (of leaves): retained green throughout the winter. Evergreen leaves vary greatly in length of life from one complete year to 2–3 years in Scots pine, 3–4 in holly, 6–7 in Norway spruce, and up to 15 in monkey-puzzle.

Fat-body: a fatty or oily swelling on the surface of a seed, often attractive to ants.

Form (in plant classification): a minor genetic variant from the normal, often differing merely in a single feature such as angle of branching (fastigiate or weeping forms), flower colour (white-flowered forms), or the colour or shape of leaves (copper- or cut-leaved forms).

Fruit: the structure developed from the ovary or ovaries of a flower, following pollination and fertilization, and enclosing the ripe seeds. The term is often extended to include other associated parts, as in the "fruits" of strawberry, rose, or fig. Fruits may be dry or fleshy, may open to release the seeds or remain closed, and may in some instances be winged, plumed, or covered with spines or prickles.

Gland: a small, usually translucent and often more or less spherical container for oil, resin, or some other liquid secretion. Many leaves, like those of bay laurel, have internal glands which appear as shining dots against the light; and there are glands at the junction of leaf-stalk with blade in guelder rose and some plums, cherries, and poplars.

Inferior (of an ovary): surmounted by perianth and by stamens, if present. If the ovary is **superior** these other parts of the flower are attached round the base of the ovary or at the edge of a cup which arises below the base of the ovary.

Inflorescence: a flowering branch, or the flowering upper end of a main stem above the uppermost normal foliage leaves.

Leaf shapes: see diagrams, p. 209

Monocotyledon: see Seed-leaves

Mutant: an individual differing genetically from its parents because of a newly-arisen genetic change.

Nectary: a nectar-secreting gland, usually at the base of a flower but sometimes on the blades or stalks of leaves.

Node: the level of attachment of one or more leaves to the parent stem.

Panicle: a branching inflorescence.

Perianth: a collective term for all the parts of a flower outside the stamens and ovaries. It may consist of distinct sepals and petals or, as in some magnolias, the perianth segments may be much the same in size, shape, and colour.

Pollen: the dust of small grains, usually yellow in colour, formed inside the anther-lobes of a stamen. Each pollen grain can germinate on the stigma of the appropriate kind of flower and give rise to a pollen-tube which conveys 2 male sexual cells, one of which may fertilize the egg inside an ovule.

Raceme: a narrowly conical inflorescence in which stalked flowers are borne, usually in the axils of bracts, on an unbranched axis, the youngest at the top and successively older ones lower down.

Rugose (of the surface of a leaf, etc.): wrinkled or markedly uneven.

Seed-leaves: the leaves of the embryo plant within a seed, technically termed "cotyledons". The flowering plants are divided into 2 sub-classes—the dicotyledons with 2 seed-leaves and the monocotyledons with only 1. The monocotyledons commonly have long narrow leaves and the parts of their flowers in threes.

Sepals: the outer set of perianth-segments of a flower, often green and firm and protecting the flower in bud.

Spike: an inflorescence like a raceme but with unstalked flowers.

Stamen: the parts of a flower between perianth and ovary. Each stamen usually has a slender stalk or **filament** and a pair of **anther-lobes** that split open to release the pollen.

Stigma: the sticky end of the style, or of each of its branches, on which pollen is caught and into which the pollen-tube passes.

Stipules: the pair of small and variously shaped appendages standing one on each side of the base of the leaf-stalk or leaf in some but not all plants. In many trees and shrubs the bud-scales are stipules. **Stipulate:** having stipules.

Style: the slender stalk, of variable length and sometimes absent, between the top of an ovary and the stigma or stigmas.

Sucker: a leafy shoot growing from a bud borne on a root.

Switch-plant: a plant with green stems and small leaves which may be scale-like and not green or may fall early. Many brooms are switch-plants.

Tomentose: densely covered with short velvety hairs.

Umbel: a cluster of stalked flowers all springing from the same point on the parent stem. Umbels may be flat-topped but are not necessarily so.

Umbo: that part of the end of a pine-cone scale that was formed during the first year's growth of the cone. In 5-needle pines it forms the tip of the mature cone-scale but in other pines it is central on the scale-end and is usually rhombic.

Unisexual (of a flower): having only stamens or only ovaries, not both. Some unisexual flowers appear to be bisexual but either the stamens or the ovary being non-functional they are effectively unisexual.

Whorl: a set of 3 or more leaves (or other plant-organs) all borne at the same level on the parent axis. The parts of flowers are commonly but by no means invariably in whorls.

linear elliptic oblong lanceolate ovate oblanceolate obovate rhombic deltoid

palmate pinnate heart-shaped (cordate) truncate rounded wedge-shaped asymmetric ciliate gland

Terms used to describe leaf shapes and base of leaf shapes

LIST OF BOOKS FOR FURTHER READING

Identification and Description of Native British Trees and Shrubs

CLAPHAM, A. R., TUTIN, T. G., & WARBURG, E. F., *Flora of the British Isles**, 2nd edn. 1962. Cambridge University Press, Cambridge.

EDLIN, H. L., *British Woodland Trees*, 2nd edn. 1945. Batsford, London.

MEIKLE, R. D., *British Trees and Shrubs* (The Kew Series) 1958. Eyre & Spottiswoode, London.

PRIME, C. T., & PEACOCK, R. J., *Trees and Shrubs—Their Identification in Summer or Winter*, 1970. Heffer, Cambridge.

Identification and Description of Cultivated Trees
Conifers

DALLIMORE, W., & JACKSON, A. B., *Handbook to Coniferae**, 4th edn., revised by S. G. Harrison. 1966. Arnold, London.

EDLIN, H. L., *Know Your Conifers* (Forestry Commission Booklet No. 15). 1970.

MITCHELL, A. F., *Conifers in the British Isles* (Forestry Commission Booklet No. 33). 1972.

Flowering Plants

EDLIN, H. L., *Know Your Broadleaves* (Forestry Commission Booklet No. 20). 1968.

General

BEAN, W. J., *Trees and Shrubs Hardy in the British Isles**, 8th edn. 1970. Transatlantic, London.

Hillier's Manual of Trees and Shrubs. 1972. Hillier & Sons, Winchester.

MITCHELL, ALAN, *A Field Guide to the Trees of Britain and Northern Europe*. 1974. Collins, London.

REHDER, ALFRED, *Manual of Cultivated Trees and Shrubs**, 2nd edn. 1940, Macmillan, New York.

British Woodland Ecology

PEARSALL, W. H., *Mountains and Moorlands* (New Naturalist Series and Fontana Library), 2nd edn., revised by Winifred Pennington. 1971. Collins, London.

TANSLEY, A. G., *Britain's Green Mantle*, 2nd edn., revised by M. C. F. Proctor. 1968. Allen & Unwin, London.

STEVEN H. M., & CARLISLE, A., *The Native Pinewoods of Scotland*. 1959. Oliver & Boyd, Edinburgh.

Other Books

EDLIN, H. L., *Woodland Crafts in Britain*. 1949. Batsford, London.

MORRIS, M. G., & PERRING, F. H. (ed.), *The British Oak*. 1974. Botanical Society of the British Isles.

PENNINGTON, WINIFRED, *History of British Vegetation*. 1969. The English Universities Press, London.

POLLARD, E., HOOPER, M. D., & MOORE, N. W., *Hedges* (New Naturalist Series). 1971. Collins, Glasgow.

"R.B.A.", *Roadside Planting*. 1930. Country Life, London.

*large comprehensive works

ACKNOWLEDGEMENTS

We are especially grateful to Mr. H. G. Hillier for his kindness to the artist in giving her the run of his gardens and arboretum at Ampfield, and to his Curator Mr. Roy Lancaster for his cheerful and unfailing help with the identification and collection of specimens.

We thank Mr. Alan Mitchell and the Forestry Commission at Alice Holt and Westonbirt for specimens and advice on location of introduced species. Our thanks are also due to the National Trust at Stourhead, Wiltshire, where the artist painted 52 of the trees illustrated; and to Mr. Peter Ward, Forester, for great help with specimens and location of planted forest trees.

It is a pleasure to express our deep gratitude to Professor C. D. Pigott, of the University of Lancaster, who has always been ready to discuss ecological matters in the light of his intimate knowledge and understanding of British vegetation and who has helped us greatly by directing us to good examples of various types of woodland, especially in North-western England.

The artist is grateful in addition to the many people who gave access to their gardens and helped collect specimens.

INDEX

The numbers in heavy type refer to illustrations

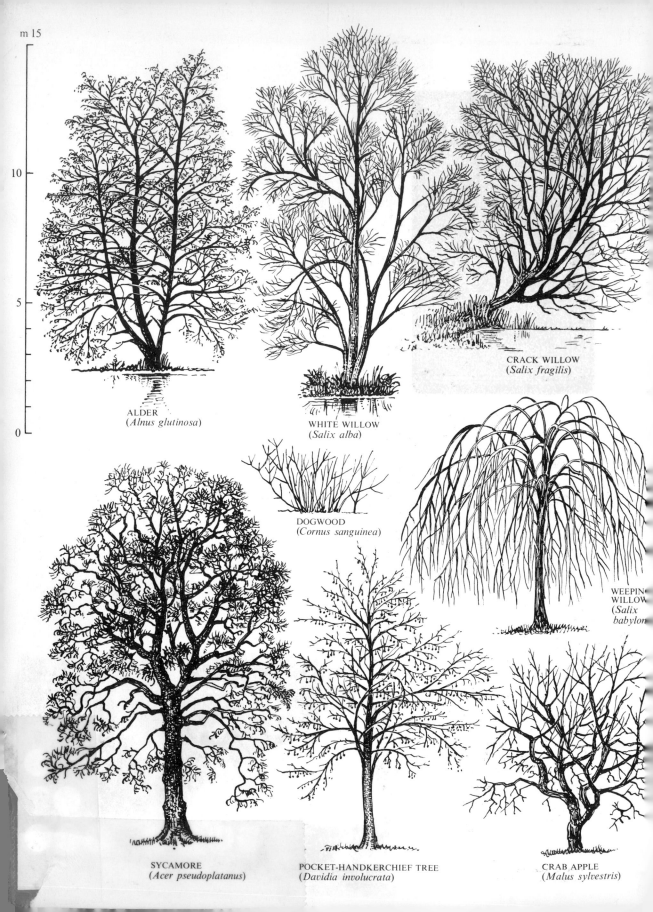

m 15

10

5

0

ALDER
(*Alnus glutinosa*)

WHITE WILLOW
(*Salix alba*)

CRACK WILLOW
(*Salix fragilis*)

DOGWOOD
(*Cornus sanguinea*)

WEEPING
WILLOW
(*Salix
babylon*

SYCAMORE
(*Acer pseudoplatanus*)

POCKET-HANDKERCHIEF TREE
(*Davidia involucrata*)

CRAB APPLE
(*Malus sylvestris*)